A Guide to Prayer for
  All Who Seek God

A Guide to Prayer
for
All Who Seek God

Norman Shawchuck
Rueben P. Job

Sunday Scripture Readings from
The Revised Common Lectionary

UPPER
ROOM BOOKS®
NASHVILLE

A Guide to Prayer for All Who Seek God
© 2003 by Norman Shawchuck and Rueben P. Job
All rights reserved.

Unless noted otherwise, scripture quotations are from the New Revised Standard Version Bible, copyright 1989, Division of Christian Education of the National Council of the Churches of Christ in the United States of America. Used by permission. All rights reserved. Scripture noted KJV is from the King James Version of the Bible. Additional scripture notices on pages 427-28.

Lectionary tables from *The Revised Common Lectionary.* Copyright © 1992 The Consultation on Common Texts (CCT), P. O. Box 340003, Room 381, Nashville, TN 37203-0003. All rights reserved. Reprinted with permission.

ACKNOWLEDGMENTS on pages 416 ff. constitute a continuation of the copyright page. While every effort has been made to secure permissions, we may have failed in a few cases to trace or contact the copyright holder. We apologize for any inadvertent oversight or error.

Book Design: Bruce Gore
Deluxe Edition First Printing: 2003
Printed in the United States of America

LIBRARY OF CONGRESS CATALOGING-IN-PUBLICATION DATA
A guide to prayer for all who seek God / [collected by] Norman Shawchuck, Rueben P. Job.
     p. cm.
"Sunday Scripture readings from the Revised common lectionary."
  ISBN 0-8358-0999-4
  1. Devotional exercises. 2. Meditations. I. Shawchuck, Norman, 1935-
II. Job, Rueben P. III. Common lectionary (1992)
     BV4832.3.G85 2003
     242'.3--dc21   2003009892

NOTE ON LANGUAGE: While effort has been made to select and edit material to be inclusive, some texts retain original language that uses male nouns and pronouns in reference to humanity and to God.

For all who pray

Contents

Preface

This *Guide to Prayer for All Who Seek God*, like the two *Guides to Prayer* that preceded it, found birth and life in our own daily experience of seeking to walk with God in an ever more faithful and fruitful way. Special efforts were made to reach back and mine the treasures of the first centuries of our faith. We have included material from some of the well-known and some unknown mothers and fathers of the faith. Their message seems as relevant today as it was a thousand years ago. We have sought this kind of timeless message in both the ancient and contemporary material we have selected for reflection. While every reading is new, the revolutionary element in this guide, as in the others, is the invitation to incorporate the simple daily office into your daily life. Living for a week, a month, a year, or a lifetime with the sacred writing of scripture along with ancient and contemporary spiritual guides is to live a transformed life. We seek this transformed life for ourselves and commend it to you for daily practice.

We offer our gratitude to the many lay- and clergy-persons who pointed us toward books and articles that provided nourishment for their own spiritual lives and have found their way into this volume.

Such a volume could never be produced without the competence and commitment of skilled editors. We offer a special word of gratitude to JoAnn Miller and Sarah Schaller-Linn for their patient and gentle guidance of the entire project. We are deeply grateful for their tireless efforts to move toward our goal of helping this volume serve as a window to God.

Autumn 2002
Norman Shawchuck
Rueben P. Job

How to Use This Guide to Prayer

This *Guide to Prayer* follows the Christian calendar and the *Revised Common Lectionary*. You may know that when you pray with the guide you are keeping a tradition that has nourished the prayers of God's people for some two thousand years. The Christian calendar is a spiritual calendar, a calendar of spiritual experience. It does not follow the Gregorian calendar.

Note that you need not follow this *Guide to Prayer* by rote or strict sequence. From time to time God may lead you into a particular season of spiritual experience in which God desires that you "linger awhile." When facing such a situation, you may wish to spend time in those sections of the *Guide to Prayer* that more pointedly address the particular experience into which God is leading you. Then, when you feel ready to move on, you may return to the appropriate week in the guide and proceed with your daily prayer discipline from that point.

Keeping a Spiritual Journal

In addition to the daily use of the guide, we urge you to keep a daily journal of your spiritual experience. Apart from daily meditation upon the scriptures and prayer, perhaps no activity proves as beneficial to your spiritual journey as keeping a written journal of your spiritual experience. We recommend that at the beginning of each new year, you take time to reflect upon the entries you have made in your journal. You will almost certainly gain much insight into the way God has led you over the past year(s).

The Prayer of Examen

The prayer of examen, which includes the examination of consciousness and the examination of *conscience*, emerges as a most important spiritual discipline. Richard Foster says that the examen of consciousness permits us to "prayerfully reflect on the thoughts, feelings and actions of our days to see how God has been at work among us and how we responded. . . . In the examen of conscience we are inviting the Lord to search our hearts to the depths. Far from being dreadful, this is a scrutiny of love."* A simple search yields many variations of the prayer of examen. For example, you will find a model of the examen in the book *Leading the Congregation* by Norman Shawchuck and Roger Heuser, 51-56. Also, the book *Sleeping with Bread*, by Dennis Linn, offers simple models of the examen. Richard Foster's book *Prayer: Finding the Heart's True Home* provides helpful material regarding the prayer of examen.

* Richard J. Foster, *Prayer: Finding the Heart's True Home* (San Francisco: HarperSanFrancisco, 1992), 28, 29.

Lectionary Readings in This *Guide to Prayer*

We have included the Sunday readings from the *Revised Common Lectionary* in the guide for those who wish to use them in their churches and private prayers. This guide includes the ecumenical Sunday lectionary readings, but the rest of the daily scriptures and themes have been chosen on the basis of our own experience of the growing number of resources—ancient and contemporary—that speak most poignantly to us. Finally we have arranged the weekly lectionary readings in this *Guide to Prayer* to begin with Sunday and to proceed through Saturday. In the previous guides, we arranged the lectionary readings to begin with Monday and to proceed through Sunday. However, many people found this confusing, since the calendar week begins on Sunday.

The Sunday lectionary readings are identified as "A" for Year A, "B" for Year B, and "C" for Year C. The three-year cycle then repeats itself again and again.

Calendar Year 2003 corresponds to Year B plus
　　Advent and Christmas from Year C;
Year 2004 corresponds to Year C plus
　　Advent and Christmas from Year A;
Year 2005 corresponds to Year A plus
　　Advent and Christmas from Year B;
Year 2006 corresponds to Year B plus
　　Advent and Christmas from Year C;
Year 2007 corresponds to Year C plus
　　Advent and Christmas from Year A;
Year 2008 corresponds to Year A plus
　　Advent and Christmas from Year B;
Year 2009 corresponds to Year B plus
　　Advent and Christmas from Year C;
and so on.

Introduction to the Liturgical Calendar

Before Christianity was born, the ancient Jews observed a weekly day of sabbath rest, and later the early Christians came to observe Sunday as a holy day for worship and rest. When we spend daily time with God, we create for ourselves a little sabbath, a rest and restoration of our spent inner resources.

Following the resurrection of Jesus, Sunday came to be observed as the Christian day of sabbath for the early church. Sunday's central service of worship was the breaking of the bread or "communion." Daily prayer was observed in various ways by virtually all the early Christians and Jews. For the Christians, each week's Sunday was, and is, a "little Easter."

From the beginning the Christians celebrated Easter as the anniversary of Jesus' resurrection. The Season of Easter lasted for seven weeks, culminating on the Day of Pentecost, which celebrated the giving of the Holy Spirit to the apostles and also served as a conclusion to the Easter period.

Easter became the main annual feast of the early Christian church. This feast day was a popular time for baptisms and was preceded by a forty-day period (excluding Sundays) of intensive instruction. This season of instruction, which became known as Lent, is patterned after Jesus' forty days in the wilderness.

Holy Week (Palm Sunday to Easter Day) became a time when pilgrims retraced the movements of Jesus during the last week leading up to his crucifixion and resurrection. Easter week begins with Easter Day and continues to the second Sunday of Easter.

Apparently Christmas began to be celebrated as the anniversary of Jesus' birth in the fourth century.

As it gained more importance, Christmas also acquired a preparatory period similar to Lent, which was called Advent. The Advent Season occurs at the point where the liturgical year ended, thus it soon was observed as an important time of preparation for the celebration of Jesus' birth, and as a time of looking forward to his second coming. We now consider Advent to be the first season in the liturgical calendar.

In 321 c.e. with the conversion of the Emperor Constantine, who made Christianity the official religion of the empire, the *liturgical calendar*—the calendar of participatory public worship—began to take a more final form. Several Christian festivals were added to the Christian year as early as the fourth century. By the beginning of the seventh century, the liturgical calendar was fairly well fixed as the seasons and festivals of the Christian year. However, over the centuries both the Eastern and the Western Church have made minor changes. Indeed, as late as the last half of the twentieth century, various American religious bodies made minor changes to the liturgical calendar, but these changes have not seriously altered its basic form and flow.

The Christian Calendar—
also Known as the Christian Year

Almost from its inception, the Christian church has kept time in two distinct ways. One way is the following of the secular calendar and the other is observing the calendar of the Christian year or liturgical calendar. Since its beginning, the calendar of the Christian year was intended to be a constant means of grace though which we receive God's gifts to us. This "Year of Grace" is about what God does for us.

The Christian calendar is comprised of a series of feasts and celebrations and two long seasons of Ordinary Time or Kingdomtide. The seasons (and days) of the Christian year are the following:

- the Season of Advent
- the Season of Christmas
- the Day of the Epiphany
- the Season after the Epiphany (Ordinary Time)
- the Season of Lent
- the Season of Easter
- the Day of Pentecost
- the Season after Pentecost (Ordinary Time)

Season of Advent begins the Christian Year, includes the four Sundays before Christmas, and offers a time of preparation for the coming of Christ.

Season of Christmas begins with the anniversary of the birth of Jesus Christ on December 25 and continues through the Day of the Epiphany on January 6.

The Day of the Epiphany, January 6, commemorates the Magi's visit to the baby Jesus.

Season after Epiphany: The first season of Ordinary Time begins with the Baptism of the Lord, which marks the beginning of Jesus' ministry, comprises the first Sunday after Epiphany through Ash Wednesday, and celebrates the Transfiguration of the Lord on the last Sunday.

Ordinary Time comprises the Sundays that fall between the two great Christological cycles of Advent/Christmas/Epiphany and Lent/Easter/Pentecost. The shorter period of Ordinary Time between Epiphany and Ash Wednesday is often designated as Sundays after Epiphany, and the longer period between the Day of Pentecost and Advent is often designated as Sundays after Pentecost.

Season of Lent begins with Ash Wednesday and concludes at sunset the day before Easter (Easter Eve). In ancient times, Lent was a time for religious instruction, introspection, and baptism into the church. Today Lent is regarded as a period of penitence in preparation for Easter.

Season of Easter celebrates the resurrection of the Lord, begins with Easter Day, and concludes on the Day of Pentecost, which is preceded by Ascension Sunday, the day of the Lord's ascension into heaven.

Day of Pentecost commemorates the visitation of the Holy Spirit upon Jesus' disciples as they prayed in the upper room.

Season after Pentecost: The second Season of Ordinary Time begins with the Holy Spirit's visitation upon the disciples in the upper room.

The last Sunday in Pentecost is Reign of Christ (or Christ the King) Sunday.

Following Reign of Christ Sunday comes the Season of Advent, and the Christian year starts over, new and fresh.

NOTE: For two excellent treatments of the Christian year, see Laurence Hull Stookey, *Calendar: Christ's Time for the Church* (Nashville: Abingdon, 1996) and Hoyt L. Hickman, Don E. Saliers, Laurence Hull Stookey, and James F. White, *The New Handbook of the Christian Year* (Nashville: Abingdon, 1992).

Weekly
Guidance

The Season of Advent

We do get another chance! The Season of Advent gives the church the opportunity to begin again. Once more the full story of God's grace is awaiting our discovery. Once more we shake off the failures and victories of the past, and we get a clean page on which to write the story of our companionship with God in Christ. Once more we get to listen and respond in faithfulness to the God who comes to us so humbly, intimately, and personally in the birth of Jesus. Advent marks the beginning of the church year and lays before us the pathway of faith for the year ahead. Advent initiates once again remembering, retelling, and celebrating the whole drama of God's revelation.

Four weeks is the limit to this season that declares the truth about a God whose love and resourcefulness have no limits. "Advent" has its roots in the Latin word *adventus*, or coming. This season proclaims the coming of Christ in the birth of Jesus, in the Word and Spirit, and in the final victory when God's kingdom shall be complete. *Our privilege* as Christians is to receive the gracious gifts of God's presence in Christ. *Our task* is to prepare for his coming so that we will not miss life's greatest gift.

Sometimes the hype and clichés of the season distract us. The clever marketing efforts succeed in making us desire tangible things we can hold in our hands and savor as gifts. However, marketing hype and catchy clichés cannot answer the deep questions of the heart, explain the mystery of God's presence, or help us comprehend the meaning of our existence. Yet all these gifts are promised to us in the Advent Season.

Yes, it is true that God's astounding and radical intervention in our human history cannot be contained in the tame and timid displays of Christmas lights, catchy slogans, or the exchange of gifts. Advent confronts us once again with God's unparalleled effort to communicate the message that all humankind is embraced and held close by a God of love. Jesus Christ has come, is present with us, and will come again in final victory when all darkness, pain, and evil will be no more. In Advent we begin again to try to make plain the wonderful truth of the most extraordinary good news the world has ever heard. Soon we will join the angelic chorus in singing, "Christ the Savior is born."

1: God's Preposterous Promise

Affirmation
For in [Christ] every one of God's promises is a "Yes."
For this reason it is through him that we say the
"Amen," to the glory of God (2 Cor. 1:20).

Petition
Remember your word to your servant,
    in which you have made me hope.
This is my comfort in my distress,
    that your promise gives me life (Ps. 119:49-50).

Sacred Reading: anthology or other selected reading

Daily Scripture Readings

Sunday	A.	Isaiah 2:1-5; Romans 13:11-14; Psalm 122; Matthew 24:36-44
	B.	Isaiah 64:1-9; 1 Corinthians 1:3-9; Psalm 80:1-7; Mark 13:24-37
	C.	Jeremiah 33:14-16; 1 Thessalonians 3:9-13; Psalm 25:1-10; Luke 21:25-36
Monday		Mark 1:1-8
Tuesday		Psalm 131
Wednesday		Zephaniah 3:14-17
Thursday		Isaiah 40:1-5
Friday		Isaiah 40:6-11
Saturday		Luke 12:35-38

Prayer: thanksgiving, petition, intercession, praise, and offering

Reflection: silent (listening to God), written (journaling)

God's Promise

Here is my servant, whom I have chosen,
    my beloved, with whom my soul is well pleased.
I will put my Spirit upon him,
    and he will proclaim justice to the Gentiles.
He will not wrangle or cry aloud,
    nor will anyone hear his voice in the streets.
He will not break a bruised reed
    or quench a smoldering wick
until he brings justice to victory.
    And in his name the Gentiles will hope.
        (Matt. 12:18-21).

My Response

My soul dances in delight, for God has visited me with unspeakable promise,which God alone can perform.

Readings for Reflection

❧ "If it sounds too good to be true, it is." We have all heard this with the warning about scam artists that are waiting to take our money and our property. And it is true that there are those who prey on the naive, the trusting, and the innocent. Most of us can remember hearing about that seductive bargain that turned out to be a disaster. We have seen it happen and have promised ourselves it will never happen to us.

Because we see such deception in our world, it is not unusual that we guard ourselves against the truth of the gospel story. We are afraid that it is indeed too good to be true. What if we believed and then found out it was only myth and hype? Better to keep our distance. We listen to the gospel story, let it creep into the edges of our lives, but never can bring ourselves to embrace it fully. What if it is just another cheap commercial trick that has nothing to do with our need or destiny and everything to do with the storyteller's need and fortune? Since it is better to be wise than to be a fool, we stand near the edge of the Advent story and keep all of our options open.

So often I stand on the edge of the light, afraid to believe, afraid to act, afraid that this story is too good to be true. But then in my better moments, when I listen closely to the story, move closer to the light, my fears seem to evaporate like an early morning mist, and I can believe again. I can believe that God who made all that is became clothed in our human flesh so that we might become clothed in God. I can believe that God claims me as a beloved child. I can believe that all my days are in God's strong and tender hands. I can believe that life is good, beautiful, and eternal. I can believe that not only my days but all days are in God's good and able hands. I can believe, rejoice, and wait trustingly and expectantly for the unfolding of God's promise given so many ways and most clearly in the Advent story. Thanks be to God!

We are not unlike Zechariah in the presence of God's messengers. Our questions are like his. How can this be? The angel speaks to us as to him, "Do not be afraid . . . for your prayer has been heard" (Luke 1:13). God gives the promise and God keeps the promise. So even though it does sound too good to be true, it is true! Thanks be to God it is true! Two thousand years of Christian experience and testimony declare that the preposterous promise is true. Today believe that your prayer is heard and the light and presence of God will lead you through all your days.

—Rueben P. Job

❧ Believe the Gospel, that is, believe the joyful news of divine grace through Jesus Christ. Cease from sin; manifest repentance for your past lives; submit obediently to the Word and will of the Lord; and you will become companions, citizens, children and heirs of the new and heavenly Jerusalem. . . . Walk according to the Spirit and not according to the flesh.

—From *The Complete Writings of Menno Simons c. 1496-1561*

When Luther wrote, "Faith is the yes of the heart, a confidence on which one stakes one's life," he was saying faith is a response of the whole self to God. It is not just our words: the creeds we confess, the prayers we pray, the way we argue our faith, or what we say in teaching our children. It is not just our works and deeds: our faithful attendance at church, our participation on committees, or our acts of love toward others.

This yes is an inner assent of the will. It is a willingness to receive the grace and the guidance of God. It can be so deep and far-reaching as to cause a real conversion of life, a real repentance, a turning around to go in a completely new direction. It always involves, says Luther, the daily death of the person we have been in order to fulfill our reason for being alive: to accomplish God's will in our time and place.

—From *Faith, the Yes of the Heart* by Grace Adolphsen Brame

God's apparent lack of restraint when it comes to creating things is but a symptom of a deeper "problem": God lacks restraint when it comes to loving, too. In fact, God is *most* unrestrained when it comes to loving. Put another way, God cannot love except abundantly.

We see this abundance of God's love demonstrated throughout [Hebrew Scriptures]. The Chosen People turn away from God again and again. What does God do? Does God throw up his divine hands in disgust and cry, "Enough already!" and zap those Israelites into kingdom come? No, God continues to love them, taking them back again and again and again. There seems to be no end to God's love. There is no end to God's love.

—From *Abundant Treasures* by Melannie Svoboda

"He will wipe every tear from their eyes. There will be no more death or mourning or crying or pain, for the old order of things has passed away" (Rev. 21:4).

Christmas is the promise that the God who came in history and comes daily in mystery will one day come in glory. God is saying in Jesus that in the end everything will be all right. Nothing can harm you permanently, no suffering is irrevocable, no loss is lasting, no defeat is more than transitory, no disappointment is conclusive. Jesus did not deny the reality of suffering, discouragement, disappointment, frustration, and death; he simply stated that the Kingdom of God would conquer all of these horrors, that the Father's love is so prodigal that no evil could possibly resist it.

—From *Reflections for Ragamuffins* by Brennan Manning

ॐ The world waits. History waits and labors. Something draws near, and we love its being far away there rather than here, among ourselves. Except, of course, that it is here among us too and within us as we wait for the story to begin, the story whose end we already know and yearn to know again and wish we did not know: the story whose meaning may be our meaning, as we wait for the child to be born.

For this is what Gabriel comes to announce, and Mary stands there as still as life in her blue mantle with her hands folded on her lap, and the terrible salutation is caught like a bird's wing in the golden net of the air—*Ave Maria gratia plenah. Dominus tecum.* And then she hears him say, "Behold, you will conceive in your womb and bear a son, and you shall call his name . . . ." But she knows his name before Gabriel says it, just as we also know his name, because the child who is going to be born is our child as he is her child. He is that which all the world's history and all of our own inner histories have been laboring to bring forth. And it will be no ordinary birth but a virgin birth because the birth of righteousness and love in this stern world is always a virgin birth. It is never men nor the nations of men nor all the power and wisdom of men that bring it forth but always God, and that is why the angel says, "The child to be born will be called the Son of God."

—From *The Magnificent Defeat* by Frederick Buechner

✦ There is no need to multiply examples of what is so patently an essential condition of the Christian walk. We are saved through faith—an unflagging, unwavering attachment to the person of Jesus Christ.

What is the depth and quality of your faith commitment? In the last analysis, faith is not a way of speaking or even of thinking; it is a way of living. Maurice Blondel said, "If you want to know what a person really believes, don't listen to what he says but watch what he does." Only the practice of faith can verify what we believe. Does faith permeate the whole of your life? Does it form your judgments about death, about success? Does it influence the way you read the newspaper? Do you have a divine sense of humor that sees through people and events into the unfolding plan of God? When things are turbulent on the surface of your life, do you retain a quiet calm, firmly fixed in ultimate reality? As Thérèse of Lisieux said, "Let nothing disturb you, let nothing frighten you. All things are passing. God alone remains." Does your faith shape your Advent season this year?

—From *Reflections for Ragamuffins* by Brennan Manning

2: *Nagging Questions*

Affirmation
My God, in you only do I find the answer to the questions that perplex and confuse me. Yet I know that in your good time the answer will be made to me.

Petition
Give me grace, dear God, to live with my questions until you are pleased to make my way clear.

Sacred Reading: anthology or other selected reading

Daily Scripture Readings

Sunday	A.	Isaiah 11:1-10; Psalm 72:1-7, 18-19; Romans 15:4-13; Matthew 3:1-12
	B.	Isaiah 40:1-11; Psalm 85:1-2, 8-13; 2 Peter 3:8-15; Mark 1:1-8
	C.	Malachi 3:1-4; Luke 1:68-79; Philippians 1:3-11; Luke 3:1-6
Monday		Luke 1:18-20
Tuesday		Isaiah 40:27-31
Wednesday		Luke 1:5-20
Thursday		Luke 1:21-25
Friday		Romans 8:18-25
Saturday		Galatians 5:2-6

Prayer: thanksgiving, petition, intercession, praise, and offering

Reflection: silent (listening to God), written (journaling)

God's Promise
If you listen to my word I will answer you. I will not leave you in the darkness of doubt. Always I

am seeking to converse with you, but not always do you listen.

My Response
Speak your word to me, my Lord, your servant is listening. I yearn to hear your voice and to be transformed by you.

Readings for Reflection

❧ Zechariah was a deeply religious man, a man full of years and full of experience. He was a leader in the religious life of his community, and he was filled with a question that would not go away. Even an angelic visit did not calm his fears or answer his questions. "How can I know that God's promise is true for me?"

It is easy for us to make light of Zechariah's struggle, thinking it would be different for us. If an angel visited us, we would believe. If we had received such a direct promise from God, we would trust and rejoice. But the truth is we have received a much greater and more direct promise. We have the life, crucifixion, and resurrection of Jesus to confirm the promise of God's love and provision. We have the presence and power of the Holy Spirit to assure us the companionship of God and the power of God in everyday life. We have two thousand years of experience to remind us and assure us that God can be trusted and that God will provide. But the questions are not easily put to rest. What if I am wrong and give my life to the focus of my wishful thinking and not to the living God? What if I am listening to my own desire and not the voice of God as I seek direction for my life? What if God leads me astray and into a life that is too much for me?

Zechariah is not the only one who hears the nagging questions. We hear them too. How will I know God is guiding me? How will I know God will provide for me? How will I know that God will forgive me? How will I know God loves me as an individual?

How will I know? How will I know God? These are the nagging questions that lurk close in many of our lives, and to deny them is to give them power they do not have. To face the questions honestly and directly is to see them for what they are—a response of fear to our lack of faith. So what shall we do? Continue our life as Zechariah did—praying, serving, listening. And as we continue our disciplined listening for the voice of God, we will be called to remember that God does care for us and provide for us in wonderful ways, even when we are unaware of that provision.

After living with the questions, the apostle Paul said, "I am convinced that neither death, nor life, nor angels . . . , nor anything else in all creation, will be able to separate us from the love of God in Christ Jesus our Lord" (Rom. 8:38-39). The assurance that we are enfolded in the loving arms of God can still the nagging questions and grant us the grace, peace, and serenity to live all of life fully and faithfully every day. Grant us this blessed assurance today and always.
—Rueben P. Job

❧ The power of stories is that they are telling us that life adds up somehow, that life itself is like a story. And this grips us and fascinates us because of the feeling it gives us that if there is meaning in any life—in Hamlet's, in Mary's, in Christ's—then there is meaning also in our lives. And if this is true, it is of enormous significance in itself, and it makes us listen to the storyteller with great intensity because in this way all his stories are about us and because it is always possible that he may give us some clue as to what the meaning of our lives is.
—From *The Magnificent Defeat* by Frederick Buechner

❧ The Christmas contemplative knows that hope is a gift, an undeserved gift of peace, but that it is also a call to decision—the decision to trust. . . .

Hope thrives on the difficult and challenges the

conclusion that our only contribution to the world will be, in the words of T. S. Eliot, "an asphalt driveway in front of our home and a thousand lost golf balls." Hope convinces us that in clinging to a miserable sense of security and status quo, the possibility of growth and greatness is utterly defeated. Hope says that I no longer need be dismayed over my personal dishonesty and self-centeredness and feeble life of faith. That I no longer need to feel defeated, insensitive, and superficial.

Because the question no longer is: Can *I* do it? Am *I* able? Can *I* overcome my moodiness, my laziness, my sensuality, my grudges and resentments? The only question is: Is Jesus Christ able? Can my Savior, the Lord of my life, revive my drooping spirit and transform *me* at Christmas as he transformed the world through his birth in Bethlehem?

—From *Reflections for Ragamuffins* by Brennan Manning

❧ Ironic as it is, we are always shocked when we realize that we have little control over our lives or the lives of those around us. We thought we were in charge. After all, aren't we independent and self-sufficient? But serious illness throws a wrench into our illusion of control.

What should we do when we are in the midst of circumstances beyond our control? It is wise to realize that we are helpless, to assess our support and resources, and to act to seek the help we need. . . .

Certainly, illness is a wake-up call to rely on God. The wonderful thing is that even though the situation prodding us to rely on One greater than ourselves is terrible, it also bears the wonderful fruit of faith. All we need to do is ask God for help and then be alert to God's provision.

—From *Abiding Hope* by Ann Hagmann

❧ The resurrection does not solve our problems about dying and death. It is not the happy ending to our life's struggle, nor is it the big surprise that God has kept in

store for us. No, the resurrection is the expression of God's faithfulness to Jesus and to all God's children . . . . [It] is God's way of revealing to us that nothing that belongs to God will ever go to waste. What belongs to God will never get lost—not even our mortal bodies. The resurrection doesn't answer any of our curious questions about life after death, such as, How will it be? How will it look? But it does reveal to us that, indeed, love is stronger than death. After that revelation, we must remain silent, leave the whys, wheres, hows and whens behind, and simply trust.
—From *Our Greatest Gift* by Henri J. M. Nouwen

☙ Religious energy is in the dark questions, seldom in the answers. Answers are the way out. Answers are not what we are here for. When we look for answers, we're looking to change the pattern. When we look at the questions, we look for the opening to transformation.
—From *Everything Belongs* by Richard Rohr

☙ God tells Zechariah through an angel's visit that he and his wife will know the joy of having a child, but Elizabeth comes to that knowledge without an angel or a dream or any special sign to help her believe. She knows the incredible joy of having her disgrace wiped away, but she also experiences the added joy of recognizing that God is about to do something even more wonderful, and not just for her and Zechariah personally but for the whole world. She realizes that the Messiah is about to be born.

Elizabeth asks Mary, "Why has this happened to me, that the mother of my Lord comes to me?" Her question reflects the wonder of realizing that God comes to us individually. And that reality is remarkable. God could herd us all together like flocks of sheep and redeem us in groups. God could zap whole congregations and speed up the process of saving the world. But God wants relationship with each of us and so chooses to come to us one by one. . . .

Elizabeth is overwhelmed when she realizes that the mother of the Messiah has come to her personally. A righteous and blameless person, she finds that fact of being sought by God difficult to grasp and impossible to explain. We ordinary folks who intimately know ourselves to be less than righteous and less than blameless find it even more difficult to understand that God seeks us out and wants relationship with us! Because relationships are built one person at a time, God invests time and energy in each one of us, knowing each one of us is unique and infinitely valuable.

—From *While We Wait* by Mary Lou Redding

3: God's Revolutionary Purpose

Affirmation
I cry to God Most High,
    to God who fulfills his purpose for me.
He will send from heaven and save me (Ps. 57:2-3).

Petition
Be merciful to me, O God, be merciful to me,
    for in you my soul takes refuge . . .
    until the destroying storms pass by (Ps. 57:1).

Sacred Reading: anthology or other selected reading

Daily Scripture Readings

Sunday	A.	Isaiah 35:1-10; James 5:7-10; Psalm 146:5-10; Matthew 11:2-11
	B.	Isaiah 61:1-4, 8-11; Luke 1:47-55; 1 Thessalonians 5:16-24; John 1:6-8, 19-28
	C.	Zephaniah 3:14-20; Isaiah 12:2-6; Philippians 4:4-7; Luke 3:7-18
Monday		Luke 1:26-33
Tuesday		Job 33:29-33
Wednesday		1 Samuel 3:1-10
Thursday		1 Samuel 3:11-18
Friday		Mark 9:2-8
Saturday		John 10: 1-6

Prayer: thanksgiving, petition, intercession, praise, and offering

Reflection: silent (listening to God), written (journaling)

God's Promise
"I will never leave you or forsake you" (Heb. 13:5).

My Response
My heart is steadfast, O God,
   my heart is steadfast. . . .
For your steadfast love is as high as the heavens;
   your faithfulness extends to the clouds (Ps. 57:7-10).

Readings for Reflection

꙳ Mary's song of praise must have been a shock—
even to Elizabeth and surely to everyone else who
heard it. It bordered on treason and blasphemy and
must have left every adult who heard it angry, confused, embarrassed, surprised, curious, or frightened.
And it could be that all these feelings were swirling
around in the hearts and minds of those who heard
this message of radical revolution.

First of all, here she was a simple peasant girl,
announcing that God had chosen her for great responsibility, honor, and blessing. Only Elizabeth could hear
this song without a knowing smile, attributing all this
nonsense to teenage idealism. As a matter of fact,
Mary's declaration would likely have been dismissed
as teenage daydreams if it had not all come true!

And what about this prophecy that God would
bring down the rich and powerful and lift up the weak
and powerless? Where did she get this nonsense?
Again we might say it was youthful idealism, out of
touch with reality and an absolute absurdity in
our world. We could say that—if we didn't know
about Jesus and his proclamation and practice of
the same truth.

The final straw was the youthful confidence that
God can be trusted to keep promises. Where did a mere
child get the wisdom and the faith to bear witness to
God's trustworthiness so boldly? Perhaps from the
same God who dwelt within and spoke through the

voice and actions of Jesus. Jesus trusted God as loving Abba and taught and lived his faith in a God who was absolutely trustworthy. He not only taught people to receive God's love but also taught them how to trust, love, and obey this trustworthy God.

God's promise seems no less preposterous today. Turn the values of this world upside down? Rich become weak, poor become strong? Each of us is chosen to be God's special witness to God's promise of love and justice? It does seem like a preposterous promise, until we listen carefully to the Advent story, observe the life of Jesus, and listen to the Spirit's voice today. But then we see that the promise is for us. The responsibility to tell the story is ours. And yes, the blessing and honor come to all whose lives point to Jesus Christ and God's revolutionary purpose in the world.

—Rueben P. Job

❧ Paul Tournier, the great Christian doctor, declares that life, in order to be life, must necessarily be *dialogue*. No one can find life in any real sense of the term in isolation. He must find it in contact, in dialogue, with others. The supreme dialogue of life is the dialogue with God. Paul Tournier writes: 'Jesus Christ is the dialogue re-established. He is God coming to us because we cannot go to him.' Jesus came with the good news that God is not a God who hides himself, that God is not a God whom only the philosophers may know, that God is the God who at all costs desires to be known, and who in the most costly way has revealed himself to all.

—From *The Mind of Jesus* by William Barclay

❧ The story that Christianity tells, of course, claims to give more than just a clue, in fact to give no less than the very meaning of life itself and not just of some lives but of all our lives. And it goes a good deal further than that in claiming to give the meaning of God's life among men, this extraordinary tale it tells of the love between God and man, love conquered and love conquering, of long-lost love and love that sometimes looks like hate. And so, although in one sense the story Christianity tells is one that can be so simply told that we can get the whole thing really on a very small Christmas card or into the two crossed pieces of wood that form its symbol, in another sense it is so vast and complex that the whole Bible can only hint at it. Where does the story of God and man begin, for instance? Biblically speaking, you would have to say that it begins with Genesis and the picture we get of the Spirit of God brooding over the dark waters of chaos before the great "Let there be light!" of Creation sounded. But that amounts to saying that it has no beginning in time at all. Or where do we say that it ends? With the Crucifixion perhaps, where man brings the story to an end by killing God, or with nuclear war perhaps, where man brings it to an end by killing himself. But the answer to this is, "Behold, I create new heavens and a new earth!" and "He that believeth in me, though he were dead, yet shall he live," so the Christian story is beyond time altogether.

Yet it is also in time, the story of the love between God and man. There is a time when it begins, and therefore there is a time before it begins, when it is coming but not yet here, and this is the time Mary was in when Gabriel came to her. It is Advent: the time just before the adventure begins, when everybody is leaning forward to hear what will happen even though they already know what will happen and what will not happen, when they listen hard for meaning, their meaning, and begin to hear, only faintly at first, the beating of unseen wings.

—From *The Magnificent Defeat* by Frederick Buechner

᷍ The symbol of Christmas—what is it? It is the rainbow arched over the roof of the sky when the clouds are heavy with foreboding. It is the cry of life in the newborn babe when, forced from its mother's nest, it claims its right to live. It is the brooding Presence of the Eternal Spirit making crooked paths straight, rough places smooth, tired hearts refreshed, dead hopes stir with newness of life. It is the promise of tomorrow at the close of every day, the movement of life in defiance of death, and the assurance that love is sturdier than hate, that right is more confident than wrong, that good is more permanent than evil.

—From *The Mood of Christmas* by Howard Thurman

    ❦ So we see that heeding God's call can mean leaving home and all that is familiar. It can demand our accumulated wealth and security or dare us to place our blessings, even our lives, at risk. It can also mean simply living where we are but with an entirely new set of priorities. In every case, our particular vocation in God's service arises from our response to the basic call to radical availability.

—From *Companions in Christ: Participant's Book,* Part 4 by Gerrit Scott Dawson

    ❦ "Whoever does not receive the kingdom of God as a little child will never enter it" (Mark 10:15). The natural progression of life is from childhood to old age. On the contrary, the Kingdom of God within us goes from the age of an old man to the childhood of the spiritually renewed man. This calls for two yardsticks: during the natural course of life one grows in prudence, wisdom and responsibility; but in spiritual life one grows in childlikeness, simplicity, impulsiveness, joy, clarity and unity of purpose.

—From *The Desert Journal* by Carlo Carretto

    ❦ Knowing the stories of our faith, and how they connect with our own life experiences, means that we can celebrate the faithfulness and grace-bestowing love of God that was given to Abraham and Sarah, to the Israelites in Egypt and in the wilderness, and to the disciples. We can celebrate what is given to us as we join others in claiming God's promise and rejoicing in God's love as we gather at the Lord's table. We can celebrate what will be given to us and to all creation in times yet to come because God is faithful and God keeps God's promises.

We know who we are—children of God *loved* and *forgiven* and *called* by God! And we know Whose we are—children of God who are called to be witnesses to God's love and care for all the world. We are therefore able to share in the festivity that grows out of our shared stories and visions. Our *identity* as God's beloved sons and daughters causes us to seek ways to celebrate and repeatedly affirm that we are who we are!

—From *Rituals for Resurrection* by Linda J. Vogel

❧ The whole purpose for which we exist is to be thus taken into the life of God.
—From *Mere Christianity* by C. S. Lewis

❧ "Spiritual" is not just something we *ought* to be. It is something we *are* and cannot escape, regardless of how we may think or feel about it. It is our nature and our destiny.
—From *The Divine Conspiracy* by Dallas Willard

Fourth Sunday in Advent
Sunday between December 18 and December 24

4: I Am Yours

Affirmation
You are my God, and I will give thanks to you;
    you are my God, I will extol you (Ps. 118:28).

Petition
Teach me to do your will,
    for you are my God.
Let your good spirit lead me
    on a level path (Ps. 143:10).

Sacred Reading: anthology or other selected reading

Daily Scripture Readings

Sunday	A.	Isaiah 7:10-16; Psalm 80:1-7, 17-19; Romans 1:1-7; Matthew 1:18-25
	B.	2 Samuel 7:1-11, 16; Psalm 89:1-4, 19-26; Romans 16:25-27; Luke 1:26-38
	C.	Micah 5:2-5; Psalm 80:1-7; Hebrews 10:5-10; Luke 1:39-45
Monday		Luke 1:38
Tuesday		1 Samuel 3:1-14
Wednesday		1 Samuel 3:15-21
Thursday		Psalm 10:12-18
Friday		Matthew 9:9-13
Saturday		Acts 10:34-43

Prayer: thanksgiving, petition, intercession, praise, and offering

Reflection: silent (listening to God), written (journaling)

God's Promise
For [God] has said, "I will never leave you or forsake you." Jesus Christ is the same yesterday and today and forever (Heb. 13:5, 8).

My Response
Therefore, since we are receiving a kingdom that cannot be shaken, let us give thanks, by which we offer to God an acceptable worship with reverence and awe (Heb. 12:28).

Readings for Reflection

❧ So many of the entries in my journal end, "I am yours." It appears so often because that is the way I want to live my life every day. It is also there because I know how easily I am distracted to "belong" to something or someone else. I genuinely want to belong to God fully and without qualification. But living in our culture, we easily tend to brush aside that desire.

Mary made this incredible leap of faith and offered herself without qualification to God for whatever God chose to bring into her life. At the moment of this confession, recorded in Luke 1:38, she could not have known the magnitude of her decision. Yes, the angel messenger was clear in reporting God's desire for her, but it was still a huge step to say a willing and faithful yes to whatever God would choose. The risk to her reputation, the commitment of faith to an unknown path, the simple trust that God would provide today and tomorrow were not unlike the ingredients of our decision to offer ourselves to God without qualification.

In our better moments we know that it makes little difference what others may think of us. We know deep within our hearts that pleasing God is far more important than pleasing those around us. And yet risking our reputation for God is difficult for us. It is easy to remain silent and hidden when my colleagues make decisions based on the cultural norms rather than in the way of Christ. I don't like being called "too spiritual" or "unrealistic," and so I'm tempted to remain silent when I should speak a clear and simple word of faith. Yes, "I am yours." Help me to live that way.

We like to think we can know the future, and so we make plans, make investments, and seek to determine what the future will be. Planning, investing, and preparing are wonderful practices that we should incorporate in our lives. However, these practices should not dull our readiness to hear God's call to an unknown path and our readiness to say yes to that call. "I am yours." Lead me always in your path.

We know we are entirely dependent upon God, yet we forget and try to make our own provision for tomorrow or waste our energy in anxiety and fear that we will be forsaken when tomorrow comes. Mary was able to trust her life fully to the everlasting arms, sure that she would be upheld no matter what the future brought. "I am yours." Help me to remember you provided for me as a helpless baby; you provide for me now and will provide for me through eternal ages. Help me to live as one life totally given to you.
—Rueben P. Job

❧ "Our wills are ours to make them thine," an old prayer says. Mary, in response to the angel announcing that fearful but wonderful happening within her being, simply answered, "Let it be with me according to your word" (Luke 1:38). That was a yes with profound implications.

Such a letting go of security for simplicity of life can be desperately difficult. Jesus agonized before his crucifixion: "Not my will, but thine be done" (Luke 22:42). Had such circumstances been suddenly thrust upon him, it would have been hard enough. But he knew beforehand what could happen, and he willingly walked toward it, "setting his face toward Jerusalem."
—From *Faith, the Yes of the Heart* by Grace Adolphsen Brame

❧ No matter how often we sing them, the simple words and music of Phillips Brooks's "O Little Town of Bethlehem" transport us to that night in which the Christ child came to earth. Through a gentle, quiet tune and pictures made by words, we enter the time and place when God, transcendent and unfathomable, was born into human history—in a human way, in terms a human being could best understand.

As the carol proceeds, our words become a prayer. It is a prayer that asks for something incredible: that the miracle be reproduced, and that this time, the event not simply happen in history, but in us.

—From *Faith, the Yes of the Heart* by Grace Adolphsen Brame

❧ We are destined to be conformed to the image of Christ, who is himself "the image of the invisible God" (Col. 1:15); the divine image in which we were originally created is restored to us in Jesus Christ. But this process of being reshaped according to God's intended pattern takes time. It is the work of the Holy Spirit and is called sanctification in Christian theology. After turning our hearts back to God and receiving the justification that comes through faith in Christ, then begins the work of bringing our whole character in line with that of Christ. We begin to mature in knowledge, wisdom, and love. Our growth in the Spirit is marked by movements up and down, forward and backward, and sometimes even in circles! For human beings, the spiritual life is no straight line of unimpeded progress. It is, however, by God's unwavering goodness, always undergirded by grace. This is what gives us the hope and courage to persevere.

—From *Companions in Christ: Participant's Book,* Part 1 by Rueben P. Job and Marjorie J. Thompson

❧ If there are few contemplatives in our parishes it is because most are content to remain "conventional Christians." Conventional Christians secretly assure themselves that if they attend to the prescribed externals, go regularly to church, and don't go off the deep end, they are pleasing to God (although in fact they are pleasing mostly to themselves). Nonetheless, we *are* called to "go off the deep end" by abandoning ourselves to the Lord's care and to risk everything by letting go of everything. We are invited (though never demanded) to hang over an *interior abyss* in dark trusting faith where our security blanket of control is stripped away and we stand naked and defenseless before our Creator. Such is the essential nature of the contemplative/mystical experience.

—From *Why Not Be a Mystic?* by Frank X. Tuoti

  ✦ It requires a lot of inner solitude and silence to become aware of these divine movements. God does not shout, scream or push. The Spirit of God is soft and gentle like a small voice or a light breeze. It is the spirit of love. Maybe we still do not fully believe that God's Spirit is, indeed, the Spirit of love, always leading us deeper into love. Maybe we still distrust the Spirit, afraid to be led to places where our freedom is taken away. Maybe we still think of God's Spirit as an enemy who wants something of us that is not good for us.

But God is love, only love, and God's Spirit is the Spirit of love longing to guide us to the place where the deepest desires of our heart can be fulfilled. Often we ourselves do not even know what our deepest desire is. We so easily get entangled in our own lust and anger, mistakenly assuming that they tell us what we really want.

The Spirit of love says: "Don't be afraid to let go of your need to control your own life. Let me fulfill the true desire of your heart."

—From *Here and Now* by Henri J. M. Nouwen

  ✦ Advent creates new men and women. Look up, you whose eyes are fixed on this earth, you who are captivated by the events and changes on the surface of this earth. Look up, you who turned away from heaven to this ground because you had become disillusioned. Look up, you whose eyes are laden with tears, you who mourn the loss of all that the earth has snatched away. Look up, you who cannot lift up your eyes because you are so laden with guilt. "Look up, your redemption is drawing near."

Something different than you see daily, something more important, something infinitely greater and more powerful is taking place. Become aware of it, be on guard, wait a short while longer, wait and something new will overtake you! God will come, Jesus will take possession of you and you will be redeemed people!

Lift up your heads, you army of the afflicted, the humbled, the discouraged, you defeated army with bowed heads. The battle is not lost, the victory is yours—take courage, be strong! There is no room here for shaking your heads and doubting, because Christ is coming.

—From *A Testament to Freedom: The Essential Writings of Dietrich Bonhoeffer*

❧ *Becoming the Beloved means letting the truth of our Belovedness become enfleshed in everything we think, say or do.* It entails a long and painful process of appropriation or, better, incarnation. As long as "being the Beloved" is little more than a beautiful thought or a lofty idea that hangs above my life to keep me from becoming depressed, nothing really changes. What is required is to become the Beloved in the commonplaces of my daily existence and, bit by bit, to close the gap that exists between what I know myself to be and the countless specific realities of everyday life. Becoming the Beloved is pulling the truth revealed to me from above down into the ordinariness of what I am, in fact, thinking of, talking about and doing from hour to hour.

—From *Life of the Beloved* by Henri J. M. Nouwen

❧ God created us for a purpose more astonishing and sublime than we can imagine. Every great Christian theologian and saint has borne witness to this high purpose. The human being is created in the divine image and likeness in order to have continual and intimate communion with the One who made us. We are created to love and be loved by God, born to serve and be served by Christ, destined to enjoy the vitality of the Holy Spirit and in turn receive God's delight in us forever! Such is God's good pleasure and our highest bliss.

—From *The Way of Forgiveness: Participant's Book* by Marjorie J. Thompson

The Season of Christmas

Christmas holds the key to unlocking the deepest mysteries of our lives: Who are we, where did we come from, is there meaning to our lives, and where are we going? Granted, we focus at this time on the birth of Jesus, on the exchange of gifts, and the place of joy and triumph even when days are dark and foreboding. But the enormous truth of Christmas rests in the revelation of God's self to humankind. At last we can talk about God in terms we understand, human terms. Because of Jesus, we can make sense of our lives and understand more fully who we are and where we are going.

The writer of Colossians describes the scope of this revelation when he says, "He is the image of the invisible God . . . in him all the fullness of God was pleased to dwell, and through him God was pleased to reconcile to himself all things . . ." (Col. 1:15-20).

As we learn more about the created world, we understand the unknowability of a God who has authored a creation billions of light years in size and growing. Our minds cannot grasp the vastness, the energy and the complexity of such a creation, let alone the Creator who brought it into existence. Were we left with just the creation and the sacred texts, we might feel that God is distant, uncaring, and unapproachable.

When Jesus appears as revealer of this transcendent God, God becomes near, loving, and approachable. Now we know that God understands us and that we can begin to understand God. The birth of Jesus allows an experience of God with us and within us. While Moses was told not to look on the face of God (Exod. 33), Jesus said that we see God when we see Jesus (John 14). The great mystery of God unfolds in the birth, life, death, and resurrection of Jesus. Now we know who we are—God's beloved children; to whom we belong—our faithful redeemer; and where we are going in our journey of life—to a place prepared for us. Thus the Christmas story is such good news.

5: God Clothed in Human Flesh

Affirmation
Do not be afraid; for see—I am bringing you good news of great joy for all the people: to you is born this day in the city of David a Savior, who is the Messiah, the Lord (Luke 2:10-11).

Petition
Make me worthy, Lord, to serve you and all the world's people who live and die in loneliness, hunger, poverty, and sickness. Give them through my hands this day their daily bread, and by my love, give them peace and joy.

Sacred Reading: anthology or other selected reading

Daily Scripture Readings

Sunday	A.	Isaiah 9:2-7; Psalm 96; Titus 2:11-14; Luke 2:1-14
	B.	Isaiah 62:6-12; Psalm 97; Titus 3:4-7; Luke 2:8-20
	C.	Isaiah 52:7-10; Psalm 98; Hebrews 1:1-12; John 1:1-14
Monday		Luke 2:1-14
Tuesday		Isaiah 42:1-9
Wednesday		John 3:1-16
Thursday		John 1:29-34
Friday		Matthew 1:18-25
Saturday		Romans 1:1-7

Prayer: thanksgiving, petition, intercession, praise, and offering

Reflection: silent (listening to God), written (journaling)

God's Promise
Prepare the way of the Lord,
    make his paths straight.

Every valley shall be filled,
and every mountain and hill shall be made low,
and the crooked shall be made straight,
and the rough ways made smooth;
and all flesh shall see the salvation of God (Luke 3:4-6).

My Response
They set out; and there, ahead of them, went the star that they had seen at its rising, until it stopped over the place where the child was. When they saw that the star had stopped, they were overwhelmed with joy. On entering the house, they saw the child with Mary his mother; and they knelt down and paid him homage. Then, opening their treasure chests, they offered him gifts of gold, frankincense, and myrrh (Matt. 2:9-11).

Readings for Reflection

❧ New discoveries about our universe seem to emerge every day. Telescopes in space enable us to see into the created order farther and more clearly than ever before. But even with all of this marvelous technology we have not been able to chart the boundaries of creation. And even if we could, the idea of a created order many billions of light years in depth is too much for us to comprehend. So how can we comprehend the One whom we call Creator? Clearly, an infinite God has a communication problem with finite humankind. Christians find the answer to that problem in Jesus Christ. The mystery of this magnificent universe finds resolution in the mystery of the birth in Bethlehem. Jesus Christ came and was clothed in human flesh to let us know who God is and what God is really like. In Jesus Christ we see that God is approachable, and to a degree knowable by creatures like us. God can understand our condition because God has made us. We can know God because God has been revealed in Jesus Christ.

Colossians 1:15 and 16 say it so well. "He is the image of the invisible God, the firstborn of all creation; for in him all things in heaven and on earth were created, things visible and things invisible, whether thrones or dominions or rulers or powers—all things have been created through him and for him." In Jesus we have the perfect reflection of God. While the Creator of this vast universe may seem distant and unknowable, we can see, understand, and know Jesus of Nazareth. While it may seem too much to ask the Maker of the complex creation to hear us as we pray, we remember Jesus listened to everyone. So we, you and I, can know the One who knows us and we can communicate with the One who is author of all.

Our earthly existence takes on new meaning when we remember that God chose to put on our humanity and chose to wear that humanity as an ordinary working man. Our ordinary existence is not so ordinary when we remember that God chose this existence to give us a true picture of the divine. Therefore there are no unimportant moments in any lifetime. All are precious gifts of opportunity to know and serve the One who made us and chose to stand with us and like us in the gift of life.

—Rueben P. Job

When God comes among us there are always and only two possible consequences: judgment or salvation. There is judgment if we close our eyes to his coming or refuse to receive him. In that case, we are dependent on God's justice and mercy. Or there is salvation and healing if we welcome him with faith and trust.

—From *Forty Days with the Messiah* by David Winter

He looks like anything but a king. His face is prunish and red. His cry, though strong and healthy, is still the helpless and piercing cry of a baby. And he is absolutely dependent upon Mary for his well-being.

Majesty in the midst of the mundane. Holiness in the filth of sheep manure and sweat. Divinity entering the world on the floor of a stable, through the womb of a teenager and in the presence of a carpenter.

She touches the face of the infant-God. *How long was your journey!*

This baby had overlooked the universe. These rags keeping him warm were the robes of eternity. His golden throne room had been abandoned in favor of a dirty sheep pen. And worshiping angels had been replaced with kind but bewildered shepherds.

Meanwhile, the city hums. The merchants are unaware that God has visited their planet. The innkeeper would never believe that he had just sent God into the cold. And the people would scoff at anyone who told them the Messiah lay in the arms of a teenager on the outskirts of their village. They were all too busy to consider the possibility.

Those who missed His Majesty's arrival that night missed it not because of evil acts or malice; no, they missed it because they simply weren't looking.

Little has changed in the last two thousand years, has it?

—From *God Came Near* by Max Lucado

ᴥ Is there anyone in our midst who pretends to understand the awesome love in the heart of the Abba of Jesus that inspired, motivated, and brought about Christmas? . . .

God entered into our world not with the crushing impact of unbearable glory, but in the way of weakness, vulnerability, and need. On a wintry night in an obscure cave, the infant Jesus was a humble, naked, helpless God who allowed us to get close to him.

—From *Reflections for Ragamuffins* by Brennan Manning

ᴥ I wonder, if we were to stop people at random in the street on December 24th and ask them what they want most for Christmas, how many would say, "I want to see Jesus"?

I believe that the single most important consideration during the sacred season of Advent is *intensity of desire*. Paraphrasing the late Rabbi Abraham Heschel, "Jesus Christ is of no importance unless he is of supreme importance." An intense inner desire is already the sign of his presence in our hearts. The rest is the work of the Holy Spirit.

—From *Reflections for Ragamuffins* by Brennan Manning

❴ Meantime, "Blessed are your eyes, for they see: Many Prophets and righteous men have desired to see the things you see, and have not seen them; and to hear the things that you hear, and have not heard them." You see and acknowledge the day of your visitation; such a visitation; as neither you nor your fathers had known. You may well say, "This is the day which the Lord hath made; we will rejoice and be glad therein." You see the dawn of that glorious day whereof all the Prophets have spoken. And how shall you most effectually improve this day of your visitation?

The First point is, see that you yourselves receive not the blessing of God in vain. Begin at the root, if you have not already. Now repent, and believe the gospel. If you have believed, "look to yourselves, that ye lose not what you have wrought, but that ye receive a full reward." Stir up the gift of God that is in you. "Walk in the light, as he is in the light. And while you hold fast that which you have attained go on unto perfection." Yea, and when you are "made perfect in love," still, "forgetting the things that are behind, press on to the mark for the prize of the high calling of God in Christ Jesus."

—From "Sermon 66" by John Wesley

❴ Oscar Wilde says in his *De Profundis*, there is always room in an ignorant man's mind for a great idea. It is of profoundest significance to me that the Gospel story, particularly in the Book of Luke, reveals that the announcement of the birth of Jesus comes first to simple shepherds who were about their appointed tasks. After theology has done its work, after the reflective judgments of men from the heights and lonely retreats of privilege and security have wrought their perfect patterns, the birth of Jesus remains the symbol of the dignity and the inherent worthfulness of the common man.

Stripped bare of art forms and liturgy, the literal substance of the story remains, Jesus Christ was born in a stable, he was born of humble parentage in surroundings that are the common lot of those who earn their living by the sweat of their brows. Nothing can rob the common man of this heritage—when he beholds Jesus, he sees in him the possibilities of life even for the humblest and a dramatic resolution of the meaning of God.

If the theme of the angels' song is to find fulfillment in the world, it will be through the common man's becoming aware of his true worthfulness and asserting his generic prerogatives as a child of God. The diplomats, the politicians, the statesmen, the lords of business and religion will never bring peace in the world. Violence is the behavior pattern of Power in the modern world, and violence has it own etiquette and ritual, and its own morality.

—From *The Mood of Christmas* by Howard Thurman

❧ Are you willing to believe that love is the strongest thing in the world—stronger than hate, stronger than evil, stronger than death—and that the blessed life which began in Bethlehem nineteen hundred years ago is the image and brightness of the Eternal Love? Then you can keep Christmas.

And if you keep it for a day, why not always?

—From *The Spirit of Christmas* by Henry Van Dyke

❧ I have learned how to love with great love from a little child in Calcutta. Once, there was no sugar and I do not know how that little Hindu child four years old heard in the school that Mother Teresa had no sugar for her children.

He went home and told his parents, "I will not eat sugar for three days: I will give my sugar to Mother Teresa."

His parents had never been to our house before to give anything, but after three days they brought him. He was so small, and in his hand there was a little bottle of sugar. How much can a four-year-old child eat? But the amount he could have eaten for three days, he brought. He could scarcely pronounce my name, but yet he gave and the love he put in the giving was beautiful.

I learned from that little one that at the moment we give something to him, it becomes infinite!
—From *My Life for the Poor* by Mother Teresa

❧ Rich and moist, the grain fields of Moab were the first home of Ruth's tender roots. When transplanted to Bethlehem's soil, Ruth sought to put down roots in the grain fields of "the house of bread," where she hoped to glean. Embedded in Israelite soil, the tendrils of Ruth's roots sought and found the roots of the other female ancestors of "the Son of David" and bore the fruit of loving-kindness. Intertwined together but with separate identities, the roots of Tamar, Rahab, and Ruth were strong and vital. Life flowed upward through them to the broken branches of the family tree of Israel. The branches were restored and grew and flourished, until at last they came into full bloom in the wondrous birth of Jesus the Messiah.
—From *Mother Roots* by Helen Bruch Pearson

❧ From the wilderness comes a voice crying out: "Prepare the way of the Lord, make his paths straight" (Luke 3:4). On the road ahead someone is coming toward us, someone for whom we must prepare by undertaking massive new construction. Valleys of loss and despair are to be filled with new hope. Mountains of self-assigned virtue are to be replaced by humility. Crooked minds are to be straightened through repentance, broken bodies to be healed through compassion, and misshapen ideologies graded by truth. Yet even before we have begun this great work, the visitor is among us, knowing full well the meager measure of our capacities. Here is One who will freely labor with us and for us along the wilderness road so that, eventually, "all flesh shall see the salvation of God" (Luke 3:6).

But before this expansive vision can come to pass, the road must narrow drastically. It shrinks to the width of a virgin's womb; it conforms to the proportions of a worn manger; it follows the line of a jaw set toward Jerusalem. This road shares the dimensions of a rough beam thrust on abused shoulders. It fits within the space of a grave separating old and new creations; it tapers to the time between a decision to follow or not to follow; it narrows to the distance between the One who bids us come and the One who is the end of all our seeking.

The One who sets the course of this road, and whose entry into it defines the way forward, is the same who walks beside us, flesh of our flesh, God with us. Therefore, we can trust without reservation a journey whose future turns we cannot see.

—From "Editor's Introduction" by John S. Mogabgab in *Weavings* November/December 2001

6: Reading the Signs

Affirmation

The Jews then said to him, "What sign can you show us for doing this?" Jesus answered them, "Destroy this temple, and in three days I will raise it up." . . . After he was raised from the dead, his disciples remembered that he had said this; and they believed the scripture and the word that Jesus had spoken (John 2:18-19, 22).

Petition

As [Jesus] and his disciples and a large crowd were leaving Jericho, Bartimaeus son of Timaeus, a blind beggar, was sitting by the roadside. When he heard that it was Jesus of Nazareth, he began to shout out and say, "Jesus, Son of David, have mercy on me!" . . .Jesus stood still and said, "Call him here." And they called the blind man, saying to him, "Take heart; get up, he is calling you." So throwing off his cloak, he sprang up and came to Jesus. Then Jesus said to him, "What do you want me to do for you?" The blind man said to him, "My teacher, let me see again." Jesus said to him, "Go; your faith has made you well." Immediately he regained his sight and followed him on the way (Mark 10:46-47, 49-52).

Sacred Reading: anthology or other selected reading

Daily Scripture Readings

Sunday	A.	Jeremiah 31:7-14; Psalm 147:12-20; Ephesians 1:3-14; John 1:10-18
	B.	Jeremiah 31:7-14; Psalm 147:12-20; Ephesians 1:3-14; John 1:10-18
	C.	Jeremiah 31:7-14; Psalm

	147:12-20; Ephesians
	1:3-14; John 1:10-18
Monday	James 1:2-8
Tuesday	Isaiah 9:1-7
Wednesday	Matthew 16:1-4
Thursday	Acts 2:22-24
Friday	1 Kings 3:1-9
Saturday	Hebrews 5:11-14

Prayer: thanksgiving, petition, intercession, praise and offering

Reflection: silent (listening to God), written (journaling)

God's Promise
For surely I know the plans I have for you, says the LORD, plans for your welfare and not for harm, to give you a future with hope. Then when you call upon me and come and pray to me, I will hear you. When you search for me, you will find me; if you seek me with all your heart (Jer. 29:11-13).

My Response
Great is the LORD, and greatly to be praised;
    his greatness is unsearchable. . . .
On the glorious splendor of your majesty,
    and on your wondrous works, I will meditate
        (Ps. 145:3, 5).

Readings for Reflection

☙ As Christians we believe God seeks to speak to and guide those who are the object of God's creation and constant love. It seems inconceivable that God who has created humankind and called the church into being would not communicate with all that has been created. As Christians we believe that throughout the centuries God has sought to guide the church and each individual life.

History presents examples of humankind and the church horribly missing the mark of God's will. Times when God's will was not followed, and wars, schism, hatred, and racism infected the world. There are also some examples of wonderful times when individuals and when the church listened for, heard, and obeyed the voice of God in beautiful and healing ways. Perhaps the church and individuals usually have fallen somewhere between unqualified hearing and obedience to the voice of God and ignoring the voice of God as a result of being overpowered by voices of the world.

Finding God's voice in the midst of this noisy world is not easy. So many voices clamor for our attention, and so much noise tends to shield us from the voice of the One, who as Evelyn Underhill said, "has everything to tell us and nothing to learn from us." However, millions of people have learned how to "read the signs," that is, to observe how God has acted and is acting now, to listen attentively, and to receive knowledge and direction from a source greater than they are.

The foundation for reading the signs is the desire to know God's will and the confidence that God desires that we do know, understand, and obey God's will. For some, such a desire has become a way of life. That is, there are persons who habitually ask, "Lord, what is your will in this matter? In my life, in my church?" For such persons, discernment is a way of life and an unconscious process. They do not look for special times to listen for God's voice; they simply listen, trust, and obey. These persons see all experiences, ordinary and extraordinary, as conveying God's presence and message. When such persons read the Bible or the daily paper, they are aware of another Presence speaking and guiding. These individuals experience the ordinary events of life as filled with meaning and direction from God. For them, all of life is a conversation, a dialogue with the One who made them. For them, discernment is a way of life.

—Rueben P. Job

❧ To view reality from a slightly different perspective often yields a view of things totally unlike what they appeared to be. If we take just a couple of steps in another direction, what we view as reality is often profoundly changed.
—Norman Shawchuck

❧ "Then I saw a new heaven and a new earth; for the first heaven and the first earth had passed away, and the sea was no more. And I saw the holy city, the New Jerusalem, coming down out of heaven from God, prepared as a bride adorned for her husband. And I heard a loud voice from the throne saying, 'See, the home of God is among mortals. He will dwell with them as their God; and they will be his peoples, and God himself will be with them; he will wipe every tear from their eyes. Death will be no more; mourning and crying and pain will be no more, for the first things have passed away.' And the one who was seated on the throne said, 'See, I am making all things new.' Also he said, 'Write this, for these words are trustworthy and true'" (Rev. 21:1-5).

As it was in the past, so it is today: American churches give virtually no attention through their liturgies to the fact that January 1 is the beginning of a new civil year. Yet virtually every nation on earth gives a special significance to the day.

John Wesley, never known to miss an opportunity to gather people together for prayer and worship, attributed a special significance to covenant services, and he found the celebration of the new year to be an especially propitious time to invite people to renew their covenants/promises with God.

(For examples and additional resources for use in New Year's Eve or Day services, see Hoyt Hickman et al., *The New Handbook of the Christian Year* (Nashville, Tenn.: Abingdon Press, 1992, p. 78 ff.)
—Norman Shawchuck

இ These blessed people really are the light of the world! They may only be one insignificant candle, but they give light to the entire house. When people in a dark world see the work of these citizens of the kingdom, the people give glory to God because they know there is still hope for this world!

This is who we are called to be as citizens of the kingdom of God. We may be amazed or surprised— that is exactly the response Matthew intended! The Beatitudes are not placid statements spoken softly. They are exclamations. We step out into the morning sun after a foggy night and exclaim, "Wow! Look at that sunshine!" We hear a great piece of music and come away exclaiming, "Wow! That's really Beethoven!" The Beatitudes are similar exclamations. They exclaim "Wow! Look at the happiness of those who are citizens of the kingdom of God! This is really living; we just never saw it before!"
—From *What Will You Do with King Jesus?* by James A. Harnish

இ The pattern should be clear. When serenity comes up out of anxiety, joy out of depression, hope out of hopelessness; when good is returned for evil, forgiveness replaces retaliation, and courage triumphs over fear; then we recognize the movement of something beyond the personality and mental health. Such profound manifestations of the human spirit are the faces of the fourth dimension, which I have called the Holy.
—From *The Transforming Moment* by James E. Loder

இ Now as to the quiz, do the spirits that tempt you lead to "love, joy, peace, patience, kindness, generosity, faithfulness, gentleness, and self-control"? If you can answer yes, your spirits have passed Paul's test in Galatians (5:22) for good spirits proved by their fruits. The creative venture for your generation is to determine what love means for a nation; what joy is for our civilization; what the shape of peace is among factions of ancient animosity; how patience is found for the slow processes of justice; what constitutes kindness in helping the weak, poor, and oppressed; how government can be generous without patronizing; how people can be faithful to their traditions while responsive to changes; how gentleness orders might to combat wrong; and how nations, civilizations, societies, governments, armies, peoples, and factions as well as you yourselves individually can exercise self-control in the face of enormous insecurity and competition.

The study of God and ultimate things might not be to your special taste, but it is crucial for your generation's theological task. The practice of some religious path in order to gain spiritual depth might not appeal to you now, but it is necessary for the theological task of your generation. Without knowledge and depth I fear you will become intoxicated by the wrong spirits. So many of us are tipsy and only babble.

In the long run there are no more important questions for your generation than, Which is the true God? and What spirits are the divine ones? The importance of the questions is not for your personal piety, although that too is important in its way. The importance is for your generation's calling in public life. The new cultural beginnings we inevitably will be enacting, consciously or unwittingly, need to discern divine winds of creative origins and prophetic morality. The other spirits are more tempting but toxic. So may God's Spirit rush upon you like a mighty wind and dance with flaming tongues of light and power on your heads. God bless you all. Amen.

—From *The God Who Beckons* by Robert Cummings Neville

❧ What is of God's new reality and what is of the old, dying reality? As we seek conscious and living communion with God, how do we distinguish between God's activity and the many less than benign forces in the world? "He brought me out into a broad place; he delivered me, because he delighted in me" (2 Sam. 22:20). These words, voiced by David celebrating God's help in victory over enemies, offer dramatic images for understanding the mysterious work of discerning the spirits. . . .

True discernment calls us beyond the well-tended gardens of conventional religious wisdom to the margin between the known and the unknown, the domesticated and the wild. We incur risk any time we place ourselves in the presence of that which exists beyond our control. "Without the confidence of faith," comments St. Isaac of Nineveh, "no one will rashly let his [or her] soul go into the midst of terrible and difficult things." How crucial, then, that our efforts to sift and sort the forces shaping our spiritual life be undertaken with some bedrock assurances. King David provides one which cannot be surpassed. We are guided through narrow paths and led to spacious vistas because God delights in us. Deep in the layers of history, beneath the great upheavals of infidelity that reshape the landscape of our life with God, there abides a divine pleasure in the human creature. In the fullness of time this delight overflowed the bounds of worldly prudence and swept God into our very midst, one with us in suffering and hope. It is always in the gladsome company of this God that our discernment occurs.

—From "Editor's Introduction" by John S. Mogabgab
    in *Weavings* November/December 1995

❖ Spiritual discernment asks us to pay attention. We need to attend to both what goes on around us and within us. Ideally, this attentiveness goes on much of the time, a sort of low level, constant spiritual sifting of the data of our experience. But there are times when discernment becomes much more focused, when a crossroad is reached or a choice called for. At times like these the cumulative wisdom of tradition tells us to pay attention on many levels: to consult scripture, to seek the advice of trusted advisors, to heed the *sensus fidelium* (the collective sense of the faithful), to read widely and deeply the best ancient and contemporary thinking, to pray, to attend to the prick of conscience and to the yearnings and dreamings of our hearts, to watch, to wait, to listen.

—From "Passing Angels: The Arts of Spiritual Discernment" by Wendy M. Wright in *Weavings* November/December 1995

❧ The spiritual heritage of Christianity provides us with a number of theories and techniques of discernment. Ignatian discernment (originated by the sixteenth century Spaniard Ignatius of Loyola, founder of the Jesuits) stresses the discrimination of one's affectivity—how one feels. Put simply (although Ignatian discernment both in theory and practice is not simple), one is asked to pay attention to the "consolations" or "desolations" that result as one considers possibilities or undertakes actions. In general, and in the long term, for persons already embarked on a journey of faith, the Spirit of God presents itself as consoling, as peace and goodness. Spirits of other origins tend ultimately to give rise to experiences of confusion, disharmony, and anxiety.

In the seventeenth and eighteenth centuries, The Society of Friends, or Quakers, developed a mode of communal discernment, a listening in shared silence, to the "weight" or groundedness of various alternatives proposed for consideration. The silence of the Quaker meeting itself, in its gravity or depth, was discriminated and the hearing of such depth validated by the intuitive acknowledgment of those gathered.

The writings of a sixteenth century Carmelite mystic, John of the Cross, provide us with another alternative or complementary interpretation of discernment. A poet and spiritual theologian, John wrote of the desire of the human soul for its beloved, God. He described the process of this intense desiring as a gradual, ecstatic, painful process of stripping away all objects of desire and coming to know that it is only God, in God's unfathomable, unknowable mystery, where desire's end can be found. Desire propels one into intimacy with a love whose truest dynamics are death and resurrection. John often interprets the experience of inner suffering and pain that result from responding to divine desire as a sign that the spiritual purgation or emptying necessary for divine union is taking place.

—From "Passing Angels: The Arts of Spiritual Discernment" by Wendy M. Wright in *Weavings* November/December 1995

❧ Contemplation breaks us open to ourselves. The fruit of contemplation is self-knowledge, not self-justification. "The nearer we draw to God," Abba Mateos said, "the more we see ourselves as sinners." We see ourselves as we really are, and knowing ourselves we cannot condemn the other. We remember with a blush the public sin that made us mortal. We recognize with dismay the private sin that curls within us in fear of exposure. Then the whole world changes when we know ourselves. We gentle it. The fruit of self-knowledge is kindness. Broken ourselves, we bind tenderly the wounds of the other.

—From *Illuminated Life* by Joan Chittister

❧ Spiritual discernment has always come hard for me, so hard that I once concluded that I could not do it. After all, discernment is a spiritual *gift*—and I obviously had not been given that gift. I felt I could do nothing but shrug and trudge on. And trudge I did for long periods of my life. In one instance I spent almost a year trying to discern God's will on an important matter that would affect the rest of my life. During that year I felt the intense frustration of being dragged across the cutting edge of indecision. That was a long time to be in turmoil. It was tough. My only saving grace was that I would not commit to a decision until I felt that I had clear knowledge of God's will. I now realize that my reluctance to act was an important part of the discerning process instead of an absence of discernment at work in me. But not knowing that at the time made it a year of anguish. . . .

God wants *everyone* to know God's will. God doesn't withhold grace, play games, or tease us to test our faithfulness or our worthiness to be trusted with divine insight. I am convinced that God is far more prone to human revelation than I am to divine encounter. God's will is that you and I, everyone, and our faith communities should discern and act upon God's will.

—From *Yearning to Know God's Will* by Danny E. Morris

The Season of Epiphany:
First Season of Ordinary Time*

The Season of Epiphany is the first and shortest season of Ordinary Time, beginning January 12 and continuing through the Tuesday before Ash Wednesday. Ordinary Time then resumes again at the end of the Easter Season (on the Day of Pentecost) until the beginning of Advent on the fourth Sunday before Christmas.

Ordinary Time on the Christian calendar is not mundane at all, since this is the season of weekly celebrations of the Resurrection—celebrated by the Eucharist, the preaching, the worship, and the ministry of the church carried on seven days a week.

*For an excellent treatment of Ordinary and Extraordinary Time, see Laurence Hull Stookey, *Calendar: Christ's Time for the Church* (Nashville: Abingdon Press, 1996), 133–40.

The Season of Epiphany

Patiently a friend explained a depiction of the Lord's Supper crafted in wire and steel. I tried to see the message in this piece of art, but it seemed invisible to my eyes. Only as she traced the images with her finger was I able to see the beautiful and dramatic image of Jesus gathered at table with the disciples.

Epiphany is the day and season in the church year when we patiently watch and listen as God is quietly revealed before us once again. Sometimes, even when we try hard to do so, we just don't see God in our everyday lives or in the events of our world. Epiphany gives us the time and the resources to watch, wait, listen, look, and anticipate the light, life, and truth of the Lord's presence in our midst.

Contemporary observances of Epiphany include the coming of the wise men with gifts for the Christ child and the baptism of Jesus. The season concludes with Transfiguration Sunday. Epiphany is the time when the church gathers to remember and reflect upon the mighty acts of God in the birth of Jesus Christ. As we watch and wait in the light of Christ, we begin to see the unfolding drama of the Christ child becoming prophet, healer, teacher, and savior. Much of the story is still to be told, but already we are being reminded of the direction in which this one sacred life is moving. Here was life at its very purest and very best. Life that had come from God was walking with God and was going to God (John 13:3). This life "enlightens" us as we remember that we too have come from God, are invited to walk with God, and one day will be fully at home with God.

7: *Dangerous Journey*

Affirmation
I am God, . . .
> there is no one who can deliver from my hand;
> I work and who can hinder it? (Isa. 43:13).

Petition
Be merciful to me, O God, be merciful to me,
> for in you my soul takes refuge;
in the shadow of your wings I will take refuge,
> until the destroying storms pass by (Ps. 57:1).

Sacred Reading: anthology or other selected reading

Daily Scripture Readings

Sunday	A.	Isaiah 42:1-9; Psalm 29; Acts 10:34-43; Matthew 3:13-17
	B.	Genesis 1:1-5; Psalm 29; Acts 19:1-7; Mark 1:4-11
	C.	Isaiah 43:1-7; Psalm 29; Acts 8:14-17; Luke 3:15-17, 21-22
Monday		Matthew 2:13-18
Tuesday		John 1:1-13
Wednesday		John 1:35-42
Thursday		2 Corinthians 11:1-15
Friday		2 Corinthians 11:16-30
Saturday		Matthew 10:34-39

Prayer: thanksgiving, petition, intercession, praise and offering

Reflection: silent (listening to God), written (journaling)

God's Promise
Do not fear, for I have redeemed you;
> I have called you by name, you are mine.

When you pass through the waters, I will be with you;
>   and through the rivers, they shall not overwhelm
>   you;
when you walk through fire you shall not be burned,
>   and the flame shall not consume you.
For I am the LORD your God,
>   the Holy One of Israel, your Savior (Isa. 43:1-3).

My Response
My heart is steadfast, O God,
>   my heart is steadfast. I will sing and make
>   melody (Ps. 57:7).

Readings for Reflection

❧ The Christian life is seldom described as a danger-ous journey. We are reluctant to speak of the cost of seeking God and the danger of following Christ. It is so much easier and more appealing to speak of the rewards and benefits of the journey of faith. While we must never denigrate the incomparable gifts and rewards of a life of faith, we must also look straight in the eye the cost of every decision to seek God and to fol-low Jesus Christ.

Jesus experiences the marvelous embrace of God at his baptism. To hear the voice of the One who called all things into existence name Jesus the beloved is gift and reward without comparison. It is a wonderful moment of revelation and loving affirmation. How-ever, the story does not end there, for almost immedi-ately Jesus finds himself in the desert, alone and wrestling with the darkest and fiercest forces of evil.

The earliest of prophets and the saints of this mil-lennium have all discovered that the way of faith is not always the way of ease and comfort. Determining to follow Jesus often leads us into paths we would not choose for ourselves. To say yes to God's call requires saying no to our own voice and sometimes to the voices of persons and things we love.

For Jesus the call of God had the shadow of the cross upon it. Surely Jesus' sacrifice on the cross, made for us, makes our sacrifice on the cross unnecessary. Can we then expect to escape the shadow of the cross on our journey? Probably not. But we can pray for and receive guidance and strength that will take us safely and victoriously through the dangers and risks we encounter in saying yes to the call of God in our time.
—Rueben P. Job

❧ Religion has not tended to create seekers or searchers, has not tended to create honest humble people who trust that God is always beyond them. We aren't focused on the great mystery. Religion has, rather, tended to create people who think they have God in their pockets, people with quick, easy, glib answers. That's why so much of the West is understandably abandoning religion. People know the great mystery cannot be that simple and facile. If the great mystery is indeed the Great Mystery, it will lead us into paradox, into darkness, into journeys that never cease. . . . That is what prayer is about.
—From *Everything Belongs* by Richard Rohr

❧ My Lord God, I have no idea where I am going. I do not see the road ahead of me. I cannot know for certain where it will end. Nor do I really know myself, and the fact that I think I am following your will does not mean that I am actually doing so. But I believe that the desire to please you does in fact please you. And I hope I have that desire in all that I am doing. I hope that I will never do anything apart from that desire. And I know that if I do this you will lead me by the right road, though I may know nothing about it. Therefore I will trust you always though I may seem to be lost and in the shadow of death. I will not fear, for you are ever with me, and you will never leave me to face my perils alone.
—From *Thoughts in Solitude* by Thomas Merton

❧ So grave are the dangers that attend organized religion, so powerful and so subtle are the evils resulting from the accumulation of much property (an evil which overtakes almost every well organized church sooner or later), that unless we keep this point constantly fresh in our minds, we may be in danger of repeating the old mistakes.
—From *Power Through Constructive Thinking* by Emmet Fox

❧ To find in ourselves what makes life worth living is risky business, for it means that once we know we must seek it. It also means that without it life will be valueless. More than just a few find their most valued selves despite the risk, although the majority seem to be . . . people who don't wish to make any trouble—not even the kind that's expected. The majority shrewdly stay dull to what in them is life and has meaning. A few brave souls, however, do look within and are so moved by what they find that they sacrifice, from then on, whatever is necessary to bring that self into being.
—From *Ordinary People as Monks and Mystics* by Marsha Sinetar

❧ A strange life-giver, the Holy Spirit, for the life given is compassed about by desolation. The story of Jesus bears stark testimony to this unsettling truth. At the birth of Jesus the Spirit-guided words of Simeon prophesy desolation for Israel and for the heart of Mary as well (Luke 2:34-35). Immediately after his baptism, during which God calls Jesus "my Beloved," the Spirit drives him into the wilderness of isolation, vulnerability, and temptation (Mark 1:12-13). And at the end of a life exquisitely responsive to every subtle rhythm of the Spirit's leading, Jesus chokes out the unthinkable words, "My God, my God, why have you forsaken me?" (Matt. 27:46).

Christian tradition teaches that there are times when we, like Jesus, are led into arid soulscapes that bruise and disorient us. These places seem bereft of God's presence and filled with temptations to lose heart in God's goodness, care, and sovereignty. In this harsh "winter of abandonment" (Johannes Tauler), Jesus' anguished cry of desertion becomes our own. Desert and cross—places of excruciating separation from the God we have come to know but equally unbearable intimacy with the God we are yet to know, places barren of all human possibilities but pregnant with grace. "Lord," exclaims the scorned and ill young priest in a novel by Georges Bernanos, "I am stripped bare of all things, as you alone can strip us bare, whose fearful care nothing escapes, nor your terrible love." [We discover] the riches hidden in the poverty of desert and cross, symbols of God's "terrible love." In the "fearful care" of the Holy Spirit we are stripped bare but not left naked and exposed in desert wastes.

—From "Editor's Introduction" by John S. Mogabgab
   in *Weavings* September/October 1993

&♣ One of the dangers of spiritual growth is that too much emphasis can be placed on "results," on how we are doing or how we are progressing. When we catch ourselves being anxious about the results of our prayer or wonder if we are changing fast enough, it is time to go back and ponder Ephesians 3:20. This passage tells of God's power working through us and offers the assurance that this power is "able to accomplish abundantly far more than we can ask or imagine."

—From *The Cup of Our Life* by Joyce Rupp

&♣ Today I read Acts 17:1-32, and I was deeply impressed by Paul's ability to put his thoughts and ideas into the beliefs and faith-stance of his dubious listeners. The account of this event says, Paul "argued with them." Certainly this sermon was not a one-way communication—and it brought results.

When Paul "argued" in Thessalonica, some believed and joined sides with him. Others cast the city into an uproar and set out to do harm to Jason (Paul's host) when they could not find Paul.

Wherever Paul and the others went, people were divided—some accepted, some opposed Paul's preaching. Is this not better than what we see today? Virtually no preacher or teacher can cause a riot by reason of his or her preaching or teaching today; our words and our certainties are too banal and too bland.

When I consider my own teaching, I know I am safe. No one comes into my classroom without already being convinced. My students are "on my side" from the beginning. My only problem is to keep them awake and motivated to learn.

There are no stonings or riots in my classroom. What a pity!

—Norman Shawchuck

8: *The Wisdom of Seeking God*

Affirmation
If any of you is lacking in wisdom, ask God, who gives to all generously and ungrudgingly, and it will be given you. But ask in faith, never doubting, for the one who doubts is like a wave of the sea, driven and tossed by the wind (James 1:5-6).

Petition
Teach me to do your will,
    for you are my God.
Let your good spirit lead me
    on a level path (Ps. 143:10).

Sacred Reading: anthology or other selected reading

Daily Scripture Readings

Sunday	A.	Isaiah 49:1-7; Psalm 40:1-11; 1 Corinthians 1:1-9; John 1:29-42
	B.	1 Samuel 3:1-10; Psalm 139:1-6, 13-18; 1 Corinthians 6:12-20; John 1:43-51
	C.	Isaiah 62:1-5; Psalm 36:5-10; 1 Corinthians 12:1-11; John 2:1-11
Monday		Psalm 63:1-8
Tuesday		Jeremiah 29:10-14; Isaiah 55:1-9
Wednesday		Matthew 5:1-11
Thursday		John 8:12-20
Friday		Ephesians 1:15-23
Saturday		Luke 19:1-10

Prayer: thanksgiving, petition, intercession, praise and offering

Reflection: silent (listening to God), written (journaling)

God's Promise
I love those who love me,
   and those who seek me diligently find
      me (Prov. 8:17).

My Response
As a deer longs for flowing streams,
   so my soul longs for you, O God.
My soul thirsts for God,
   for the living God.
When shall I come and behold
   the face of God?
My tears have been my food
   day and night,
while people say to me continually,
   "Where is your God?" (Ps. 42:1-3).

Readings for Reflection

❧ "Why do you spend your money for that which is not bread, and your labor for that which does not satisfy?" (Isa. 55:2) How often in my seventy plus years have I disregarded Isaiah's admonition and sought, sometimes desperately, that which is not bread and does not satisfy. Seeking God first is not just good advice; it is the only way to a joyful and faithful life in companionship with the One who made us and loves us without limit.

When I saw my first airplane as a child, I knew at once that I wanted to fly. I became a farmer, student, pastor, husband, father and still wanted to fly. Throwing caution and common sense to the wind, I joined a flying club and soon was ready for my first solo flight. I will never forget the thrill of breaking the bonds of gravity. When the aircraft broke free from the ground and slowly climbed, I was bursting with the joy of realizing a dream I had nurtured for a lifetime.

Flying still holds a thrill for me, although I have not had the controls of an aircraft for over thirty-five years. When flying club members asked why I quit flying, I responded then, "I would rather fly than eat, but my children would rather eat." It is costly to fly! Several decades later, I realize something else was going on: a growing love and desire for God and a growing awareness of stewardship. I still look up when a light plane passes overhead and for a moment feel the sensations of flight, but then I rejoice in the companionship of the One with whom we can all break bonds holding us down and rise to heights greater than we imagine.
—Rueben P. Job

❧ Nothing is real without deriving its reality from God. This was the great discovery of St. Francis when he suddenly saw the whole world in God's hands and wondered why God didn't drop it. St. Augustine, St. Teresa of Avila, St. John Vianney, and all the saints are saints precisely because for them the order of being was turned around and they saw, felt, and—above all—knew with their heart that outside God nothing is, nothing breathes, nothing moves, and nothing lives.

This makes me aware that the basis of all ministry rests not in the moral life but in the mystical life. The issue is not to live as well as we can, but to let our life be one that finds its source in the Divine life.
—From ¡Gracias! by Henri J. M. Nouwen

❧ It is unlikely that we will deepen our relationship with God in a casual or haphazard manner. There will be a need for some intentional commitment and some reorganization in our own lives. But there is nothing that will enrich our lives more than a deeper and clearer perception of God's presence in the routine of daily living.
—From "Ways of Prayer: Designing a Personal Rule" by William O. Paulsell in *Weavings* September/October 1987

❧ Since the human soul is capable of receiving God alone, nothing less than God can fill it; which explains why lovers of earthly things are never satisfied. The peace known by lovers of Christ comes from their heart being fixed, in longing and in thought, in the love of God; it is a peace that sings and loves and burns and contemplates.

—From *The Fire of Love* by Richard Rolle

❧ Simplicity and regularity are the best guides in finding our way. They allow us to make the discipline of solitude as much a part of our daily lives as eating and sleeping. When that happens, our noisy worries will slowly lose their power over us and the renewing activity of God's Spirit will slowly make its presence known.

Although the discipline of solitude asks us to set aside time and space, what finally matters is that our hearts become like quiet cells where God can dwell, wherever we go and whatever we do.

—From *Making All Things New* by Henri J. M. Nouwen

❧ Daily personal prayer, examination of conscience, and participation in a faith-sharing group: these smaller practices can be of real benefit to us in sustaining the larger practice of saying yes to life, saying no to destruction. Together, they help us to understand, judge, and evaluate our daily choices and decisions in light of their relation to our ultimate happiness, as individuals and as humans in community. If we are to enhance and build up the capacities for a good, wholesome, and holy life, we must learn to say yes to what affirms and renews wholeness and life. And we must learn to say a related no to what induces and brings about destruction and ruin. In this practice, we are invited and challenged to make a fully conscious choice about who it is we are and who it is we shall become.

—From "Saying Yes and Saying No" by M. Shawn Copeland in *Practicing Our Faith*, ed. by Dorothy C. Bass

❧ [Jesus] has said: ask and you shall receive; seek and you will find. Unfortunately we ask for the ephemeral which isn't really satisfying. We seek what is passing and will leave us empty—until we come to realize in truth we do not know what we truly want, where our true happiness lies. We need to seek a teacher, a prophetic voice—the guidance of one whom the Lord has sent, the Church who makes Jesus present to us today, Jesus who is all that our hearts seek. Until we seek and find the Truth we will in fact be in a desert chasing mirages, encountering delusions, finding all swaying and unstable.

—From *Living in the Question* by M. Basil Pennington

❧ When I was a young child of eight years old, I lived on a beautiful farm. Like my other siblings, I had chores to do after school. Mine consisted of feeding the chickens and gathering the eggs. I didn't like doing this because my free spirit wanted to be out in the grove playing or down by the creek watching tadpoles and catching minnows.

But one day all of that changed for me. I learned that I had a secret companion who always kept me company, even when I was doing the daily farm chores. Hidden away deep within my heart was a loving being named God who would always love me and would never leave me. It was at this time that a wise teacher taught me about friendship with God. She assured me that I would never be alone because I was carrying the very life of God within me. I was enthused about this discovery. I could sense that "Someone" was there. I began carrying on endless conversations with this Friend. Walking home from school, doing my chores, playing in the grove—all of these activities became opportunities to be with my "special Someone." This was the beginning of my relationship with God.

As I grew older, I recognized this inner presence as a dynamic source of guidance and consolation. I became ever more deeply rooted in the belief that this indwelling God loves me totally and unconditionally. To this day, I draw comfort and courage from the belief that I am a container holding the presence of God. This awesome and humbling gift of the Divine Indwelling constantly enlivens my spiritual path and seeds my transformation.

—From *The Cup of Our Life* by Joyce Rupp

Third Sunday after Epiphany
Sunday between January 21 and 27

9: Saying Yes to God's Call

Affirmation
[God] has said, "I will never leave you or forsake you."
So we can say with confidence,
"The Lord is my helper;
    I will not be afraid.
What can anyone do to me?" (Heb. 13:5-6).

Petition
Give me the grace to make your Word my home, that
I know you more clearly and serve you more faithfully
ever more. Amen.

Sacred Reading: anthology or other selected reading

Daily Scripture Readings

Sunday	A.	Isaiah 9:1-4; Psalm 27:1, 4-9; 1 Corinthians 1:10-18; Matthew 4:12-23
	B.	Jonah 3:1-5, 10; Psalm 62:5-12; 1 Corinthians 7:29-31; Mark 1:14-20
	C.	Nehemiah 8:1-3, 5-6, 8-10; Psalm 19; 1 Corinthians 12:12-31; Luke 4:14-21
Monday		Exodus 3:1-12
Tuesday		Jeremiah 1:1-10
Wednesday		1 Samuel 3:1-18
Thursday		Acts 9:1-9
Friday		Acts 9:10-19
Saturday		John 13:1-11

Prayer: thanksgiving, petition, intercession, praise
and offering

Reflection: silent (listening to God), written (journaling)

God's Promise
It is the LORD who goes before you. He will be with you: he will not fail you or forsake you. Do not fear or be dismayed (Deut. 31:8).

My Response
I have heard your call, my Lord, and respond with a yes that arises from the depth of my being. I know that if I follow close to you, nothing shall be able to separate me from your love. Amen.

Readings for Reflection

❧ There was a light drizzle in the air as I walked along a darkening road, hands in my pockets, head down, thinking of a task I was to do and quite oblivious to the world around me. Suddenly a voice called my name. My head came up, I looked around, and there spotted a friend who was driving by and had stopped his car to greet me. We were several thousand miles from my home and a hundred miles from his. I suspect much of my life has been like that, preoccupied with personal issues and oblivious to the voice of God calling to me every day and in every circumstance.

The Bible and saints who have gone before us give ample evidence of God's consistent call to each of us. The Bible and the saints who have traveled this road before us also make clear the universal nature of God's call to all humankind. No one is left out, exempted, or overlooked. All are of equal worth and all are called. While we may think of certain vocations as callings, God appears to consider all of life as our calling, and that includes every honorable vocation.

Regularly practicing disciplines of the holy life puts us in position to hear God's call clearly. Those disciplines include prayer, fasting, community and personal worship, acts of mercy and compassion, and faithful living.

Hearing is an important step in saying yes to God's call. But once we hear, we must still decide whether we will go where invited or sent. In other words, hearing may be the easy part of saying yes to God's call. Once we have heard and counted the cost the most difficult task remains. However, with deep faith in the living God who calls us, the only reasonable response is to say yes. For in our best moments, we know God will ask us, only us, to say yes to an invitation that is right and good for us. Listen closely, think deeply, pray fervently, and you will be lead to the right answer to God's invitational call. In my experience the right answer is always yes. The good news is that even when I was unable to give the right answer, God was patient and gave me opportunity to grow in faith until I was able to say yes and to claim another part of my inheritance as a child of God.

—Rueben P. Job

❧ Every morning at 6:45 I go to the small convent of the Carmelite Sisters for an hour of prayer and meditation. I say "every morning," but there are exceptions. Fatigue, busyness, and preoccupations often serve as arguments for not going. Yet without this one hour a day for God, my life loses its coherency and I start experiencing my days as a series of random incidents and accidents.

My hour in the Carmelite chapel is more important than I can fully know myself. It is not an hour of deep prayer, nor a time in which I experience a special closeness to God; it is not a period of serious attentiveness to the divine mysteries. I wish it were! On the contrary, it is full of distractions, inner restlessness, sleepiness, confusion, and boredom. It seldom, if ever, pleases my senses. But the simple fact of being for one hour in the presence of the Lord and of showing him all that I feel, think, sense, and experience, without trying to hide anything, must please him.

—From ¡Gracias! by Henri J. M. Nouwen

❧ For God alone my soul in silence waits; from him comes my salvation (Ps. 62:1). Thousands of years ago, a devout person, tossed about by the storms of life, knelt down before God in the silence of the Jewish Temple. Only when this sacred silence had penetrated the depths of his soul was he able to say these words: "For God alone my soul in silence waits; from him comes my salvation." Oh, you ancient singer, you appear to us like an image from a pleasant dream that we long for, yet find so distant from us. We are attracted to you, but we no longer understand you. Teach us something about the silence of the soul, the soul that waits for God.
—From *Meditating on the Word* by Dietrich Bonhoeffer

❧ Sooner or later you will have to put God first in your life, that is to say, your own true spiritual development must become the only thing that really matters. It need not, perhaps had better not, be the only thing in your life, but it must be the first thing. When this happens you will find that you have got rid of a great deal of the unnecessary junk that most people carry about; mental junk, of course, although physical junk is very apt to follow upon this. You will find that you will do a great deal less running about after things that do not matter and only waste your time and energy, when once you have put God first. Your life will become simpler and quieter, but in the true sense, richer and infinitely more worth while.
—From *Power Through Constructive Thinking* by Emmet Fox

❧ According to Niebuhr, all persons are called to be Christian. There is no distinction between the minister and the lay person with respect to this call to personal faith. Those who are called to ministry have previously been called to personal faith in Christ.

This call may come in a variety of ways. For some, faith is the result of the Spirit's activity through nurturing families, loving Sunday school teachers, and faithful Christian witnesses. For others, the call to faith is more dramatic. They may be marginal church members or outside the church when they are confronted with the gospel of Christ. This confrontation and their response in faith result in a changed life.

—From *Pastoral Spirituality* by Ben Campbell Johnson

❧ Cheap grace is the preaching of forgiveness without requiring repentance, baptism without church discipline, communion without confession, absolution without personal confession. Cheap grace is grace without discipleship, grace without the cross, grace without Jesus Christ, living and incarnate.

Costly grace is the gospel which must be *sought* again and again, the gift which must be *asked* for, the door at which a person must *knock*.

Such grace is *costly* because it calls us to follow, and it is *grace* because it calls us to follow *Jesus Christ*. It is costly because it costs us our life, and it is grace because it gives us the only true life. It is costly because it condemns sin, and grace because it justifies the sinner. Above all, it is *costly* because it cost God the life of God's Son: "you were bought at a price," and what has cost God much cannot be cheap for us. Above all, it is *grace* because God did not reckon God's Son too dear a price to pay for our life, but delivered him up for us. Costly grace is the Incarnation of God.

Costly grace is the sanctuary of God; it has to be protected from the world, and not thrown to the dogs. It is therefore the living Word, the Word of God, which God speaks as it pleases God. Costly grace confronts us as a gracious call to follow Jesus, it comes as a word of forgiveness to the broken spirit and the contrite heart. Grace is costly because it compels a person to submit to the yoke of Christ and follow him; it is grace because Jesus says: "My yoke is easy and my burden is light."

—From *A Testament to Freedom: The Essential Writings of Dietrich Bonhoeffer*

❧ What distinguishes the Christians whose faith is deep, burning, powerful, and luminous is . . . *seriousness*. Seriousness is not the opposite of joy but of superficiality. Francis of Assisi was such a lighthearted, whimsical, musical, gentle man. But that was only part of his character. On the other side was the totally dedicated, unbending, relentless search for truth and reality. A Jesus-haunted man who gave up all to obtain all. His seriousness changed him from the wealthy son of a comfortable Umbrian home into the blind ragged beggar of Mount Alvernia. It was his seriousness about what he read in the Gospel that turned his life into what it was.

—From *Lion and Lamb* by Brennan Manning

❧ In every great religious tradition the concept is clear: To be contemplative we must become converted to the consciousness that makes us one with the universe, in tune with the cosmic voice of God. We must become aware of the sacred in every single element of life. We must bring beauty to birth in a poor and plastic world. We must restore the human community. We must grow in concert with the God who is within. We must be healers in a harsh society. We must become all those things that are the ground of contemplation, the fruits of contemplation, the end of contemplation.

The contemplative life is about becoming more contemplative all the time. It is about being in the world differently. What needs to be changed in us? Anything that makes us the sole center of ourselves. Anything that deludes us into thinking that we are not simply a work in progress, all of whose degrees, status, achievements, and power are no substitute for the wisdom that a world full of God everywhere, in everyone, has to teach us. Anything that drowns out the voice of the Ultimate within must be damped.

To become a contemplative, a daily schedule of religious events and practices is not enough. We must begin to do life, to be with people, to accept circumstances, to bring good to evil in ways that speak of the presence of God in every moment.

—From *Illuminated Life* by Joan Chittister

❧ So what am I supposed to do now? This question arises for many of us after we accept Christ's invitation to follow him in the journey of the spiritual life. After we have read the scriptures, meditated on them, and prayed, the new day stretches out before us. What do Christians do? . . .

Each of us has a unique combination of personality traits and gifts. When we are able to put into practice the design that God has put within us, we find high levels of energy, fulfillment, and purpose. Ideally, what we are to do as Christians is to live in loving service to God in the world, according to the way we were created. We share in the ministry of Jesus who gave himself completely to us.

—From *Companions in Christ: Participant's Book,* Part 4 by Gerrit Scott Dawson

❧ The Christian is proud to be a fool for Christ. Such a fool is obedient, yet free; under law, yet walking by grace; sinful, yet forgiven; unlovable, yet unconditionally loved; a believer, but with a healthy skepticism; certain, but only by making the ultimate gamble. The Christian claims that God is definitively revealed in Christ, yet is still the Hidden One; knows deeply, but in a cloud of unknowing; believes, but only by faith; and acknowledges that while all things have been made new, everything remains much the same.

—From *The Art of Spiritual Direction* by W. Paul Jones

❧ Even though we may not fully understand where this response will take us and even though some of us will resist, still God waits for our yes. . . .

When Mary said yes, she could not have known about the silent night of birth in a stable or the angelic hosts singing and praising God. Would she have known about the visit to the Temple with twelve-year-old Jesus? Could she have foreseen that her son would willingly place himself in harm's way for the sake of others? Would she have said yes if she had known about the betrayal of her son that would lead to his public scourging or his trip to Calvary and crucifixion? Mary only knew for certain that if she said yes to God, everything would change. And so it will be with our yes.

An old age may end and a new age begin with the yes we speak. In the places where we give birth to our holy imaginations, God may take root in our hearts. Impregnated by God's Holy Word, the wombs of radical hope may yet blossom and bless our efforts to build a world of justice and peace. Each time we say yes, the Holy Spirit overshadows us and something new comes to birth in us.

As Christians, our roots are intertwined with the female ancestors of Jesus and planted deep in the soil of his family tree. Tamar, Rahab, Ruth, Bathsheba, and Mary courageously disturbed the air around them. Heirs to their faithfulness, we are called to do the same when we answer yes. Perhaps not yet fully comprehending what our yes may mean, but in faith that surpasses our knowledge and trusting God with our very lives, may be boldly say with Mary: "Here am I, the servant of the LORD; let it be with me according to your word." So be it. Amen.

—From *Mother Roots* by Helen Bruch Pearson

Fourth Sunday after Epiphany
Sunday between January 28 and February 3
(If this is the last Sunday after Epiphany, use Week 15.)

10: Come and Rest Awhile

Affirmation
The beloved of the LORD rests in safety—
the High God surrounds him all day long—
> the beloved rests between his shoulders (Deut.
> 33:12).

Petition
Hear my cry, O God;
> listen to my prayer.
From the end of the earth I call to you,
> when my heart is faint.
Lead me to the rock
> that is higher than I;
for you are my refuge,
> a strong tower against the enemy.
Let me abide in your tent forever,
> find refuge under the shelter of your wings (Ps.
61:1-4).

Sacred Reading: anthology or other selected reading

Daily Scripture Readings
Sunday	A.	Micah 6:1-8; Psalm 15; 1 Corinthians 1:18-31; Matthew 5:1-12
	B.	Deuteronomy 18:15-20; Psalm 111; 1 Corinthians 8:1-13; Mark 1:21-28
	C.	Jeremiah 1:4-10; Psalm 71:1-6; 1 Corinthians 13:1-13; Luke 4:21-30
Monday		Jeremiah 6:1-16
Tuesday		Matthew 11:25-30
Wednesday		Psalm 116:1-7

Thursday	Isaiah 40:27-31
Friday	Mark 6:30-42
Saturday	Hebrews 4:1-11

Prayer: thanksgiving, petition, intercession, praise and offering

Reflection: silent (listening to God), written (journaling)

God's Promise
And you will have confidence, because there is hope;
    you will be protected and take your rest in safety.
You will lie down, and no one will make you afraid;
    many will entreat your favor (Job 11:18-19).

My Response
So then, a Sabbath rest still remains for the people of God; for those who enter God's rest also cease from their labors as God did from his. Let us therefore make every effort to enter that rest, so that no one may fall (Heb. 4:9-11).

Readings for Reflection

❧ Hunger and thirst for God are universal. We have been created to yearn for God, our true home. And the Bible reminds us that God yearns for relationship with us, our coming home to God. Why then does our hunger and thirst so often go unsatisfied? If God does indeed yearn for us and we yearn for God, why does my life often feel unattached and empty?

My mother insisted that my two brothers and I be at the table before anyone began to eat. She always called me in ample time so that I could be washed and ready when the meal was prepared. But more often than she liked, I was late because I was preoccupied with catching frogs in the nearby spring, filling my stomach with chokecherries from a nearby grove, or just not listening.

God's yearning for us is more intense than any mother's desire for her children, and our world offers more enticing distractions than frogs and chokecherries. So how do we bring God's yearning and our hunger and thirst together? Jesus is our best example. Even though his journey toward God was without blemish, he found it necessary to go aside to rest and to pray again and again. And in the midst of the great needs of the people around them, Jesus called the disciples to come away by themselves to rest. From that time of rest they were thrust back into the ministry of caring for the needs of the crowds that followed Jesus.

Decide today to establish a way of life that includes time for daily prayer, reflection, and regular worship in a congregation. Set aside a day every month when you will "come apart" to read, reflect, and pray in a leisurely and concentrated way. John Wesley was right: don't wait, begin today!

—Rueben P. Job

✤ The still dwelling upon God is the quietest but the most potent action of all.

—From *Power Through Constructive Thinking* by Emmet Fox

✤ Solitude is the furnace of transformation. Without solitude we remain victims of our society and continue to be entangled in the illusions of the false self. Jesus himself entered into this furnace. There he was tempted with the three compulsions of the world: to be relevant ("turn stones into loaves"), to be spectacular ("throw yourself down"), and to be powerful ("I will give you all these kingdoms"). There he affirmed God as the only source of his identity. ("You must worship the Lord your God and serve him alone.") Solitude is the place of the great struggle and the great encounter—the struggle against the compulsions of the false self, and the encounter with the loving God who offers himself as the substance of the new self. . . .

. . . Solitude is not a private therapeutic place. Rather, it is the place of conversion, the place where the old self dies and the new self is born, the place where the emergence of the new man and the new woman occurs.

—From *The Way of the Heart* by Henri J. M. Nouwen

❧ When you feel invited to remain in silence at our Lord's feet like Magdalen just *looking at Him* with *your heart*, without saying anything, don't cast about for any thoughts or reasonings but just remain in loving adoration. . . . if He invites you to beg, beg; if to be silent, remain silent; if to show your misery to God, just do so. Let Him play on the fibres of your heart like a harpist, and draw forth the melody He wishes.

—From *Union with God* by Dom Marmion

❧ Spirituality includes seeing our work as more than making a living (as important as that is); work becomes a genuine opportunity for service, a way of contributing to other people's lives. Spirituality is the responsibility we show our surroundings and our environment, the respect we have for our forests, mountains, rivers, lakes and seashores. It especially involves our attitude toward our everyday life, the way we spend our time. Are we merely wasting or killing time, or are we attempting to discover the sacred dimensions of life all around us?

In a basic sense spirituality is about the quality of our relationships, the ways we care for each other, including the ways we welcome those who are different from us into our lives and families. All the great spiritual traditions agree that spirituality encompasses all those dimensions of our lives that make us human; that is, not only prayer and worship, but our work, play, sexuality, gifts, talents, and limitations too.

Spirituality is influenced for the Christian in a most significant way by the person and ministry of Jesus; the Sacred Scriptures, which tell his story; and the life of the ongoing community that bears his name. Through Jesus we have been given an awareness that our time on this earth is sacred, that we share a sacred journey, that our God has entered human history and taken on a human face. Christian spirituality includes the many ways throughout history that Christian individuals and communities have responded and continue to respond to the awareness of God's transforming love.

—From *Mentoring* by Edward C. Sellner

⁂ There are two movements which must be plainly present in every complete spiritual life. The energy of its prayer must be directed on the one hand towards God; and on the other towards [people]. The first movement embraces the whole range of spiritual communion between the soul and God; in it we turn toward Divine Reality in adoration, bathing, so to speak, our souls in the Eternal Light. In the second we return, with the added peace and energy thus gained, to the natural world; there to do spiritual work for and with God for [others]. Thus prayer, like the whole of [the] inner life, "swings between the unseen and the seen." Now both these movements are of course necessary in all Christians; but the point is that the second will only be well done where the first has the central place. The deepening of the soul's unseen attachments must precede, in order that it may safeguard, the outward swing towards the world.

—From *Concerning the Inner Life* by Evelyn Underhill

⁂ One of the early Methodist preachers was "withering." He wrote to John Wesley about it, and Wesley's response has become a classic quote in our tradition: "O begin! Fix some part of every day for private exercises. You may acquire the taste which you have not: what is tedious at first will afterward be pleasant. Whether you like it or not, read and pray daily. It is for your life; there is no other way: else you will be a trifler all your days." Wesley's letter to John Trembath was not a legalistic requirement; it was sound spiritual guidance. It was the way to spiritual renewal. It still is.

Some of our predecessors had a phrase for it: "You have to be at the spout where the glory comes out." They meant that if we are going to actually drink of the Water of Life, we have to be at the places where it flows. Wesley's counsel to Trembath was ancient wisdom captured in a few words. Reading and praying daily comprise the two central acts of Christian devotion. While there are other means of grace and spiritual disciplines to make use of in our formation, these stand at the center regardless of which particular tradition you are part of.

—From *Prayer and Devotional Life of United Methodists* by Steve Harper

❧ Learning to listen within our hearts may not come easily. We muse, Does God call ordinary people like us? And if so, to what? How can we distinguish God's voice from all of the other voices that clamor at us— those of our culture, peer pressure, our careers, our egos? Amid our secular lives, where can we find support for our calls? And how can we remain faithful and accountable?

Christians have always struggled to understand what God would have them do. In 1835, Søren Kierkegaard wrote in his journal, What I really lack is to be clear in my mind *what I am to do, not* what I am to know. . . . The thing is to understand myself, to see what God really wishes *me* to do. . . . What good would it do me to be able to explain the meaning of Christianity if it had no deeper significance *for me and for my life?*"

—From *Listening Hearts* by Suzanne G. Farnham et al.

Fifth Sunday after Epiphany (Ordinary Time)
Sunday between February 4 and 10
(If this is the last Sunday after Epiphany, use Week 15.)

11: My Beloved

Affirmation
And just as he was coming up out of the water, he saw
the heavens torn apart and the Spirit descending like
a dove on him. And a voice came from heaven, "You
are my Son, the Beloved; with you I am well pleased"
(Mark 1:10-11).

Petition
O LORD, I have heard of your renown,
  and I stand in awe, O LORD, of your work.
In our own time revive it;
  in our own time make it known;
  in wrath may you remember mercy (Hab. 3:2).

Sacred Reading: anthology or other selected reading

Daily Scripture Readings

Sunday	A.	Isaiah 58:1-12; Psalm 112:1-10; 1 Corinthians 2:1-16; Matthew 5:13-20
	B.	Isaiah 40:21-31; Psalm 147:1-11; 1 Corinthians 9:16-23; Mark 1:29-39
	C.	Isaiah 6:1-13; Psalm 138; 1 Corinthians 15:1-11; Luke 5:1-11
Monday		Luke 3:21-22
Tuesday		2 Peter 1: 16-21
Wednesday		Psalm 18:1-6
Thursday		Psalm 18:17-19
Friday		1 John 3:1-3
Saturday		Psalm 127:1-2

Prayer: thanksgiving, petition, intercession, praise
and offering

Reflection: silent (listening to God), written (journaling)

God's Promise
As the Father has loved me, so I have loved you; abide in my love. If you keep my commandments, you will abide in my love, just as I have kept my Father's commandments and abide in his love. I have said these things to you so that my joy may be in you, and that your joy may be complete (John 15:9-11).

My Response
I love you, O LORD, my strength.
The LORD is my rock, my fortress, and my deliverer,
    my God, my rock in whom I take refuge,
       my shield, and the horn of my salvation, my
           stronghold (Ps. 18:1-2).

Readings for Reflection

❦ To hear God call our name awes us. To consider facing such an experience without trembling knees is unthinkable. To stand before the One, the author of all that exists, stretches our imaginations to the breaking point. Then to have that One speak our name transforms and changes life. Jesus, too, heard the voice from heaven saying what he already knew. He was God's beloved. What a wonderful message! To be the beloved child of the Creator. To know one is loved like that transforms and prepares us for anything. Perhaps that is why the Gospels tell us that Jesus left the baptismal service and God's affirming voice to go into the desert to be tempted by Satan. Jesus prevailed because he remembered the voice; he remembered who he was and who was with him.

    The biblical record clearly affirms the fact that God knows us and calls us by name as well. We are not strangers or aliens to God. We are each and all God's beloved. We have as our lover the Creator and Master of all that exists. The One who calls us beloved is also the one who knows us so intimately and well that even the number of hairs on our head is known.

To remember who creates us and recreates, who calls us again and again, who knows us completely, and who loves us unconditionally is to be prepared, as Jesus was, for all that is to come. We need have no fear of today or anxiety about tomorrow. We belong to God who claims us as beloved children and holds us close in the embrace of strength and love. Listen and remember today that God calls your name and be transformed and sustained in all that awaits you.

—Rueben P. Job

❧ Don't you often hope: "May this book, idea, course, trip, job, country or relationship fulfill my deepest desire." But as long as you are waiting for that mysterious moment you will go on running helter-skelter, always anxious and restless, always lustful and angry, never fully satisfied. You know that this is the compulsiveness that keeps us going and busy, but at the same time makes us wonder whether we are getting anywhere in the long run. This is the way to spiritual exhaustion and burn-out. This is the way to spiritual death.

Well, you and I don't have to kill ourselves. We are the Beloved. We are intimately loved long before our parents, teachers, spouses, children and friends loved or wounded us. That's the truth of our lives. That's the truth I want you to claim for yourself. That's the truth spoken by the voice that says, "You are my Beloved."

Listening to that voice with great inner attentiveness, I hear at my center words that say: "I have called you by name, from the very beginning. You are mine and I am yours. You are my Beloved, on you my favor rests. I have molded you in the depths of the earth and knitted you together in your mother's womb. I have carved you in the palms of my hands and hidden you in the shadow of my embrace. I look at you with infinite tenderness and care for you with a care more intimate than that of a mother for her child. I have counted every hair on your head and guided you at every step. Wherever you go, I go with you, and wherever you rest, I keep watch. I will give you food that will satisfy all your hunger and drink that will quench all your thirst. I will not hide my face from you. You know me as your own as I know you as my own. You belong to me. I am your father, your mother, your brother, your sister, your lover and your spouse . . . yes, even your child . . . wherever you are I will be. Nothing will ever separate us. We are one."

—From *Life of the Beloved* by Henri J. M. Nouwen

♣ Becoming the Beloved is the great spiritual journey we have to make. Augustine's words: "My soul is restless until it rests in you, O God," capture well this journey. l know that the fact that I am always searching for God, always struggling to discover the fullness of Love, always yearning for the complete truth, tells me that I have already been given a taste of God, of Love and of Truth. I can only look for something that I have, to some degree, already found. How can I search for beauty and truth unless that beauty and truth are already known to me in the depth of my heart? It seems that all of us human beings have deep inner memories of the paradise that we have lost. Maybe the word "innocence" is better than the word "paradise." We were innocent before we started feeling guilty; we were in the light before we entered into the darkness; we were at home before we started to search for a home. Deep in the recesses of our minds and hearts there lies hidden the treasure we seek. We know its preciousness, and we know that it holds the gift we most desire: a life stronger than death.

—From *Life of the Beloved* by Henri J. M. Nouwen

♣ One evening at sunset, as I sat by the Sea of Galilee, I was meditating on the Beatitudes, on the poor in spirit, those who mourn, the meek, those who hunger

and thirst for justice, the merciful, the pure in heart, the peacemakers, those who suffer for justice, on Jesus calling them "blessed" and saying "theirs is the kingdom of heaven." I felt drawn by the purity and simplicity of following Jesus, almost as if he found me there meditating and said, "Follow me." I was touched by joy then. It was the turning point. It was "the bread of the Coming One." It was a taste of heart's desire, I mean, a foretaste of Someone or Something still to come, an aftertaste of Someone or Something already come. I felt twenty centuries drop away between me and Jesus. I felt I was no longer a disciple at secondhand but a disciple at firsthand like Peter and John and Mary Magdalene. I thought again of the old man and his question, and I asked myself "Have you met Jesus?" and I found I could say "Yes!"
—From *The Homing Spirit* by John S. Dunne

* This enlargement of the human person cannot be achieved solely by our own efforts. Under our own steam, we cannot contain and bear the deep coincidence of opposites that we are. But they are borne within us when we give ourselves to God. For Henri, the Eucharist is the inspiration and source of all self-giving. The Eucharist carries us into and beyond ourselves so that we can give happily and gratefully even when our egos press upon us to hold back. The Eucharist, he often said, means thanksgiving, and thanksgiving means celebration. Without the Eucharist, we are preoccupied with personal survival, categorizing our experience into pleasure and pain, and doing whatever we can to extend our life-spans, to maximize pleasure. The communal eating of bread and wine is a celebration in which we realize that life and death are intertwined, that "fear and love, joy and sorrow, tears and smiles exist together. Life and death kiss each other at every moment of our existence."
—Robert A. Jonas from *Henri Nouwen: Writings Selected with an Introduction by Robert A. Jonas*

❧ The word "radical" means going to the root, getting down to essentials. People who get down to essentials and stay with them, no matter what the changes around them, are and remain radical. They are rooted in something that endures. The most radical element of our faith is the unconditional love of God. The more we internalize this truth, the greater the transformation that happens within us. Transformation has to do with freedom, freedom to live and love like Christ.
—From *Free to Pray, Free to Love* by Max Oliva, S.J.

❧ My way is all of trust and love, I don't understand souls who are afraid of so loving a Friend. Sometimes, when I read spiritual treatises, in which perfection is shown with a thousand obstacles in the way and a host of illusions round about it, my poor little mind grows very soon weary, I close the learned book, which leaves my head muddled and my heart parched, and I take the Holy Scripture. Then all seems luminous, a single word opens up infinite horizons to my soul, perfection seems easy; I see that it is enough to realize one's nothingness, and give ourself wholly, like a child, into the arms of the good God.

Leaving to great souls, great minds, the fine books I can't understand, I rejoice to be little because "only children, and those like them, will be admitted to the heavenly banquet." I am so happy that "in the kingdom of God there are many mansions," for if there were but the one, . . . I could not get in.
—From *Collected Letters: St Thérèse of Lisieux*

Sixth Sunday after Epiphany (Ordinary Time)
Sunday between February 11 and 17
(If this is the last Sunday after Epiphany, use Week 15.)

12: When All Our Systems Fail

Affirmation
Though the Lord may give you the bread of adversity
and the water of affliction, yet your Teacher will not
hide himself any more, but your eyes shall see your
Teacher. And when you turn to the right or when you
turn to the left, your ears shall hear a word behind you,
saying, "This is the way; walk in it" (Isa. 30:20-21).

Petition
O Lord, the night is so dark and my light so dim. Stay
with me through the dark night; bring me to a new and
brighter day.

Sacred Reading: anthology or other selected reading

Daily Scripture Readings

Sunday	A.	Deuteronomy 30:15-20; Psalm 119:1-8; 1 Corinthians 3:1-9; Matthew 5:21-37
	B.	2 Kings 5:1-14; Psalm 30; 1 Corinthians 9:24-27; Mark 1:40-45
	C.	Jeremiah 17:5-10; Psalm 1; 1 Corinthians 15:12-20; Luke 6:17-26
Monday		Mark 14:32-42
Tuesday		Ezekiel 37:1-6
Wednesday		Psalm 69:1-3
Thursday		Mark 15:25-32
Friday		Matthew 28:1-10
Saturday		James 1:12-18

Prayer: thanksgiving, petition, intercession, praise
and offering

Reflection: silent (listening to God), written (journaling)

God's Promise
Do not fear, for I am with you,
    do not be afraid, for I am your God;
I will strengthen you, I will help you,
        I will uphold you with my victorious right hand
            (Isa. 41:10).

My Response
Surely God is my salvation;
    I will trust, and will not be afraid,
for the LORD God is my strength and my might;
    he has become my salvation (Isa. 12:2).

Readings for Reflection

❧ His closest companions, those he trusted the most, could not keep awake with him for one hour. His hour of agony was lonely and hard. The cross loomed large and the resurrection still only a promise. The darkness of the night was superceded only by the darkness of the promise for tomorrow. This is where Jesus found himself in the garden of Gethsemane, praying his heart out to God the Father who he knew loved him but permitted him to be in this lonely valley of decision making without light or support. It appeared that all his systems of support had failed. It seemed that nothing worked and everything had failed.

Some would call the experience the dark night of the soul. Others would call it betrayal in the worst possible way. And those who have gone before tell us that if we live long enough, most of us will know what it is like to have our comfortable and trusted support systems evaporate like a morning fog. When they do, we are often left with empty hands, aching hearts, and troubled minds. Is it the end when all our systems fail? Or is it the mark of a new beginning? When we are the ones with empty hands, troubled hearts, and confused minds, it is hard to think of new beginnings. When the reality of brokenness and darkness is so pervasive, clinging to hope and light can be nearly impossible.

And yet if our feeble faith can reach out to the living God and remember a little of the two thousand years of Christian experience, we discover much that remains strong and sure even after all our systems have failed. Perhaps this is the time when, with anxious hearts and empty hands, we are ready to receive the presence and the power of the One who raised Jesus from the dead. The One who earlier had inspired Mary to say, "Here am I, the servant of the Lord; let it be with me according to your word" (Luke 1:38). The same One who brought Jesus from the tomb and called Lazarus to life seeks to bring new hope and life to us even when that seems an impossible feat, even for God.
—Rueben P. Job

ᣈ It should be the work of Christians who believe in the paschal mystery to help people when they are being led into the darkness and the void. The believer has to tell those in pain that this is not forever; there is a light and you will see it. This *isn't* all there is. Trust it. Don't try to rush through it. We can't leap over our grief work. Nor can we skip over our despair work. We have to feel it. That means that in our life we have some blue days or dark days. Historic cultures saw it as the time of incubation, transformation, and necessary hibernation. It becomes sacred space, and yet this is the very space we avoid. When we avoid darkness, we avoid tension, spiritual creativity, and finally transformation. We avoid God who works in the darkness--where *we* are not in control! Maybe that is the secret.
—From *Everything Belongs* by Richard Rohr

ᣈ When life is very difficult, people sometimes lay hold of resources that they never knew they had. The easy-going, self-centered exterior is cast off and a person of heroic stature emerges. Under pressure, false and foolish facades slip away. A new person emerges, or rather the one who has lain dormant these many years, tyrannized by an outward image bearing little resemblance to what was within. Suffering causes the mirror to crack. As the pieces fall away, we see what is hidden behind.

In the culture of the industrialized Western world, it is difficult to accept suffering. We are led to expect that it should not occur. If we lack acceptance or love of self-confidence, perhaps some consumer item will redeem the situation. Like some vast pharmacy, our technological society offers a remedy for almost every ailment. We come to believe it is not right to experience pain. We are encouraged to block it out, to forget our misery, to act "normally." Millions of people walk around pretending to be "normal."
—From *Toward God* by Michael Casey

❧ To be afraid is to have more faith in evil than in God.
—From *Power Through Constructive Thinking* by Emmet Fox

❧ Perhaps at first they talked of little things that spring evening. The upper room was dim with lamplight as Jesus sat with the twelve and remembered. Then quietly he said, "There is one here whose kiss will bring me betrayal by and by." They did not look at Judas, but each man murmured, "Master, is it I?" Each one looked inward, frightened, lest he find shifting sand where he had dreamed of rock. None placed the guilt on any other guest who had partaken of that gracious meal.

When hungry children dwell on my street, when I see tears or hear a heart's cry because someone failed to keep faith, may I too murmur, "Master, is it I?"
—Norman Shawchuck

❧ A beautiful illustration of the faith and love to be developed in the disciple is provided by the Old Testament figure Joseph. His story is found in Genesis

37–50. Out of a sense of blessedness that was with him from childhood, he remained completely faithful to God.

Attacked and sold into slavery by his envious brothers (37:18-36), then buried and forgotten for years in prison on false charges deriving precisely from his moral rectitude (39:7-23), he remained sure of the goodness of his own life before God. Later on, after becoming the governor of all of Egypt, he could say to his brothers concerning their betrayal of him, "You intended to do evil to me, but God meant for it to achieve good" (Gen. 50:20).

It is confidence in the invariably overriding intention of God for our good, with respect to all the evil and suffering that may befall us on life's journey, that secures us in peace and joy. We must be sure of that intention if we are to be free and able, like Joseph, to simply do what we know to be right.

—From *The Divine Conspiracy* by Dallas Willard

❧ You put me under the wing of a saint, and I have stayed there. You used his hands to bear me up, and the result has been grace upon grace. I asked for instruction in religion: he made me get down on my knees and make my confession and sent me straight away to Holy Communion. When I think of it, I cannot stop myself from crying: and I do not want to stop the tears running down for, O God, they are so justified. What streams of tears should flow from my eyes at the remembrance of so many mercies! How good you have been—how happy I am! What have I done to deserve it?

—From *Spiritual Autobiography of Charles de Foucauld* as reprinted in *Charles de Foucauld: Writings Selected with an Introduction by Robert Ellsberg*

❧ Defend me from all temptation, that I may ever accept the right and refuse the wrong. Defend me from myself, that in your care my weakness may not bring me to shame. May my lower nature never seize the upper hand.

Defend me from all that would seduce me, that in your power no tempting voice may cause me to listen, no tempting sight fascinate my eyes.

Defend me against the chances and changes of this life, not that I may escape them but that I may meet them with firm resolve; not that I may be saved from them but that I may come unscathed through them.

Defend me from discouragement in difficulty and from despair in failure, from pride in success, and from forgetting you in the day of prosperity.

Help me to remember that there is no time when you will fail me and no moment when I do not need you.

Grant me this desire: that guided by your light and defended by your grace, I may come in safety and bring honor to my journey's end by the defending work of Jesus Christ my Lord. May it always be so!
—Norman Shawchuck

Seventh Sunday after Epiphany (Ordinary Time)
Sunday between February 18 and 24
(If this is the last Sunday after Epiphany, use Week 15.)

13: The Temptation of Jesus

Affirmation
Because you have kept my word of patient endurance,
I will keep you from the hour of trial that is coming on
the whole world to test the inhabitants of the earth
(Rev. 3: 10).

Petition
My times are in your hand;
>　deliver me from the hand of my enemies and
>　　persecutors.
Let your face shine upon your servant;
>　save me in your steadfast love (Ps. 31:15-16).

Sacred Reading: anthology or other selected reading

Daily Scripture Readings

Sunday	A.	Leviticus 19:1-2, 9-18; Psalm 119:33-40; 1 Corinthians 3:10-11, 16-23; Matthew 5:38-48
	B.	Isaiah 43:18-25; Psalm 41; 2 Corinthians 1:18-22; Mark 2:1-12
	C.	Genesis 45:3-11, 15; Psalm 37:1-11, 39-40; 1 Corinthians 15:35-38, 42-50; Luke 6:27-38
Monday		Matthew 4:1-11
Tuesday		James 4:1-10
Wednesday		Psalm 91:1-16
Thursday		Luke 22:24-30
Friday		1 Corinthians 10:1-13
Saturday		Hebrews 4:14-16

Prayer: thanksgiving, petition, intercession, praise
and offering

Reflection: silent (listening to God), written (journaling)

God's Promise
No testing has overtaken you that is not common to everyone. God is faithful, and he will not let you be tested beyond your strength, but with the testing he will also provide the way out so that you may be able to endure it (1 Cor. 10:13).

My Response
My heart is steadfast, O God, my heart is steadfast; . . .
For your steadfast love is higher than the heavens,
 and your faithfulness reaches to the clouds
  (Ps. 57:7, 10).

Readings for Reflection

❧ Even in my seventh decade powerful temptation causes me to turn aside and think, speak and act contrary to what I believe and seek to practice. Why is temptation still with me after all these years of prayer and effort to live a life worthy of my baptism? The simple answer must be that I am tempted because I am alive. Temptation seems to be a part of life, and none of us escapes. Why should I be surprised by the subtle nibbling at my commitment or the outright onslaught on my integrity? Do I think myself better than Jesus?

Jesus rises from the water of baptism with God's affirming voice ringing in his ears. He witnesses assurance that he is God's beloved son. It can't get much better than that. But then immediately he is led into the wilderness (Matt. 4:1). There temptation in its most raw and appealing form confronts Jesus. We identify with each invitation the devil offers. We know our own hungers and we would like to feed the world. Who of us has escaped the desire just once to be noticed as a hero or at least to be able to fly? And many of us have thought if we just had a chance to manage the world, the church, or the community, all problems would be solved. The temptation to have just a little more of the world's goods, if not all we can see, always lurks close by, ready to pounce on our first interest in what others have accumulated.

The wilderness was a place to which Jesus was led, and few of us are led to escape it. Jesus left hungry but strengthened rather than diminished because he remembered his baptism. He remembered who he was. Matthew says that the moment Jesus rejected the devil's invitation, the angels came to wait upon him. Because I want temptation powerless to turn me away from God, I remember my baptism and reject the subtle and not-so-subtle invitations to turn from God.
—Rueben P. Job

&* Temptation is what distracts us, beguiles us or bullies us off the path. Temptation is what makes real life different from the world of our dreams. We dream a world which is wax under the moulding of our ambitions or of our aspirations; we meet a world which faces us with trials we have not the character to surmount, and with seductions we have not the virtue to resist.
—From *A Celebration of Faith* by Austin Farrer

&* We must not expect baptism to free us from the temptations of our persecutor. The body that concealed him made even the Word of God a target for the enemy; his assumption of a visible form made even the invisible light an object of attack. Nevertheless, since we have at hand the means of overcoming our enemy, we must have no fear of the struggle. Flaunt in his face the water and the Spirit. In them will be extinguished all the flaming darts of the evil one.

Suppose the tempter makes us feel the pinch of poverty, as he did even to Christ, and taking advantage of our hunger, talks of turning stones into bread: we must not be taken in by him, but let him learn what he has still not grasped. Refute him with the word of life, with the word that is the bread sent down from heaven and that gives life to the world.

He may try to ensnare us through our vanity, as he tried to ensnare Christ when he set him on the pinnacle of the temple and said: "Prove your divinity: throw yourself down." Let us beware of succumbing to pride, for the tempter will by no means stop at one success. He is never satisfied and is always pursuing us. Often he beguiles us with something good and useful, but its end is always evil. That is simply his method of waging war.

—From "Homily 40" by Gregory Nazianzen in *Journey with the Fathers, Year A*

❧ If the tempter tries to overthrow us through our greed, showing us at one glance all the kingdoms of the world—as if they belonged to him—and demanding that we fall down and worship him, we should despise him, for we know him to be a penniless impostor. Strong in our baptism, each of us can say: "I too am made in the image of God, but unlike you, I have not yet become an outcast from heaven through my pride. I have put on Christ; by my baptism I have become one with him. It is you that should fall prostrate before me." At these words he can only surrender and retire in shame; as he retreated before Christ, the light of the world, so will he depart from those illumined by that light. Such are the gifts conferred by baptism on those who understand its power; such the rich banquet it lays before those who hunger for the things of the Spirit.

—From "Homily 40" by Gregory Nazianzen in *Journey with the Fathers, Year A*

❧ We are living in a world that rejects love and that affirms selfishness as the ultimate value. The pressure from society is constantly insinuating itself through our upbringing, education, and culture. Society as a whole is saturated with the non-God.

First we have to affirm our interior freedom to be who we are or who we want to be in the face of all worldly enticements, including the worldly enticements associated with the spiritual journey. We bring the false self with us into the spiritual journey and into our relationship with God. Perhaps for many years our relationship with God might be termed co-dependent because we deal with God in the magical way that is characteristic of children. An important fruit of contemplative prayer is to be purified of our childish ideas about God. As our idea of God expands, there is no word, no way, no gesture, that can articulate it anymore. Hence we fall into silence, the place we should have been in the first place.

God's first language is silence. There is no word in the Trinity except the Eternal Word, and that one Word contains everything. As Saint John of the Cross writes: "It was said once, and said in absolute silence. And it is only in silence that we hear it."

—From *Intimacy with God* by Thomas Keating

➴ There is a danger in the contemplative life. The danger is that contemplation is often used to justify distance from the great questions of life. Contemplation becomes an excuse to let the world go to rot. It is a sad use of the contemplative life and, at base, a bogus one. If contemplation is coming to see the world as God sees the world, then see it clearly we must. If contemplation means to become immersed in the mind of God, then we must come to think beyond our own small agendas. If contemplation is taking on the heart of God in the heart of the world, then the contemplative, perhaps more than any other, weeps over the obliteration of the will of God in the heart of the universe.

—From *Illuminated Life* by Joan Chittister

➴ The pitfall of the religion of perfection is self-righteousness, that cancer of the soul that requires more of others than it demands of itself and so erodes its own fibre even more. It is an inner blindness that counts the sins of others but has no eye for itself. The self-righteous soul, the soul that preens on its own virtue, denies itself the self-knowledge that enables God to ignore what is lacking in us because our hearts are on the right way. It blocks the spirit of life from filling up the gaps within us that we ourselves are helpless to repair because the soul is not ready to receive.

Real contemplatives receive the other with the open arms of God because they have come to know that for all their emptiness God has received them.

—From *Illuminated Life* by Joan Chittister

❧ Like many, Luther's behavior did not always reflect his theology. Still, his discovery in scripture that people by God's grace can have a right relationship with God vastly changed his outlook on life. Having that fundamental relationship secured, he believed that a joyful and loving life would follow.

During a period in 1527 when he suffered from dizziness and from a disease occasioned both by high fever and physical weakness, Luther succumbed to a feeling of psychological abandonment. The prayers of his wife and friends sustained him in his despair. During this time he composed, "A Mighty Fortress Is Our God." A clue to his faith lay in his admission that "the prince of darkness grim" raged in his life. Luther surmounted these personally trying times with the assurance that he need not fear the devil's onslaughts because "one little Word shall fell him." That Word is Jesus Christ. The reformer survived his rough moments by naming and clinging to Jesus Christ.

—From *Spiritual Guides for the 21st Century* by K. James Stein

14: Denying Our Mortality

Affirmation

For I know that my Redeemer lives,
> and that at the last he will stand upon the earth;
and after my skin has been thus destroyed,
> then in my flesh I shall see God,
whom I shall see on my side,
> and my eyes shall behold, and not another (Job
> 19:25-27).

Petition

Hold me up, that I may be safe
> and have regard for your statutes continually
> (Ps. 119:117).

Sacred Reading: anthology or other selected reading

Daily Scripture Readings

Sunday	A.	Isaiah 49:8-16; Psalm 131; 1 Corinthians 4:1-5; Matthew 6:24-34
	B.	Hosea 2:14-20; Psalm 103:1-13, 22; 2 Corinthians 3:1-6; Mark 2:13-22
	C.	Isaiah 55:10-13; Psalm 92:1-4, 12-15; 1 Corinthians 15:51-58; Luke 6:39-49
Monday		Mark 8:31-38
Tuesday		Matthew 16:24-28
Wednesday		Luke 12:13-21
Thursday		Psalm 84:1-12
Friday		Matthew 16:21-23
Saturday		John 5:19-24

Prayer: thanksgiving, petition, intercession, praise and offering

Reflection: silent (listening to God), written (journaling)

God's Promise
Even to your old age I am he,
     even when you turn gray I will carry you.
I have made, and I will bear;
     I will carry and will save . . . (Isa. 46:4).
And everyone who lives and believes in me will never
die. Do you believe this? (John 11:26).

My Response
Even though I walk through the darkest valley,
     I fear no evil;
for you are with me;
     your rod and your staff—they comfort me
          (Ps. 23:4).

Readings for Reflection

❧ Many of us spend a lifetime denying our mortality. Our culture gives us more than enough help in this effort, an effort that so often keeps us at least one step away from fully trusting in God's desire or ability to provide for us. Even the church has helped us in our denial. So rarely do we hear teaching or preaching that fully celebrates the glorious gift of life and honestly reminds us that birth and death are each a necessary and irreplaceable part of life.

Peter did not want Jesus to die, and he could not remain silent when Jesus reminded him that death waited in Jerusalem. Peter did not yet fully understand that life was larger than this world and relationship with God was life-giving and unending. We are like him in that we do not want to face the reality of death. Perhaps he understood that reality a little better after the resurrection. Perhaps we do too, but we so easily forget that life in God is eternal and our passing from this world to the next does not conclude our existence.

I have watched many autumns come on the heels of summer and leave with the tug of winter. Each one reminds me of my mortality and of the promise of resurrection. When autumn comes, the farmers are busy gathering the harvest and storing its richness for the long winter ahead. But before the last kernel is put away, the true farmer is already planning for spring planting and the new life it promises. We are mortal. We are born and we shall all die. The person who is in communion with God wears mortality comfortably. To be with God is to be at home in this world and the next.

—Rueben P. Job

≈ How then can a lifetime be described in the language of absolute truth? . . . It seems to me that it is a good thing to have constantly in mind the shortness of our life on earth.

—From *The Way* by a Priest

≈ The fact that I believe God will enfold me when I die and that the pattern . . . will be recreated in another dimension does not alter the fact that I have had a good life which I shall be sorry to leave. I console myself with the knowledge that in every ending there is a new beginning, and that out of death comes redemption, resurrection and renewal.

—From *Absolute Truths* by Susan Howatch

≈ We die; indeed we have to die in order to be resurrected, restored and renewed. We die and we die and we die in this life, not only physically—within seven years every cell in our body is renewed—but emotionally and spiritually as change seizes us by the scruff of the neck and drags us forward into another life. We are not here simply to exist. We are here in order to become. It is the essence of the creative process; it is in the deepest nature of things.

—From *Absolute Truths* by Susan Howatch

❧ Jesus has gone before us. In the words of John 13:1, he has made the crossing from this world toward the Father and summons us to come after him. We will do this definitively when, at the hour of our death, we will have to summon up whatever resources we have in order to cast ourselves into the arms of God. We need to remember, however, that the quality of this supremely personal act is not manufactured at the last moment. It is the fruit of countless small choices made from infancy onward which have given shape to our will. To the extent that our decisions have centered on feeding self we will find it very hard to change course in that awesome hour. On the other hand, if life and providence have taught us to reach beyond self to other persons and to God, then the grace of God will empower us to follow Christ and so enter into glory.

The ultimate truth of human life is that all our searching leads to God. In Saint Augustine's timeless words, "You have made us for yourself [O God] and our hearts are restless until they rest in you." This is something we know about every human being. He or she is made for God; there will always be an incompleteness until a person arrives at God.
—From *Toward God* by Michael Casey

❧ Holding my father's hands as his life slipped away, I realized that these were the hands that had held my newborn life and felt the pulse of my heart at birth. There is a time when hearts begin to beat, and there is a time when they stop. So begins and ends our allotted time on earth.

The mystery of death is intimately connected to the miracle of birth. Each is a gift. Each is part of the same continuum. One cannot embrace one without taking hold of the other.

My father had learned this lesson long ago. Death was never a stranger to his life: his entrance into adulthood began with the death of his father. Death introduced him to obligations—his duty to care for his mother and siblings, his responsibility to manage the family farm—that lasted a lifetime. His years were marked with other deaths as well: the death of his mother, the failure of crops and businesses, the death of livestock and horses.

But for every death there was also a birth. My father witnessed birth each year as the seeds he had sown burst into green and growing life. He rejoiced at the new life that came with the birth of his children. He saw his efforts as a father give birth to confident and responsible adults.

My father embraced it all—birth, death, and everything that came between. And he died as he had lived, with quiet faith in a loving God who had promised to lead him "beside still waters" and restore his soul.
—From *Unspoken Wisdom* by Ray S. Anderson

❧ And if we trust what Jesus said out of his own direct consciousness of God we shall share his belief in the future life. This belief is supported by the reasoning that a God of infinite love would not create finite persons and then drop them out of existence when the potentialities of their nature, including their awareness of [God], have only just begun to be realized.
—From *The Center of Christianity* by John Hick

❧ Death stood at the door. This dear old man hovered in the valley of the shadow. I had been called to his bedside by the family to be present for his final hours. His sister-in-law, who had kept a constant vigil of love, told me he had made a death wish some months ago. "As I get near the end," he had said, "I have my doubts about many things in life. But I hope I can leave this earth with dignity . . . my faith in God is stronger than ever."

She showed me a picture of him from earlier years. He seemed so vibrant and full of life then, and now so forlorn and hopeless, gasping for that final breath. Then he was gone. I held his hand until his hold ended, almost symbolic of giving up and letting go. But he died in dignity. No respirator kept him from his date with destiny or his meeting with the God he loved. There was the sadness of farewell, but also gratitude that his wish had been granted.

We all proceed every day to our final destiny. If we are wise, we will accept its finality with gratitude; if we are sensible we prepare for it now. If we are blessed, we will depart, as Simeon prayed, in peace . . . and dignity.

—From *Autumn Wisdom* by Richard L. Morgan

15: Listening to God

Affirmation

And all of us, with unveiled faces, seeing the glory of the Lord as though reflected in a mirror, are being transformed into the same image from one degree of glory to another; for this comes from the Lord, the Spirit (2 Cor. 3:18).

Petition

But someone has testified somewhere,
> "What are human beings that you are mindful of them,
> or mortals, that you care for them?" (Heb. 2:6).

Sacred Reading: anthology or other selected reading

Daily Scripture Readings

Sunday	A.	Exodus 24:12-18; Psalm 2; 2 Peter 1:16-21; Matthew 17:1-9
	B.	2 Kings 2:1-12; Psalm 50:1-6; 2 Corinthians 4:3-6; Mark 9:2-9
	C.	Exodus 34:29-35; Psalm 99; 2 Corinthians 3:12–4:2; Luke 9:28-36
Monday		Matthew 17:1-8
Tuesday		Isaiah 42:1-9
Wednesday		Romans 12:1-2
Thursday		Romans 12:9-13
Friday		Romans 12:14-21
Saturday		Colossians 3:12-17

Prayer: thanksgiving, petition, intercession, praise and offering

Reflection: silent (listening to God), written (journaling)

God's Promise
I am the resurrection and the life. Those who believe in me, even though they die, will live, and everyone who lives and believes in me will never die. Do you believe this? (John 11:25-26).

My Response
Listen, I will tell you a mystery! We will not all die, but we will all be changed, in a moment, in the twinkling of an eye, at the last trumpet. For the trumpet will sound, and the dead will be raised imperishable, and we will be changed (1 Cor. 15:51-52).

Readings for Reflection

❧ What does the voice of God sound like? The voice from heaven reported in Matthew 17:1-8 suggests that when we listen to Jesus, we hear the voice of God. The voice the disciples heard was understandable and it directed them to listen to Jesus, the beloved son. It is not that difficult to read the words of Jesus. To listen to and obey those words is more demanding.

As Christians we share the good news that God can be heard, understood, and obeyed. We have scriptures, nature, history, and the stories of our lives that speak God's truth. Further we have the capacity to "hear" God's voice deep within our own souls. Through the centuries faithful listeners have discovered ways to sharpen their listening skills. Practices and disciplines increase our desire and capacity to be faithful to what we hear and know to be the voice of God. John Wesley called these practices means of grace, that is, practices that mediate God's love, will, presence, and power in very special ways.

A complete list of the means of grace likely includes all things. A God for whom all things are possible may use any and all things to address us. And yet it seems most often the voice and message of God are heard and the presence and power of God are felt when people quietly, fervently, and faithfully pray, worship, witness, and serve humankind. Do you want to hear God speak to you? Polish up your practices of prayer, worship, witness, and service, and you will be amazed at what you hear.

—Rueben P. Job

❧ We do not come to be with Jesus because we are righteous or strong. The people gathered around Jesus because they were needy. In his sermon Jesus begins to explain the profound difference between the religious leaders' teaching about attaining righteousness through their interpretation of the Law and traditions and the greater righteousness that moves beyond the Law to a relationship with God in Jesus Christ.

Our sinful, restricted self is uncomfortable and fights being revealed. But deeper within us is the longing for God, placed within our true self by God. We come to God as we are: caught by sin and longing for God; and we are always met by God's grace and mercy.

—From *Learning to Listen* by Wendy Miller

❧ Much of our world's noise and activity seems designed to silence the hungers and longings of our heart. Maybe we are unaware of these deep, inner hungers. They are there, but perhaps no one has encouraged us to pay attention. Jesus speaks to the hungers of our heart, to our inner longings.

If we listen to Jesus, we will discover that these longings are the doorways through which we come to God and through which God comes to us. Jesus says that the people with these longings are "blessed"— are welcomed into God's family, are brought into God's kind and gracious presence, are connected to one another.

—From *Learning to Listen* by Wendy Miller

❧ The Word of God is always sacramental. In the book of Genesis we are told that God created the world, but in Hebrew the words for "speaking" and for "creating" are the same word. Literally translated it says, "God spoke light and light was." For God, speaking is creating. When we say that God's word is sacred, we mean that God's word is full of God's presence. On the road to Emmaus, Jesus became present through his word, and it was that presence that transformed sadness to joy and mourning to dancing. This is what happens in every Eucharist. The word that is read and spoken wants to lead us into God's presence and transform our hearts and minds. Often we think about the word as an exhortation to go out and change our lives. But the full power of the word lies, not in how we apply it to our lives after we have heard it, but in its transforming power that does its divine work as we listen.

—From *With Burning Hearts* by Henri J. M. Nouwen

❧ The Word of God is not a word to apply in our daily lives at some later date; it is a word to heal us through, and in, our listening here and now.

The questions therefore are: How does God come to me as I listen to the word? Where do I discern the healing hand of God touching me through the word? How are my sadness, my grief, and my mourning being transformed at this very moment? Do I sense the fire of God's love purifying my heart and giving me new life? These questions lead me to the sacrament of the word, the sacred place of God's real presence.

—From *With Burning Hearts* by Henri J. M. Nouwen

❧ There are few things that help so much for conversing with Christ as silence. The silence I speak of is, obviously, the inner silence of the heart without which the voice of Christ will simply not be heard. This inner silence is very hard to achieve for most of us: close your eyes for a moment and observe what is going on within you. The chances are you will be submerged in a sea of thoughts that you are powerless to stop—talk, talk, talk (for that is what thinking generally is, me talking to myself)—noise, noise, noise: my own inner voice competing with the remembered voices and images of others, all clamoring for my attention. What chances does the subtle voice of God stand in all this din and bustle? . . .

Your tolerance of silence is a fairly good indicator of your spiritual (and even intellectual and emotional) depth.

—From *Contact with God* by Anthony de Mello

  ❧ Read quietly, slowly, word for word to enter into the subject more with the heart than the mind. . . . From time to time make short pauses to allow these truths time to flow through all the recesses of the soul and to give occasion for the operation of the Holy Spirit who, during these peaceful pauses and times of silent attention, engraves and imprints these heavenly truths in the heart . . . . Should this peace and rest last for a longer time it will be all the better. When you find that your mind wanders resume your reading and continue thus, frequently renewing these same pauses.

—From *The Sacrament of the Present Moment* by Jean-Pierre de Caussade

  ❧ The *how* of the role of scripture in spiritual formation is not so much a body of information, a technique, a method, a model, as it is a mode of being in relationship with God that we bring to the scripture. . . .

I suggest that your top priority be to listen for God. Seek to allow your attention and focus to be on listening for what God is saying to you as you read . . . . Listen for God to speak to you in and through, around and within, over and behind and out front of everything that you read. Keep asking yourself, "What is God seeking to say to me in all of this?" By adopting this posture toward the text you will begin the process of reversing the learning mode that establishes *you* as the controlling power who seeks to master a body of information. Instead, you will begin to allow the text to become an instrument of God's grace in your life. You will begin to open yourself to the possibility of God's setting the agenda for your life through the text. Not only will this exercise begin to transform your approach to reading (and prepare you for the role of scripture in spiritual formation), it will also begin to transform your whole mode of being in relationship with God in a way that will enhance genuine spiritual formation.

—From *Shaped by the Word* by M. Robert Mulholland Jr.

❧ In solitude, we come to know the Spirit who has already been given to us. The pains and struggles we encounter in our solitude thus become the way to hope, because our hope is not based on something that will happen after our sufferings are over, but on the real presence of God's healing Spirit in the midst of these sufferings.

—From *Making All Things New* by Henri J. M. Nouwen

❧ Every time you listen with great attentiveness to the voice that calls you the Beloved, you will discover within yourself a desire to hear that voice longer and more deeply.

—From *Life of the Beloved* by Henri J. M. Nouwen

❧ Attentiveness to God's spirit requires deeply receptive, prayerful listening. Practicing the art of attending to the Spirit involves us in contemplative listening. Such listening is quite distinct from the various ways in which we generally listen to another. . . .

It is holy listening, rooted in silence. It seeks emptiness in order to be filled with the Spirit. It is permeated by humility. Such listening assumes that the Spirit is active among us and works through us. So it makes space for that movement. It is primarily receptive, patient, watchful, and waiting. Yet it does not fear action when acton is called for. Such listening is generously flexible, hospitable, and warm. It embraces the widest possible spectrum of life's beauty and pain. It acknowledges the creation of all people in the image and likeness of God. It approaches life as a mystery into which we joyously and generously live. While in one sense a gift, such listening is generally cultivated over the years as we prayerfully attend to the Spirit in our own lives and as others listen to us in the same grace-filled way.

—From *Companions in Christ: Participant's Book*, Part 5 by Wendy M. Wright

❧ Ask God to make you aware of divine nudges in your life. What has God said to you through recent incidents? What was God saying to you in that unexpected phone call? in that flat tire? in that moving television program? in that bout of anxiety? in that "coincidence"? In silence discover where God seems to be directing your attention.

Now pay attention to your hunches, your impulses. Obviously, not every hunch or impulse is a message from God, but God does sometimes choose to communicate this way. What do you feel an urge to do? Call an old friend? Take a nap? Go for a walk in the park? Read a certain book? Play with your kids? Offer forgiveness to someone who hurt you? Record your impulse in your journal.

If your impulse is not patently foolish, will not hurt anyone, and seems consistent with the gospel, try following it. See what happens. Discover what you feel. What other hunches are you aware of?

—From *Ashes Transformed* by Tilda Norberg

❧ Never let anyone tell you the desert is barren. It is teeming with life. Agile reptilian creatures lurked under stones, tenacious plants clung to life in the thin, sandy topsoil, minute wildflowers, nearly invisible unless viewed from close range, dotted the desert floor. All of it was cradled in the vast embrace of a silence so deep it calmed all thought and feeling. Life in the palm desert pulsed so deep it calmed all thought and feeling. Life in the palm desert pulsed with all the rustle and restless sounds of wind, trees, oceans, or rivers. . . . The deep silence entered me and taught me to listen, to see, to hear, to become attentive to the noiseless substrata beneath all that is.

Conversion, the desert ascetics assure us, is forged in such a place, a place of listening awareness where one becomes attentive to the silence of God. There, in the vast stillness of desert solitude, we are gradually converted, unmade, and remade. We become a fresh beginning.

—From *The Time Between* by Wendy M. Wright

The Season of Lent

The Season of Lent is like a roller coaster ride with emotions that are down and up again and again as the story of our salvation makes plain our sinful ways and the cost of our redemption. We begin with Ash Wednesday where we roughly bump up against our own mortality. Here we know that sin and death are real, and they are real not just for someone else. Sin and death are real for us. This is where we begin the Lenten Season, with our face pressed hard against the reality of our sin and our death. If we did not know how the story ends, this would be a dark and depressing journey. But we do know how the story ends and therefore in the midst of austerity and fasting we remember our faithful Savior and the Easter declaration that life is always victorious over death, always!

In the forty days of Lent (not counting Sundays) we experience the temptations of Jesus and remember our own. We recognize in the rapidly rising hopes of a triumphal entry some of our own expectations and hopes for a world of peace and love. But then comes Holy Week, and we see so many of those hopes dashed to their death. A somber time to be sure, but even in Lent we remember that each Sunday of the year is a little Easter. Therefore we take courage, our hearts grow strong, and once again we determine to throw our lives into the struggle on the side of peace, justice, and love.

Historically Lent was a time of preparation and instruction for catechumens as they prepared for their baptism and welcome into the body of Christ on Easter Sunday. Today baptism, confirmation, and reaffirmation of baptismal vows are often included within the Easter celebration. Certainly it is a time for reflection on the central truths of the redemption story.

A season that begins with ashes pressed upon our heads ends with the fragrance, sight, and touch of flowers racing through our senses and inviting us to join the triumphant song "Christ the Lord Is Risen Today!" Now we know as never before that our mortality will put on immortality (1 Cor. 15:53). Death and resurrection are now claimed as our own. Fear has given way to inexpressible joy, and doubt has given way to triumphant hope. Christ is risen!

First Sunday in Lent

16: Discipleship: Serving with Jesus

Affirmation
And he appointed twelve, whom he also named apostles, to be with him, and to be sent out to proclaim the message, and to have authority to cast out demons (Mark 3:14-15).

Petition
Peter answered him, "Lord, if it is you, command me to come to you on the water.". . . But when he noticed the strong wind, he became frightened, and beginning to sink, he cried out, "Lord, save me!" (Matt. 14:28, 30).

Sacred Reading: anthology or other selected reading

Daily Scripture Readings

Sunday	A.	Genesis 2:15-17, 3:1-7; Psalm 32; Romans 5:12-19; Matthew 4:1-11
	B.	Genesis 9:8-17; Psalm 25:1-10; 1 Peter 3:18-22; Mark 1:9-15
	C.	Deuteronomy 26:1-11; Psalm 91:1-2, 9-16; Romans 10:8-13; Luke 4:1-13
Monday		Luke 22:24-30
Tuesday		Isaiah 41:8-10
Wednesday		Luke 16:10-13
Thursday		Matthew 12:15-21
Friday		1 Corinthians 4:1-5
Saturday		John 15:12-16

Prayer: thanksgiving, petition, intercession, praise and offering

Reflection: silent (listening to God), written (journaling)

God's Promise

And he said to them, "Go into all the world and proclaim the good news to the whole creation. The one who believes and is baptized will be saved; but the one who does not believe will be condemned. And these signs will accompany those who believe: by using my name they will cast out demons; they will speak in new tongues; they will pick up snakes in their hands, and if they drink any deadly thing, it will not hurt them; they will lay their hands on the sick, and they will recover" (Mark 16:15-18).

My Response

Take, Lord, and receive all my liberty, my memory, my understanding, and my entire will—all that I have and call my own. You have given it all to me. Lord, I return it. Everything is yours; do with it what you will. Give me only your love and your grace. This is enough for me.

Readings for Reflection

❧ Being a disciple was becoming stressful. The pace clearly had quickened during this three-year course in discipleship. The crowds had grown larger and demanded more. The lessons to be learned often seemed over the heads of the disciples. Jesus talked more and more about his own death and what was to follow. Frankly the disciples did not understand it, and the more confused they became, the more frustrated they became. We appreciate that phenomenon. It happens to us. When we are under a heavy load for a long period of time, we often become frustrated, impatient, and sometimes not very nice to be around. We even begin to compare ourselves to others and begin to think that we deserve a little bigger slice of the reward pie than even our closest friend.

That kind of reaction to stress may explain why the disciples began arguing about who was to be regarded as the greatest among those who followed Jesus. Jesus shattered their hopes of achieving special status or special reward (Luke 22:26).

The world's system of reward has nothing to do with the disciple's system of reward. A disciple of Jesus Christ is called first to be servant of all, and the leader is to take the lowliest position of service. This system turns the world's concept of leadership upside down. The first disciples found it hard to understand and even more difficult to live by such a value system. But Jesus seems to say there is no other way. Disciples serve.

—Rueben P. Job

⸮ The Church, then, both washes the feet of Christ and wipes them with her hair, and anoints them with oil, and pours ointment upon them, because not only does she care for the wounded and cherish the weary, but also sprinkles them with the sweet odour of grace; and pours forth the same grace not only on the rich and powerful, but also on men of lowly estate. She weighs all with equal balance, gathers all in the same bosom, and cherishes them in the same lap.

Christ died once, and was buried once, and nevertheless He wills that ointment should daily be poured on his feet. What, then, are those feet of Christ on which we pour ointment? The feet of Christ are they of whom He Himself says; "What ye have done to one of the least of these ye have done to Me." These feet that woman in the gospel refreshes, these feet she bedews with her tears; when sin is forgiven to the lowliest, guilt is washed away, and pardon granted. These feet he kisses, who loves even the lowest of the holy people. These feet he anoints with ointment, who imparts the kindness of his gentleness even to the weaker. In these the martyrs, in these the apostles, in these the Lord Jesus Himself declares that He is honoured.

—From "Letter 41" by Saint Ambrose

❧ My God, in these quiet moments I caught a glimpse of your vision for me. Inspire me, my God, to carry into the everydayness of my life all to which I aspire at such a moment as this. May my faith have feet and hands, a voice and a heart, that it may minister to others—that the gospel I profess may be seen in my life.

I go this hour to encounter the routine of duty with a new vision. Equip me for my common tasks, that I may this day apply myself to them with fidelity and devotion. And not for myself alone do I pray:

Bless homemakers, mothers, and servants, who minister in the home and who maintain sacred sanctuaries to which tired persons return at the end of day.

Bless doctors and nurses. May their work reflect God's love and pity to those who leave this earth today.

Bless the teachers, the school administrators, and those who labor to keep school buildings clean and pleasant for those who study and learn there.

Bless coal miners and all who toil in grime and darkness, that we may enjoy clean and pleasant lives.

May your blessing rest upon all men and women who minister to others. May each one come to know the joy of partnership with you.

I give this prayer to you who inflames my soul with vision and desire, that I may be a faithful laborer in the fields you have assigned to my stewardship. Help me to be a good and faithful steward.

—Norman Shawchuck

❧ When I was growing up, I thought the greatest Christian must be the person who walks around with shoulders thrown back because of tremendous inner strength and power, quoting Scripture and letting everyone know he has arrived. I have since learned that the most mature believer is the one who is bent over, leaning most heavily on the Lord, and admitting his total inability to do anything without Christ. The greatest Christian is not the one who has *achieved* the most but rather the one who has *received* the most.

God's grace, love, and mercy flow through him abundantly because he walks in total dependence.
—From *Fresh Faith* by Jim Cymbala

❧ Goodness and Faithfulness—we think of them as the supreme virtues of plain people. Yet they, too, are the fruits of the Spirit. In the long run we cannot really manage them without God. The good citizen, good employer, good artist, good worker—the faithful husband or wife or mother—in these, too, Divine Love, selfless charity, is bringing forth its fruits within the natural order and on the natural scale: proclaiming the dignity and possibilities of our human life on all levels, disclosing the full meaning of the Word made flesh. Another lesson in not being high-minded; another invitation to come off our self-chosen spiritual perch, whatever it may be, and face the facts of human life.
—From *The Fruits of the Spirit* by Evelyn Underhill

❧ Faithfulness is consecration in overalls. It is the steady acceptance and performance of the common duty and immediate task without any reference to personal preferences—because it is there to be done and so is a manifestation of the Will of God. It is Elizabeth Leseur settling down each day to do the household accounts quite perfectly (when she would much rather have been in church) and saying, "The duties of my station come before everything else." It is Brother Lawrence taking his turn in the kitchen, and Saint Francis de Sales taking the burden of a difficult diocese and saying, "I have now little time for prayer—but I do what is the same."

The fruits of the Spirit get less and less showy as we go on. Faithfulness means continuing quietly with the job we have been given, in the situation where we have been placed; not yielding to the restless desire for change. It means tending the lamp quietly for God without wondering how much longer it has got to go on.
—From *The Fruits of the Spirit* by Evelyn Underhill

❧ The church is the worshiping community. We are that body of people who are learning together to repent, pray, and serve in the light of our history and an imagination that is teaching us to do so. The focus of our history and imagination is Jesus Christ, in whom we see what it means to live in repentance, prayer, and service. We seek to follow him, to be his disciples, and to undertake the disciplines that such a life requires.

As we follow him, we see that we cannot be the church and remain a closed system of intimate and exclusive social relationships through which we are protected from the world. To the extent that we actually are being transformed in repentance, prayer, and service, we find that we must continually strive to rupture our own boundaries. The church is just not the church except as it seeks to incorporate within its mutuality enemies and strangers. Its repentance, prayer, and service is for all people, for the world as such, and not just for others as Christians. In the church we are impelled by the very dynamics of what it means to be the church to meet the enemies and strangers of our lives.

—From *Vision and Character* by Craig R. Dykstra

❧ Take, Lord, and receive all my liberty, my memory, my understanding, and my entire will—all that I have and call my own. You have given it all to me. To you, Lord, I return it. Everything is yours; do with it what you will. Give me only your love and your grace. That is enough for me.

—From *The Spiritual Exercises of St. Ignatius*

17: The Cost of Discipleship

Affirmation

Therefore, since we are surrounded by so great a cloud of witnesses, let us also lay aside every weight and the sin that clings so closely, and let us run with persever-ance the race that is set before us, looking to Jesus the pioneer and perfecter of our faith, who for the sake of the joy that was set before him endured the cross, dis-regarding its shame, and has taken his seat at the right hand of the throne of God (Heb. 12:1-2).

Petition

Save me, O God,
> for the waters have come up to my neck.
I sink in deep mire,
> where there is no foothold;
I have come into deep waters,
> and the flood sweeps over me.
I am weary with my crying;
> my throat is parched.
My eyes grow dim with waiting for my God (Ps. 69:1-3).

Sacred Reading: anthology or other selected reading

Daily Scripture Readings

Sunday	A.	Genesis 12:1-4; Psalm 121; Romans 4:1-5, 13-17; John 3:1-17
	B.	Genesis 17:1-7, 15-16; Psalm 22:23-31; Romans 4:13-25; Mark 8:31-38
	C.	Genesis 15:1-12, 17-18; Psalm 27; Philippians 3:17–4:1; Luke 13:31-35
Monday		Matthew 16:24-28
Tuesday		Acts 14:21-23
Wednesday		2 Timothy 2:8-13
Thursday		Romans 6:5-11

| Friday | 1 Thessalonians 3:1-13 |
| Saturday | Luke 14:25-33 |

Prayer: thanksgiving, petition, intercession, praise and offering

Reflection: silent (listening to God), written (journaling)

God's Promise
No one shall be able to stand against you all the days of your life. As I was with Moses, so I will be with you; I will not fail you or forsake you. . . . Only be strong and very courageous, being careful to act in accordance with all the law that my servant Moses commanded you (Josh. 1:5, 7).

My Response
Now I know that the LORD will help his anointed;
    he will answer him from his holy heaven
    with mighty victories by his right hand.
Some take pride in chariots, and some in horses,
    but our pride is in the name of the LORD our God.
They will collapse and fall,
    but we shall rise and stand upright (Ps. 20:6-8).

Readings for Reflection

❦ Salvation is free, but the cost of discipleship is enormous. I try to hide from the truth, but when I read the Gospels and seek to live in communion with God, I discover both parts of the statement are dead-center truth. I can do nothing to earn my salvation. My redemption is a pure gift of grace, a gift offered to me without qualification or reservation. I am God's child and no one or no thing can change that fact. Jesus Christ lived, died, and lives again to bring this gift of salvation to me in all of its fullness. My faith can appropriate this gift, but even my greatest doubt cannot change its reality. I am God's beloved, embraced in

God's love for now and eternity. All words are inadequate to describe the extravagance and grandeur of the gift of salvation. Our hymns of praise and gratitude fall lifeless before the immensity of this gift. We simply and humbly offer all that we are to the One who offers us the option of becoming more than we are.

In offering ourselves as fully as we can, we discover the cost of discipleship. For to bind our lives to Jesus Christ requires that we try to walk with him into the sorrows and suffering of the world. Being bound to Jesus Christ, we see barriers broken down and we are led to places we have never been before and to carry loads we have not even seen before. Having offered ourselves to Jesus Christ, we may expect to become the eyes, ears, voice, and hands of Jesus Christ in the world and in the church. The cost of salvation? It is completely free and without cost. The cost of discipleship? Only our lives—nothing more and nothing less.
—Rueben P. Job

❧ For the Christians are distinguished from other [persons] neither by country, nor language, nor the customs which they observe. For they neither inhabit cities of their own, nor employ a peculiar form of speech, nor lead a life which is marked out by any singularity. The course of conduct which they follow has not been devised by any speculation or deliberation of inquisitive [persons]; nor do they, like some, proclaim themselves the advocates of any merely human doctrines. But, inhabiting Greek as well as barbarian cities, according as the lot of each of them has determined, and following the customs of the natives in respect to clothing, food, and the rest of their ordinary conduct, they display to us their wonderful and confessedly striking method of life. They dwell in their own countries, but simply as sojourners. As citizens, they share in all things with others, and yet endure all things as if foreigners. Every foreign land is to them as their native country, and every land of their birth as a land of strangers. They marry, as do all (others); they beget children; but they do not destroy their offspring. They have a common table, but not a common bed. They are in the flesh, but they do not live after the flesh. They pass their days on earth, but they are citizens of heaven. They obey the prescribed laws, and at the same time surpass the laws by their lives. They love all [persons], and are persecuted by all. They are unknown and condemned; they are put to death, and restored to life. They are poor, yet make many rich; they are in lack of all things, and yet abound in all; they are dishonoured, and yet in their very dishonour are glorified. They are evil spoken of, and yet are justified; they are reviled, and bless; they are insulted, and repay the insult with honour; they do good, yet are punished as evil-doers. When punished, they rejoice as if quickened into life; they are assailed by the Jews as foreigners, and are persecuted by the Greeks; yet those who hate them are unable to assign any reason for their hatred.

—From "Epistle to Diognetus" by Mathetes

 ❧ We need not wonder about the cost of discipleship. We need only look upon Jesus on the cross. There we see the awful cost of the ministry that is offered in the life, nature, and spirit of Jesus.

The cost is awful indeed. But if our work introduces men and women to Jesus and to God's love, this cost must be accepted. In our own self-emptying, those who gaze upon us may see Jesus. In our conviction, people may be convinced to look upon the cross of Jesus and say, "Truly this is the Son of God."

We have heard it said, "We can never wear the crown until we bear the cross," but for those who willingly enter into the sufferings of Jesus, the cross is their crown, and they wear it with dignity and submission.

—Norman Shawchuck

 ❧ The Christian way is different: harder, and easier. Christ says, "Give me All. I don't want so much of your

time and so much of your money and so much of your work: I want You. I have not come to torment your natural self, but to kill it. No half-measures are any good. I don't want to cut off a branch here and a branch there, I want to have the whole tree down. . . . Hand over the whole natural self, all the desires which you think innocent as well as the ones you think wicked—the whole outfit. I will give you a new self instead. In fact, I will give you Myself: my own will shall become yours."
—From *Mere Christianity* by C. S. Lewis

❧ All of God's life is available to each of us already, but not yet. Ordinary suffering will not be taken away, nor the suffering we must face when we bear witness to God's love and are met with the world's hostility and scorn. But our suffering will have meaning, will be lifted up, transformed by the unceasing love of God.
—Robert A. Jonas from *Henri Nouwen: Writings Selected with an Introduction by Robert A. Jonas*

❧ O, begin! Fix some part of every day for private exercises. . . . Whether you like it or no, read and pray daily. It is for your life; there is no other way: else you will be a trifler all your days. . . . Do justice to your own soul; give it time and means to grow. Do not starve yourself any longer.
—From "Letter to Mr. Jonathan Maskew" by John Wesley

❧ A cup is a container for holding something. Whatever it holds has to eventually be emptied out so that something more can be put into it. I have learned that I cannot always expect my life to be full. There has to be some emptying, some pouring out, if I am to make room for the new. The spiritual journey is like that—a constant process of emptying and filling, of giving and receiving, of accepting and letting go.
—From *The Cup of Our Life* by Joyce Rupp

❧ Fully immersed in this world, Christians belong to no world. Instead, while teased by each hope and every vision, they know them to be only hints of the new heaven and the new earth rooted in divine promises. And our yearning to become lost in God only intensifies our tears over the thought of leaving this life. Christian existence is a joyful nonsense. In a culture of self-realization, the Christian's call is to renounce self; in the face of noise, silence is the preference; in a world of competition, the Christian's declaration is that the winners will be losers and the losers winners; in a culture whose economy is intent on consumption, the Christian insists on simplicity; in a culture structured by possessions, the Christian insists upon a high standard of life; and at every point, the Christian exposes the emptiness of fullness for the sake of the gospel's fullness of emptiness.

—From *The Art of Spiritual Direction* by W. Paul Jones

18: Living the Transformed Life

Affirmation
And all of us, with unveiled faces, seeing the glory of the Lord as though reflected in a mirror, are being transformed into the same image from one degree of glory to another; for this comes from the Lord, the Spirit (2 Cor. 3:18).

Petition
This is my prayer, that your love may overflow more and more with knowledge and full insight to help you to determine what is best, so that in the day of Christ you may be pure and blameless, having produced the harvest of righteousness that comes through Jesus Christ for the glory and praise of God (Phil. 1:9-11).

Sacred Reading: anthology or other selected reading

Daily Scripture Readings

Sunday	A.	Exodus 17:1-7; Psalm 95; Romans 5:1-11; John 4:5-42
	B.	Exodus 20:1-17; Psalm 19; 1 Corinthians 1:18-25; John 2:13-22
	C.	Isaiah 55:1-9; Psalm 63:1-8; 1 Corinthians 10:1-13; Luke 13:1-9
Monday		Matthew 5:13-16
Tuesday		2 Corinthians 4:16-18
Wednesday		2 Corinthians 5:1-10
Thursday		Matthew 15:10-20
Friday		Philippians 3:1-11
Saturday		John 16:25-33

Prayer: thanksgiving, petition, intercession, praise and offering

Reflection: silent (listening to God), written (journaling)

God's Promise
I will give them one heart, and put a new spirit within
them; I will remove the heart of stone from their flesh
and give them a heart of flesh, so that they may follow
my statutes and keep my ordinances and obey them.
Then they shall be my people, and I will be their God
(Ezek. 11:19-20).

My Response
I want to know Christ and the power of his resurrection and the sharing of his sufferings by becoming like
him in his death. . . . Beloved, I do not consider that I
have made it my own; but this one thing I do: forgetting what lies behind and straining forward to what
lies ahead, I press on toward the goal for the prize of the
heavenly call of God in Christ Jesus (Phil. 3:10, 13-14).

Readings for Reflection

ᨆ When we think of models of the transformed life, we
naturally turn to the saints of the past or look at more
contemporary heroes of faithfulness like Mother Teresa
or Douglas Steere. Because we do, we often overlook
those near us who daily claim the power of God to live
life at a higher level than it could be lived alone.

Living a transformed life is not possible on our
own. Most of us do not live up to the best that we know
how to live. Deep within we know that there is room
for improvement. We can do better. Connecting our
desire to do and be better with God's amazing grace
creates a partnership that leads to transformation.

We know that living a transformed life means living at God's direction with grace-given capacity. This
is more than we can do on our own, and, in fact, living
the transformed life does not mean trying harder. It
means trusting more and staying close to the only One
who can make us more than we are.

As we learn to put our trust and faith in God, we
become open and available to receive God's forming

and transforming power in our own lives. In our better moments we know that it is God at work within us that provides the transformation. This is the day to claim God's presence and help as you live the transformed life.

—Rueben P. Job

✥ Here, O God, I pray for a realization of my condition in your eyes. Help me to see and know myself as you see and know me. Give me clear insight into my relationship with you. Let me know myself as you know me.

Give me assurance that I belong to you. Remove from me those nagging doubts and needless fears that I may not be good enough to be numbered with the great company of heaven.

On the other hand, if I am living in separation from you, if I am more a creature of evil than a child of God, O Great Physician, use your convicting scalpel on me. Perform within me the surgery necessary to heal me of all soul-sickness.

Christ, I abandon myself to you. Do with me every necessary thing to assure my entrance into eternal life—and the heaven already prepared for me.

—Norman Shawchuck

✥ Nothing will give us so much strength as being fully known and fully loved by fellow human beings in the Name of God. That gives us the courage to drink our cup to the bottom, knowing it is the cup of our salvation. It will allow us not only to live well but to die well. When we are surrounded by loving friends, death becomes a gateway to the full communion of saints.

—From *Can You Drink the Cup?* by Henri J. M. Nouwen

✥ Our questions can serve us well in a time such as this, a time of grave uncertainty, of soaring potential, of fragile yet resilient hope. Our questions and questing are crucial, because they can help us live into the answer of the future. I am certain of one thing: the love that is God is at the heart of the answer, just as it is at the heart of each moment—past, present, and future. Faith today, tomorrow, and always seeks to live, to love, and to be loved fully. It seeks the Holy and waits (though not always patiently) to be found; it nurtures and activates wisdom and compassion. It chooses to embrace hope and to be embraced by hope, even when overwhelmed by despair; it seeks life even in the face of death. We act in faith, knowing that we see only dimly. But living in faith, we act anyway, choosing and doing the best we can. We act and live in confidence that someday we will see face to face, that we will live into the answers. For God's grace embraces our questions as well as our answers and our blindness as well as our vision, just as the sun shines steadily through the night, waiting to illumine the sky at dawn.

—From *Wrestling till Dawn* by Jean M. Blomquist

❧ Action, just as silence and the word, can help us to claim and celebrate our true self. But here again we need discipline, because the world in which we live says, "Do this, do that, go here, go there, meet him, meet her." Busyness has become a sign of importance. Having much to do, many places to go, and countless people to meet gives us status and even fame. However, being busy can lead us away from our true vocation and prevent us from drinking our cup.

—From *Can You Drink the Cup?* by Henri J. M. Nouwen

❧ It is not easy to distinguish between doing what we are called to do and doing what we want to do. Our many wants can easily distract us from our true action. True action leads us to the fulfillment of our vocation. Whether we work in an office, travel the world, write books or make films, care for the poor, offer leadership, or fulfill unspectacular tasks, the question is not "What do I most want?" but "What is my vocation?" The most prestigious position in society can be an expression of obedience to our call as well as a sign of our refusal to hear that call, and the least prestigious position, too, can be a response to our vocation as well as a way to avoid it.

—From *Can You Drink the Cup?* by Henri J. M. Nouwen

❧ Probably our journey of forgiveness will be impossible unless we realize we cannot do it alone. We are not the source of our healing. Truly the kingdom of God is within us as Jesus told us. But that kingdom is *God's* presence, and we need God's help to experience that inner glory.

As with any deep healing and release, the empowered mercy of God within and around us is ours to claim. We must face the facts: we are vulnerable (woundable); we have been hurt; we need to name our hurt and our deep needs as clearly and fully as we can. Little can change until we have faced where we actually are.

—From *Forgiveness, the Passionate Journey* by Flora Slosson Wuellner

❧ When we were traveling in India, . . . we had the unforgettable experience of talking with Mother Teresa. We remember savoring that time: the sunlight on the balcony, her wise and wrinkled face with piercing eyes, the sisters in the courtyard below doing laundry, and her parting words, "Please pray for us that we will be faithful, and not interfere with God's work."

In the immediacy of that moment, we were given a gift—and that gift involved what we should and could do (be "faithful"), and what we shouldn't do ("interfere with God's work"). She truly believed that she and her sisters—whose devotion to God and care of the rejected and dying ones in our world is legendary—needed to be aware of this possibility and to guard against getting in the way of God's work. Those who criticize Mother Teresa for not attacking the systemic problems that cause persons to be sick and hungry and dying on the streets of Calcutta and Chicago may be called to do that very thing. But Mother's calling was to share compassion and love and to feed and hold the dying. Each of us must discern and answer our own unique call.

Mother Teresa's request presupposes that God is active and that we only muck up the situation when we forget that our understanding is partial. We must avoid the temptation to play God!

—From *Sacramental Living* by Dwight W. Vogel and Linda J. Vogel

❧ The shalom bringers spread a sense of warmth, comfort, hope, and well-being even before a word is spoken. They themselves are the interlinking, not just their words and actions. They do not talk about religion all the time. They are not constantly telling us to cheer up and look on the bright side. They may not say anything special at all, but when we are with them we feel understood, accepted, welcomed.

When we think of these men and women in our lives, we feel as if God is reaching out to us through them. We know that if God is like them—only much more so—then the universe is in safe hands. The glory of God shines through their faces and touches us through their hands.

We call them the children of God.

—From *Forgiveness, the Passionate Journey* by Flora Slosson Wuellner

19: Why Do We Drift Away?

Affirmation

Beloved, do not believe every spirit, but test the spirits to see whether they are from God; for many false prophets have gone out into the world. By this you know the Spirit of God: every spirit that confesses that Jesus Christ has come in the flesh is from God, and every spirit that does not confess Jesus is not from God. And this is the spirit of the antichrist, of which you have heard that it is coming; and now it is already in the world. Little children, you are from God, and have conquered them; for the one who is in you is greater than the one who is in the world (1 John 4:1-4).

Petition

Beloved, do not imitate what is evil but imitate what is good. Whoever does good is from God; whoever does evil has not seen God (3 John 11).

Sacred Reading: anthology or other selected reading

Daily Scripture Readings

Sunday	A.	1 Samuel 16:1-13; Psalm 23; Ephesians 5:8-14; John 9:1-41
	B.	Numbers 21:4-9; Psalm 107:1-3, 17-22; Ephesians 2:1-10; John 3:14-21
	C.	Joshua 5:9-12; Psalm 32; 2 Corinthians 5:16-21; Luke 15:1-3, 11-32
Monday		James 1:12-16
Tuesday		Ezekiel 34:1-6
Wednesday		Galatians 5:8-20
Thursday		1 Corinthians 11:17-22
Friday		Mark 6:1-6
Saturday		3 John 2-12

Prayer: thanksgiving, petition, intercession, praise and offering

Reflection: silent (listening to God), written (journaling)

God's Promise
And this is the testimony: God gave us eternal life, and this life is in his Son. Whoever has the Son has life; whoever does not have the Son of God does not have life (1 John 5:11-12).

My Response
But you, beloved, build yourselves up on your most holy faith; pray in the Holy Spirit; keep yourselves in the love of God; look forward to the mercy of our Lord Jesus Christ that leads to eternal life (Jude 20-21).

Readings for Reflection

❧ The twelve all had a good beginning with Jesus. Their signs of loyalty, fidelity, and faithfulness came often in their brief time with Jesus. And yet in many of the crucial times for Jesus and for them, the truth is that they drifted astray. They lost sight of Jesus and his way and focused on themselves and their way.

A good beginning is wonderful to experience and to observe. Even more wonderful is to see a woman or a man full of years and still full of goodness and faith. To observe a marriage that is marked by fidelity and unqualified love after a half century of living brings hope and encouragement to all who desire strong families and strong communities. Faithfulness is a wonderful thing to experience and to observe.

Some congregations have remarkable and almost miraculous beginnings. Beginnings that are marked by rapid growth and transformation of nearly every life that enters their sphere of ministry. These congregations' transforming ministry touches every part of their community, and that community is forever changed.

Faithfulness is a wonderful thing to experience and to observe.

There are denominations that carry a precious part of the gospel's treasure in such faithful ways that the world is a better place because God has given them life. Their faithfulness in good times and bad, in wealth and poverty, provides direction and encouragement for all who choose to live a life of goodness and holiness. Faithfulness is a wonderful thing to experience and to observe.

The bad news is that individuals, congregations, and denominations can drift astray. It happens so easily. It happens the moment we take our eyes off Jesus Christ. The moment we lose our center we begin to lose our way. We know it does not have to be that way because every day we can keep our eyes upon Jesus Christ and ask for guidance and grace to remain faithful. The good news Christians share is that Jesus Christ is able and willing to guide and enable us on our journey toward our true home with God.
—Rueben P. Job

～ As I listen to myself and to other Christians, I notice that after some years of following Jesus we tend to suffer from various symptoms of drifting away.

When we were young in our faith, we were eager to give sacrificially of our time and resources to alleviate the pains of the poor; we were eager to take time for daily reading of the scripture and prayer. Fasting was a spiritual delight, and we would plow through snow up to our belt buckles to get to church on Sunday. Then, after some years, we began to drift away from the spiritual disciplines that sustained us in earlier times.

John labeled three deadly conditions that cause us to drift away from our earlier spiritual disciplines (1 John 2:16): lust of the flesh, lust of the eyes, and the pride of life (or, if you will, lustful desires, wandering eyes, and greedy eyes—a false sense of security in our material possessions). John insisted that if we follow in these ways, we certainly will come to spiritual and ethical shipwreck.

Most Christians, I suppose, don't come to such extreme conditions. But for many, after some years of faithful practice, spiritual rigor mortis sets in—and all is lost. Paul suggests an antidote for drifting away: "'Sleeper, awake! Rise from the dead, and Christ will shine on you.' Be careful then how you live, not as unwise people but as wise, making the most of the time, because the days are evil. So do not be foolish, but understand what the will of the Lord is. Do not get drunk with wine, for that is debauchery; but be filled with the Spirit, as you sing psalms and hymns and spiritual songs among yourselves, singing and making melody to the Lord in your hearts, giving thanks to God the Father at all times and for everything in the name of our Lord Jesus Christ" (Eph. 5:14-20).
—Norman Shawchuck

  We have an inborn persisting tendency to attribute to ourselves the successes of our spiritual life, the resistance we offer to temptation, the devotion we achieve, the discipline we keep and the good works we do. Surely we thank God for all that, but in our heart of hearts we congratulate ourselves on our exploits, and secretly worship our sword and our bow. We take as done by us what is done by God in us; even obvious graces from heaven stick to the soul and seem after some time to be connatural to us and springing from us. That is spiritual pride of the worst kind, and if it really takes hold of a soul, it is enough to stop any spiritual progress at all. The disease is as dangerous as it is common.
—From *Faith for Justice* by Carlos G. Valles

  Unfortunately, our error is "to want to do it our way," "to feel ourselves to be somebody," "to trust in our own plans," "not to give due weight to the Father's plan." It's frightening, my sister, the extent to which hidden pride burns the soul and dries up everything. And pride is all the greater in spiritual people: in us. I can understand why Jesus took a bitter line when dealing with us (the professionally religious): sinners and prostitutes will take their place ahead of us.

It's because we don't want to be little! On the excuse that the religious life is a great, very great thing, we no longer dream *of becoming nothing, nothing, nothing.*

—From *Letters to Dolcidia: 1954–1983* by Carlo Carretto

☙ After a while, this Sabbath-less way of living might even become a point of honor with us. We begin bragging about being so busy that we "have not had a vacation in years." What we fail to realize is that this is already a public declaration of our spiritual poverty. Whether we mean it to be or not, it is also a way of making others feel guilty about honoring the time they need for marginality. In this way, we begin to perpetuate the destructive equation of ministry with work.

—From *The Journey from Misery to Ministry* by Francis Dorff

☙ As our insensitivity to our own feelings grows, our lives often begin leaking all kinds of negative emotions. Without even realizing it, we go about feeling frustrated, unappreciated, resentful, exploited, lonely, put upon, needy, angry, and acting in ways that let these negative emotions overflow toward others. If we were in touch with our feelings, these emotions could be moments of truth for us, warning us that we are heading for trouble. They could be the raw material for soul-searching and meditative exploration of what is going on in our lives. When we are out of touch with our hearts, however, we fail even to notice our feelings, much less to receive and act on their important messages.

—From *The Journey from Misery to Ministry* by Francis Dorff

❧ On all days and seasons, indeed, dearly-beloved, some marks of the Divine goodness are set, and no part of the year is destitute of sacred mysteries, in order that, so long as proofs of our salvation meet us on all sides, we may the more eagerly accept the never-ceasing calls of God's mercy. But all that is bestowed on the restoration of human souls in the divers works and gifts of grace is put before us more clearly and abundantly now, when no isolated portions of the Faith are to be celebrated, but the whole together. For as the Easter festival approaches, the greatest and most binding of fasts is kept, and its observance is imposed on all the faithful without exception; because no one is so holy that he ought to not be holier, nor so devout that he might not be devouter. For who, that is set in the uncertainty of this life, can be found either exempt from temptation, or free from fault? Who is there who would not wish for additions to his virtue, or removal of his vice? seeing that adversity does us harm, and prosperity spoils us, and it is equally dangerous not to have what we want at all, and to have it in the fullest measure. There is a trap in the fullness of riches, a trap in the straits of poverty. The one lifts us up in pride, the other incites us to complaint. Health tries us, sickness tries us, so long as the one fosters carelessness and the other sadness. There is a snare in security, a snare in fear; and it matters not whether the mind which is given over to earthly thoughts, is taken up with pleasures or with cares; for it is equally unhealthy to languish under empty delights, or to labour under racking anxiety.

—From "Sermon 49" by Leo the Great

❧ A desert father was asked for a word of wisdom by one of his disciples. "Go to the cemetery and curse the dead," said the old man. The disciple went off and stood among the graves and shouted: "You cowardly, sinful brood! The stench of your sins is an offence to Heaven. I curse you with all the power at my command. May you never see the light!" The young man went back to his master and told him that he had completed the task. "Did the dead say anything to you?" the old man asked. "Not a word!" answered the disciple. "Now go to the cemetery and praise the dead." The young man ran off, stood among the graves, and began a great eulogy: "You are greater than the apostles. Your good deeds rise up to Heaven like the incense. You inspire those you have left behind to great deeds. Such is your power, you glorious saints!" The young man hurried back to his master's cell. "Well," said the old man, "how was it this time? Did the dead have anything to say?" The disciple answered, "They were as silent as before." After a period of silence, the old man said, "That is how you have to be—like the dead; beyond cursing and praise, unaffected by the opinions of others."

—From *Soul Making* by Alan W. Jones

❧ Within the body of Christ we need to be intentional about the seeds we sow, about how our behavior with friends should be preparing us for service out in the world. We need each other to draw us out of our self-centeredness. We need others to hold us accountable, to be like a mirror to help us see our lives and our doing of our faith more clearly. We need each other for mutual encouragement, to push further into serving the world than we might if left alone.

—From *Yours Are the Hands of Christ* by James C. Howell

❧ At times my heart is drawn away from your loving purpose and way. My spirit leans toward the unloving thought, the unloving word. I am prone to turn away from you and to embrace those things I know to be wrong and harmful.

As long as I continue to fight against those things with the power to destroy my life, I know that you are with me and living in my heart. I want you to take complete control of every aspect of my life.

What a strange thing to be new and old at the same time, to be recreated by your love and yet continue to struggle with my old self. You have freed me from the guilt and power of my own brokenness, but inner healing requires a long process of divine therapy.
—From *Praying in the Wesleyan Spirit* by Paul W. Chilcote

20: A Notorious Hope

Affirmation
Though he slay me, yet will I trust in him: but I will
maintain mine own ways before him (Job 13:15, KJV).

Petition
Show me thy ways, O LORD; teach me thy paths. Lead
me in thy truth, and teach me: for thou art the God of
my salvation; on thee do I wait all the day. Remember,
O LORD, thy tender mercies and thy loving kindnesses;
for they have been ever of old (Ps. 25:4-6, KJV).

Sacred Reading: anthology or other selected reading

Daily Scripture Readings

Sunday	A.	Ezekiel 37:1-14; Psalm 130; Romans 8:6-11; John 11:1-45
	B.	Jeremiah 31:31-34; Psalm 51:1-12; Hebrews 5:5-10; John 12:20-33
	C.	Isaiah 43:16-21; Psalm 126; Philippians 3:4-14; John 12:1-8
Monday		John 1:1-5
Tuesday		Hebrews 11:1-3
Wednesday		1 Peter 1:13-21
Thursday		Hebrews 6:13-20
Friday		Galatians 5:2-6
Saturday		Acts 23:6-11

Prayer: thanksgiving, petition, intercession, praise
and offering

Reflection: silent (listening to God), written (journaling)

God's Promise
But they that wait upon the LORD shall renew their

strength; they shall mount up with wings as eagles; they shall run, and not be weary; and they shall walk, and not faint (Isa. 40:31, KJV).

My Response
The LORD was ready to save me: therefore we will sing my songs to the stringed instruments all the days of our life in the house of the LORD (Isa. 38:20, KJV).

Readings for Reflection

❧ As Christians we live by faith in God, and we carry within us the notorious hope that a life of faithfulness is indeed the best way to live. Our hope is that fidelity and faithfulness will result in a holy life and the comforting companionship of Jesus Christ. The rewards of peace and assurance of continued companionship with God in the life to come belong to every faithful Christian.

We hope for that which we do not see. The reward of holy living today is merely a hope for tomorrow. The rewards of peace and assurance may be ours today, but they are only a hope for tomorrow. The companionship of Jesus Christ is experienced today but is only a hope for tomorrow. The promise that this ordinary life can be invested in the extraordinary reign of God today and tomorrow is the hope that encourages us to do what we can where we are to make God's will known and real.

When disease, disaster, death, or triumph strike, we are filled with hope because our ultimate trust is in God. Our worlds and wealth may crumble; disease and disaster may lay hold on what and whom we value; but followers of the Christian way continue to be hopeful. We hold onto hope because we are filled with faith that God is able to consummate the promise made to redeem and transform all who turn their lives toward God.
—Rueben P. Job

❧ Present-centeredness describes this important prerequisite of contemplation. Too often we find ourselves "distracted" or "abstracted," that is, not all there. Both terms are derived from two Latin words: *trahere* meaning "to be yanked or pulled" and *de* or *ab* meaning "from." When we are distracted or abstracted, we have been pulled from the present by some concern, thought, or action. Often it is guilt and regret over the past or concerns and worries about the future that keep us from living in the present. Dwelling in the past and projecting ourselves into the future both have the same result; they fragment our consciousness, leaving us unfocused. With one foot in the past and the other in the future, this bifurcated way of being splits our attention and ruins our ability to appreciate fully what is occurring before our very eyes.

—From *The Enduring Heart* by Wilkie Au

❧ It has been said that Charles Wesley's hymns always begin on earth and end in heaven. So it is with John Wesley's theology. He was firmly convinced of the coming day of Christ, which is not yet, but toward which humankind, with the whole creation, is moving. For Wesley, it was necessary to stress God's ultimate victory; but it was also important to affirm the penultimate reality of God's presence, now experienced as life that is drawn to God in increasingly focused love. John Wesley had a doctrine of final things, an eschatology, in which God's kingdom is being presently realized even as it points toward a consummating future. The Christian lives with the lively hope that God, who has begun a good thing, will fulfill it in the day of Jesus Christ.

—From *Practical Divinity* by Thomas A. Langford

❧ Do you have any wild hopes,
    or tame ones for that matter?
    The possibility of acorns becoming towering oaks,
    or caterpillars blossoming into butterflies,

or that dawn will chase away midnight fears?
Wild hopes!
That all creation will learn the dance of joy,
and all humanity might taste the wine of peace,
and that our loving God will become transparent
    through love.

"Recast the earth, O Lord,
and move our hearts with wild hopes."
—From *Resurrection to Pentecost* by Robert F.
    Morneau

❧ Many of our tame hopes are fulfilled on a daily basis:
the hope that the sun will shine, or that the pay check
will arrive as planned, or that we will get sufficient
nourishment for the day. Though one is disappointed
once in awhile, our anticipation of these "small" things,
though not insignificant, is frequently realized.

By contrast, some of these same issues for people
in other cultures are "wild hopes." Many of our sisters and brothers do not receive a salary nor do they
get three meals a day nor does the sun of freedom
shine in their lives. Born into poverty or oppressed
by social systems, these people find little joy and
peace. If they are fortunate in avoiding violence they
still must struggle with resentment and bitterness in
their awareness of the consumption and materialism
of the wealthy.

We must pray like Jesus that hope might be
restored and that the earth might be recast. Only the
gift of the Holy Spirit can empower us to trust in the
future and to assume our rightful responsibility
for the common good. Renewing the face of the
earth is the work of the Holy Spirit through those people who say yes to being the Spirit's agents of knowledge, love, and kindness. Our hope, wild or tame, is
grounded in God's promise of presence. Herein is our
joy and peace.
—From *Resurrection to Pentecost* by Robert F. Morneau

❧ But the Lord stood by me, and strengthened me" (2 Tim. 4:16). This then he now predicts: "Through your supplication and the supply of the Spirit of Jesus Christ, according to my earnest expectation and hope," for thus do I hope. For that he may persuade us not to leave the whole matter to the prayers made for us, and contribute nothing ourselves, behold how he lays down his own part, which is Hope, the source of all good, as the Prophet says. "Let thy mercy, O Lord, be upon us, according as we have hoped in Thee" (Ps. 33:22). And as it is written in another place, "Look to the generations of old and see, did any one hope in the Lord, and was made ashamed?" (Eccles. 2:10). And again, this same blessed one says, "Hope putteth not to shame" (Rom. 5:5). This is Paul's hope, the hoping that I shall nowhere be put to shame.

"According to my earnest expectation and hope," says he, "that in nothing shall I be put to shame." Do you see how great a thing it is to hope in God? Whatever happens, he says, I shall not be put to shame, i.e. they will not obtain the mastery over me, "but with all boldness, as always, so now also, Christ shall be magnified in my body."

—From "Homily 3 on Philippians" by Saint Chrysostom

Hymn: We Are Yours, O God Most Holy

> We are Yours, O God most holy,
> We belong alone to You;
> You have told us what our names are,
> and You know us through and through.
> Alleluia! Alleluia!
> Joyful song we raise to you.
>
> May your love and spirit fill us,
> May you be our all and all;
> May Your holy will possess us,
> may we ever heed Your call.

Alleluia! Alleluia!
At your feet in praise we fall.

We rejoice to be Your servants,
To the world You send us forth;
We would be to each a blessing,
Sharing grace with all the earth.
Alleluia! Alleluia!
Grace that brings true life to birth.
—William Boyd Grove

❧ Christian existence . . . involves a life of incredible rhythms, of highs and lows, whether in a concert hall hearing Beethoven's Ninth Symphony or in a Memphis dive trumpeting the blues. Its antinomies include a hunger for community, yet a taste for the silence of aloneness. The yearning is for intimacy, but the embrace occurs on a windswept hill called Golgotha. There is an emptying out of all thought and imagery in order to lose oneself in the Unknown and Unknowable. Yet there is an excitement over the play-fulness of imagination and the intensity of mind. Christians are claimed by a past that hopes for the future by drinking deeply of the present. They are daring persons for whom belief is etched with faith-ful doubts. They hold tenaciously to what has been bequeathed, yet they gamble on the new being born.
—From *The Art of Spiritual Direction* by W. Paul Jones

❧ If wakeful Christians harbor a wish for heaven to fulfill, they wish not for an escape from reality, but for a deeper acquaintance with reality. When wakeful Christians lament this life, they grieve this world's trivialization of itself that obscures the more profound reality of the kingdom of God in our midst. Yet, more often wakeful Christians celebrate life, finding the mark of God's hand in this world and beginning their praise with the discovery of the holy here. "Holy, holy, holy is the Lord of hosts; the whole earth is full of his glory" (Isa. 6:3), the seraphim sang. Wakeful visions of other worldly praise reveal angels singing of God's reign on earth as it is in heaven.

—From *A Wakeful Faith* by J. Marshall Jenkins

Palm Sunday or the Passion of Christ

A serious reflection on the scripture references for Palm Sunday remind us that Jesus did not take a leisurely ride to town along a path strewn with palm branches. That first Palm Sunday saw the final ride on the high road of principle, obedience, and faith that would lead to the death of Jesus. The disciples may have wished otherwise, but deep in their hearts they must have known that this ride was like no other Jesus had taken and would bring the end of the life they knew as his followers.

We can be sure that Jesus knew that the shouts of "Hosanna" would give way to the cry of "Crucify." He knew because he was fully human and was well acquainted with the temptation to follow the path of political correctness and the easiest way out. He also knew the shouts would change from "Hosanna" to "Crucify" because he was fully divine and could see clearly that his journey of incarnation was near the end. The coming humiliation and execution were now undeniable. His desire to be faithful was so over-whelmingly strong that he rode on in confidence and ultimate trust in God whom he knew intimately as Abba. There was no looking back with the question, "What if?" His focus remained on God and God's will as he moved forward, propelled and sustained by his deep faith in God's goodness and love.

Palm Sunday invites us to search deeply in our own souls for the answer to the question *What words would have been on my lips that day?* This day also invites us to consider our own course for today and tomorrow. We too can move forward in obedience and faith as we place our ultimate trust in God who has been made known to us in Jesus Christ. The peace and confidence of Jesus can be ours as we place our ulti-mate trust in God.

21: The Prince of Peace

Affirmation
The Lord will rescue me from every evil attack and save me for his heavenly kingdom. To him be the glory forever and ever. Amen (2 Tim. 4:18).

Petition
Turn to me and be gracious to me,
    for I am lonely and afflicted . . .
Consider how many are my foes,
    and with what violent hatred they hate me.
O guard my life, and deliver me;
    do not let me be put to shame, for I take refuge in
        you (Ps. 25:16, 19-20).

Sacred Reading: anthology or other selected reading

Daily Scripture Readings

Sunday	A.	Isaiah 50:4-9; Psalm 31:9-16; Philippians 2:5-11; Matthew 27:11-54
	B.	Isaiah 50:4-9; Psalm 31:9-16; Philippians 2:5-11; Mark 15:1-39
	C.	Isaiah 50:4-9; Psalm 31:9-16; Philippians 2:5-11; Luke 23:1-49
Monday		Mark 11:1-11
Tuesday		Zechariah 9:9-10
Wednesday		John 12:12-19
Thursday		Isaiah 62:10-12
Friday		Matthew 21:1-11
Saturday		Luke 19:29-39

Prayer: thanksgiving, petition, intercession, praise and offering

Reflection: silent (listening to God), written (journaling)

God's Promise

Very truly, I tell you, unless a grain of wheat falls into the earth and dies, it remains just a single grain; but if it dies, it bears much fruit. Those who love their life lose it, and those who hate their life in this world will keep it for eternal life. Whoever serves me must follow me, and where I am, there will my servant be also. Whoever serves me, the Father will honor (John 12:24-26).

My Response

"Now my soul is troubled. And what should I say— 'Father, save me from this hour'? No, it is for this reason that I have come to this hour. Father, glorify your name." Then a voice came from heaven, "I have glorified it" (John 12:27-28).

Readings for Reflection

❧ A prince is identified with privilege, rank, and special benefits, but Jesus, the Prince of Peace, comes into Jerusalem riding on a donkey, a symbol of lowliness. His entrance is greeted with affirmation and acclamation. There is a joyous mood in the crowd as the people anticipate the promise of the prophets before them.

> Rejoice greatly, O daughter of Zion!/Shout aloud, O daughter Jerusalem!/Lo, your king comes to you; triumphant and victorious is he,/humble and riding on a donkey,/on a colt, the foal of a donkey./He will cut off the chariot from Ephraim and the war horse from Jerusalem;/and the battle bow shall be cut off, /and he shall command peace to the nations; his dominion shall be from sea to sea,/and from the River to the ends of the earth (Zech. 9:9-10).

The promise of peace for a people plagued by war and strife was wonderful news. Perhaps now their long agony would come to an end. The promise of peace is enough to make any suffering people celebrate. Do you suffer today? Sometimes the wars within are as devastating as the wars without. At some time in our lives, most of us will know the darkness of loneliness, disappointment, and despair. When the Prince of Peace comes to offer release, redemption, help, and hope, we are also filled with joy and the "hosannas" burst from our lips as well.

Jesus chose the way of peace in a violent world. He taught his disciples to do the same. Just for a moment Peter forgot, and because of that, one in the arresting party lost an ear. But still Jesus rebuked Peter and courageously continued his journey as the Prince of Peace on the way to his own death.

—Rueben P. Job

❧ Peacemaking must be the primary focus of all political leaders, whether in or out of power. But the temptations to personal power are too intense to be overcome by our insistently self-centered egos. Therefore, the peace must be God's peace, a peace that is freely available when we turn inwardly to Jesus. Jesus is the model of the ultimate peacemaker, always pointing to Abba as the ultimate source of peace, justice, goodness, mercy, love, and creativity. In order to claim peace, we must relinquish our own private agendas and let ourselves be claimed by God.

—Robert A. Jonas from *Henri Nouwen: Writings Selected with an Introduction by Robert A. Jonas*

❧ When Jesus was in his excruciating moment in the Garden of Gethsemane he needed his disciples to *be* with him while he prayed. He longed for the comfort of their presence and was pained by their inability to provide this for him. Jesus didn't need Peter to slice off an ear of his enemy. He just needed Peter and the others to be there with him as he faced his enemies (Lk 22:39-46).

—From *The Cup of Our Life* by Joyce Rupp

❧ The ass was the beast on which kings rode when they came in peace; only in war did they ride upon horses. The entry of Jesus was the claim to be King.

But at the same time it was the claim to be the King of peace. It was upon the ass of peace and not upon the horse of war that Jesus came. He came deliberately refusing the role of the warrior Messiah and claiming to be the Prince of peace. He was appealing for a throne, but the throne was in the hearts of men. In that entry into Jerusalem Jesus, in a dramatic symbolic action which spoke more loudly than any words, was making one last appeal to men, and saying to them: "Will you not, even now, even yet, accept me as your Lord and King, and enthrone me within your hearts?"

Jesus' entry into Jerusalem was an action of supreme courage; it was an assertion of royalty and an offer of love; it was at one and the same time royalty's claim and love's appeal.

—From *The Mind of Jesus* by William Barclay

❧   Peace, troubled Heart, be calm, be still,
    Till thy Desire appears.
The Lamb shall all my Sorrows heal,
    And wipe away my Tears.

    . . . .

Entering on Life's Meridian Stage
    I see the Shades appear,
And feel Anticipated Age,
    Death's welcome Harbinger.

    . . . .

Beneath that Load I now stand up
    And wait the End to see,
Hold fast my comfortable Hope
    Of Immortality.

On Earth I shall not always live
    Afflicted & opprest,
My Saviour will at last receive
    His Mourner to his Breast.

Here then I rest my fainting Soul,
    And calm expect the Day
That speaks my Suffering Measure full
    And summons me away.

Patient of Life, for thy dear sake
    Who liv'dst & diedst for me,
Lo from thy Hand the Cup I take
    And live & die for Thee.
—From *The Unpublished Poetry of Charles Wesley*,
    Vol. 1

❧ Is it possible that our world still knows better how
to deal with a bandit, a murderer, an insurrectionist
than it knows what to do with the Prince of Peace?
There is a sense in which an assassin's attempt on the
pope's life is less shocking to our world than the pope's
forgiveness of him. Is it possible that we would rather
deal with raw power that rides on a stallion than with
this one who comes on a donkey, with the weapons of
love, patience, suffering, and peace? Given the choice,
isn't it possible that we would take Barabbas, too?
—From *What Will You Do with King Jesus?* by James
    A. Harnish

❧ The final pictures in Matthew's gospel are not only
a bold affirmation of faith in the triumph of the kingdom of God, they are also a daring challenge to the disciples. The only logical response to this Gospel is the
Great Commission: "Go into all the world and make
disciples of all nations, for I am with you always, even
to the end of time."

One of the most courageous witnesses for Christ in
recent years was Archbishop Oscar Romero, the leader
of the Roman Catholic Church in El Salvador, who was
killed on March 24, 1980, while celebrating Mass in a
hospital chapel in San Salvador.

With unflinching courage, he applied the message
of liberation and justice to the political and social struggles of his homeland. In his last homily on March 23,

he acknowledged "the risk that is run by our poor station for being the instrument and vehicle of truth and justice," but he went on to say that, in the context of the Lenten season, "all of this is preparation for our Easter, and Easter is a shout of victory. No one can extinguish that life which Christ revived. Not even death and hatred against him and against his Church will ever be able to overcome it. He is the victor!"

—From *What Will You Do with King Jesus?* by James A. Harnish

❧ You've heard the saying "Sticks and stones may break my bones but words can never hurt me." Well, that's not true, is it? Words *can* hurt. . . . They make us feel small and exposed. They make us feel *shame*.

Revenge is *bitter*sweet—after the sweetness wears off, the bitter taste remains in your mouth. In place of revenge, civil rights leaders taught *nonviolent* ways of confronting people who are putting you down. Your first response to humiliating treatment needs to be claiming your own dignity as a person created in the image of God. This awareness sets you free to respond to injustice in creative rather than violent ways.

—From "Justice" in *Way to Live* edited by Dorothy C. Bass and Don C. Richter

The Season of Easter

The Lord is risen; the tears of grief have given way to tears of joy; and the followers of Jesus Christ now try to live in this world where evil, darkness, and death itself have been unconditionally conquered. Evil conquered? Yes! Death conquered? Yes! To live in a world where evil holds no fear and death holds no threat requires a radical shift in understanding and attitude. Such a world is no longer under the dominant control of darkness but is already showing signs of the healing and life-giving presence of light, God's light. The truth that darkness can never extinguish the light gives us confidence and hope in this season and in all seasons.

Courage now flourishes where fear once dominated. We no longer tremble before powers of darkness and evil for we know that their ultimate defeat already has occurred, and we can face them unafraid. What is there that can really do us harm? We now know the assurance that Paul declared: "In all these things we are more than conquerors through him who loved us. . . . I am convinced that neither death, nor life, . . . nor anything else in all creation, will be able to separate us from the love of God in Christ Jesus our Lord" (Rom. 8:37-39).

The Season of Easter is set within the fifty days following our Lord's resurrection. Forty days after the resurrection we observe our Lord's ascension; fifty days after the resurrection, and ten days after we observe Ascension, we observe Pentecost, marking the end of the Easter Season. We then embark on the longest season of the church year, which is identified by various names: Ordinary Time, Kingdomtide, Whitsuntide, the Season of Pentecost.

Easter Sunday

22: Jesus Christ Is Alive

Affirmation
No one has greater love than this, to lay down one's life for one's friends. You are my friends if you do what I command you. I do not call you servants any longer, because the servant does not know what the master is doing; but I have called you friends, because I have made known to you everything that I have heard from my Father (John 15:13-15).

Petition
Breathe on me, Breath of God,
Fill me with life anew,
That I may love what Thou dost love,
And do what Thou wouldst do.
—Edwin Hatch (1835–89)

Sacred Reading: anthology or other selected reading

Daily Scripture Readings

Sunday	A.	Jeremiah 31:1-6; Psalm 118:1-2, 14-24; Colossians 3:1-4; John 20:1-18
	B.	Isaiah 25:6-9; Psalm 118:1-2, 14-24; 1 Corinthians 15:1-11; Mark 16:1-8
	C.	Acts10:34-43; Psalm 118:1-2, 14-24; 1 Corinthians 15:19-26; John 20:1-18
Monday		Matthew 28:1-10
Tuesday		Revelation 1:12-20
Wednesday		Luke 24:1-12
Thursday		Acts 17:16-21
Friday		Luke 20:27-40
Saturday		Philippians 3:7-11

Prayer: thanksgiving, petition, intercession, praise and offering

Reflection: silent (listening to God), written (journaling)

God's Promise

You did not choose me but I chose you. And I appointed you to go and bear fruit, fruit that will last, so that the Father will give you whatever you ask him in my name. I am giving you these commands so that you may love one another (John 15:16-17).

My Response

I know, O Lord, that if I follow close to you nothing shall be able to separate me from your endless life and love. Give me the grace to make your word my home, that I may know you more intimately and follow you more closely—evermore.

Readings for Reflection

❧ At this very moment when I write and at the very moment when you read these words, *you and I are in the presence of the living Christ.* To remember this truth is to be shaped constantly by the presence of God in Christ in our lives. We often forget this central truth of the Christian faith, and when we do, we are easily overcome by the troubles of the world.

For me, what I write will pass before the eyes of the One about whom I write. As I write, I hope that my ordinary life and ordinary capacity will be energized, directed, and used by the One who gives me life and has called me to this ministry. If I allow myself to think that this ministry and this project are all up to me, I risk feelings from despair to arrogance. However, if I remember that I am not alone, but think, work, and live in the presence of the living Christ, I remain hopeful that even the most simple and ordinary task carried out in that presence and with the assistance of Jesus Christ is sacred, meaningful, and useful.

For you, what you read comes not from the word processor of someone full of years and short of energy or imagination. For these words are now read and heard in the presence of Jesus Christ who is able to use the most simple and ordinary words and events to enlighten, comfort, heal, and direct the seeking heart.

The risen Christ is with us and therefore we need not fear the events of this day or any day that lies in our future. We know that each day will be lived in companionship with the only One who is able to rescue, redeem, save, keep, and companion us though every experience of this life and the next.

This realization does not take away the pain or uncertainty that life holds. But it does give us strength, wisdom, guidance, and most of all, a Companion to travel through each of these experiences with us. Easter Sunday and every Sunday are gentle yet dramatic reminders that we *are not alone or on our own*. As followers of Jesus, we walk with God in Christ, and that makes the journey rich in meaning, joy, and peace no matter where it leads. Jesus Christ is alive and reads with you now words that are intended to turn your eyes, heart, and life more fully toward God.

—Rueben P. Job

᪥ On Easter Sunday, 1980, I was living in Boise, Idaho, and had boarded a plane destined for Fargo, North Dakota. I was feeling sorry that I had to travel on Easter, yet I was reflecting and praising God for resurrection—the true meaning of Easter.

As the wheels of the airplane left the runway, the voice of the captain broke into my lonely silence. "Good morning, ladies and gentlemen," he said, "and Happy Easter. It's going to be a bit choppy on our climb-out today, but we're expecting it to be somewhat smoother when we reach our assigned altitude at thirty-one thousand feet. The weather at our destination is beautiful. The temperature there is a balmy fifty degrees."

I forgot my self-pity as I thought, *He just told us the entire Christian story, including Easter, in that brief announcement.* Our life in Christ is similar: For a time we have to suffer various trials, so that the genuineness of our faith—though being tested by fire—may be found to result in praise, glory, and honor when Jesus Christ is revealed (see 1 Pet. 1:6-7).

The truth is we never were promised a smooth flight through life, but we have been promised Christ's presence and provision for the journey. In my airplane seat, I scrambled for my Bible, as in rapid succession various scripture passages invaded my memory: 2 Corinthians 1:4; Ephesians 3:13-21; 2 Corinthians 4:8-11; Hebrews 12:2.

While we never were promised a smooth *flight*, we are expecting a much smoother journey when we reach our "assigned altitude." For we are assigned to live in the spirit and life of Christ (1 Pet. 1:3). God is our captain, and we will rise above the choppiness that is now our momentary experience. This is the hope and promise of Resurrection power at its fullest and best. This is the glory of Easter (1 Pet. 1:4).

Then I read Ezekiel 37:1-14, and there I saw a picture of life lived without Christ—a life of death, dryness, weeping (vv. 1, 2, 11). I read on and saw that living in "graves" is not our assigned altitude. No indeed! We are assigned to live on a much higher plane. God promises, "I will bring you back to the land of Israel. And you shall know that I am the LORD, when I open your graves, and bring you up from your graves. I will place you on your own soil; then you shall know that I, the LORD, have spoken and will act" (vv. 12-14).

This is the altitude God has assigned to us for the living of our lives—God has assigned us to live in God's spirit. This is the secret of resurrection life.

As we neared our destination, the captain's voice broke into my musing: "We can expect a fair amount of turbulence as we begin our descent into Fargo." *Our troubles are not over yet,* I thought, *but we have hope, and Easter assures us of arrival at our final destination.*

So in all the ups and downs of our life we greatly rejoice (1 Pet. 1:6), and we can take our cue from Peter, who experienced more than a few ups and downs. Simply saying "In this you rejoice" was not enough, so Peter said it again: "Although you have not seen him, you love him; and even though you do not see him now, you believe in him and rejoice with an indescribable and glorious joy; for you are receiving the outcome of your faith, the salvation of your souls" (v. 8). This is the meaning and spirit of Easter.
—Norman Shawchuck

❧ That light which far outshines the day and sun, first pledge of resurrection, and renovation of bodies long since dissolved, the divine token of promise, the path which leads to everlasting life—in a word, the day of the Passion—is arrived, best beloved doctors, and ye, my friends who are assembled here, ye blessed multitudes, who worship him who is the author of all worship, and praise him continually with heart and voice, according to the precepts of his holy word.
—From "The Oration of the Emperor Constantine" by Eusebius

❧ Everything that is comes alive in the risen Christ—who, as Chesterton reminded, is standing behind us. Everything—great, small, important, unimportant, distant, and near—has its place, its meaning, and its value. Through union with Him (as Augustine said, He is more intimate with us than we are with ourselves), nothing is wasted, nothing is missing. There is never a moment that does not carry eternal significance—no action that is sterile, no love that lacks fruition, and no prayer that is unheard. "We know that by turning *everything* to their good God cooperates with all those who love [God]" (Rom. 8:28, emphasis added).
—From *Abba's Child* by Brennan Manning

❧ As we practice the Art of Passingover, we begin to personify the truth of this saying of Jesus. Again and again, we willingly die by "letting-go" and "letting-be," only to discover the rich harvest that awaits us in "letting-be" and "letting-grow."

To face death with such willingness is revolutionary in this culture. Our culture is largely based on the denial of death in any of its forms. For most of us, death is the opposite of life, so we deny it in order to live in peace. In the Art of Passingover, however, we experience death and life as organically related parts of a larger whole; we experience them as inextricably wedded to one another within the messianic process of growth and creativity. So, rather than deny death, we affirm it by creatively living through it; in order to become what we are not, we willingly die to what we are. That is how it is in the Art of Passingover.

As we begin to experience the on-going interrelatedness of life and death in practice, our whole approach to human growth, and to how life unfolds, changes. Formerly, we may have thought that the cycle of human life begins with physical birth and ends with physical death. Given the bias of our culture, we may even have graded the stages along the way on the basis of how close they came to death. So, we gave youth a decided "plus," middle age a perplexed "plus-minus with a question mark," and old age a definite "minus," if we considered it at all.

—From *The Art of Passingover* by Francis Dorff

❧ The holiest of men still need Christ, as their Prophet, as "the light of the world." For he does not give them light, but from moment to moment: The instant he withdraws, all is darkness. They still need Christ as their King; for God does not give them a stock of holiness. But unless they receive a supply every moment, nothing but unholiness would remain. They still need Christ as their Priest, to make atonement for their holy things. Even perfect holiness is acceptable to God only through Jesus Christ.

—From "Christian Perfection" by John Wesley

❧   Christ, whose glory fills the skies,
     Christ, the true, the only light,
     Sun of Righteousness, arise,
     Triumph o'er the shades of night.
     —From "Christ, Whose Glory Fills the Skies" by
      Charles Wesley

❧ In a word, earthly life is but the first, very short stretch of the journey to be done; it is very far from completing it.

This is the time of "the grain of wheat that dies in the earth"; it lasts the space of a day as against the thousand thousand years of God.

—From *Journey Without End* by Carlo Carretto

❧ The great spiritual teachers are not concerned about domination and power in the sense our culture uses it. Their power is in descent, not ascent. I find, in fact, my deepest power is what Jesus visualizes on the cross as powerlessness. We Christians believe that the crucifixion of Christ—utter powerlessness—is his moment of greatest power. This recognition is at the core of all spiritual teaching. It is a recognition that dramatically turns one's reality upside down. It is a paradox, a dilemma, and finally becomes a choice.

—From *Everything Belongs* by Richard Rohr

❧ "I am with you always." This is the eternal source of our daily life of prayer. This is no technique. We are in deep waters of the most intimate of all possible relationships that flow to us—forever fresh and new—from minute to minute. And, as with all that lives, our relationship with the ultimate Person is organic, open-ended, unexpected, asymmetrical, and unfolding. . . .

You might think of or picture yourself walking with Jesus or sitting across from him. Ask him as you might a beloved friend, "What can I do each day to respond from my heart to your presence? What is best and most real for me?" You may wish to ask these questions of the living Jesus Christ each day: "How can I best experience your transforming friendship today? What way can we best share and talk together today?" How do you feel like responding at this moment?

It may appear that each day will differ. Or you may feel the inner suggestion to have one main way of prayer for a period of time. Whatever suggestion surfaces will be in rhythm with the type of person you essentially are—because that is the person God created and loves.

—From *Feed My Shepherds* by Flora Slosson Wuellner

23: Jesus Meets Us on the Way

Affirmation

When Jesus came to the place, he looked up and said to him, "Zacchaeus, hurry and come down; for I must stay at your house today.". . .Then Jesus said to him, "Today salvation has come to this house, because he too is a son of Abraham. For the Son of Man came to seek out and to save the lost" (Luke 19:5, 9-10).

Petition

Now on that same day two of them were going to a village called Emmaus. . . . While they were talking and discussing, Jesus came near and went with them. . . . As they came near the village . . . he walked ahead as if he were going on. But they urged him strongly, saying, "Stay with us, because it is almost evening and the day is now nearly over." So he went in to stay with them (Luke 24:13-15, 28-29).

Sacred Reading: anthology or other selected reading

Daily Scripture Readings

Sunday	A.	Acts 2:14, 22-32; Psalm 16; 1 Peter 1:3-9; John 20:19-31
	B.	Acts 4:32-35; Psalm 133; 1 John 1:1–2:2; John 20:19-31
	C.	Acts 5:27-32; Psalm 118:14-29; Revelation 1:4-8; John 20:19-31
Monday		Luke 24:13-27
Tuesday		Luke 24:28-35
Wednesday		John 21:1-14
Thursday		Matthew 28:16-20
Friday		Acts 2:22-36
Saturday		Genesis 32:22-32

Prayer: thanksgiving, petition, intercession, praise and offering

Reflection: silent (listening to God), written (journaling)

God's Promise
Listen! I am standing at the door, knocking; if you hear my voice and open the door, I will come in to you and eat with you, and you with me. . . . See, I am coming soon; my reward is with me, to repay according to everyone's work (Rev. 3:20, 22:12).

My Response
Amen. Come, Lord Jesus! (Rev. 22:20).

Readings for Reflection

❧ There are times when all of us long for the companionship of Christ. When we are facing some deep loneliness that seems to darken the brightest day, some great sorrow that has broken our heart and changed our lives, or some heavy burden that comes through no action or fault of our own. At times like these we long for the presence of one who speaks our name, understands our plight, and can break the hold of loneliness, sorrow, despair, and burdens we bear.

There are other times when we are at the peak of our powers and all is going well that we want someone to walk with us, to share the challenge, excitement, and reward of the path we have chosen. We desire a companion who can appreciate the challenge and victory of life in the days when all is well.

There are still other times when we need a companion to whom we can say thank you. There are those times when we are overwhelmed with gratitude. We know that the goodness we enjoy is not just the result of our good work but that someone else had a hand in our well-being, comfort, and success.

At times like these it is good to remember that the risen Christ walks beside us—awaiting our invitation to stay with us, break bread with us, interpret life for us, give us hope, and share in our thanksgiving.

May we, like the disciples before us, have our eyes opened to recognize Christ as he comes to walk beside us this day.

—Rueben P. Job

❧ Living in the awareness of the risen Jesus is not a trivial pursuit for the bored and lonely or a defense mechanism enabling us to cope with the stress and sorrow of life. It is the key that unlocks the door to grasping the meaning of existence. All day and every day we are being reshaped into the image of Christ. Everything that happens to us is designed to this end. Nothing that exists can exist beyond the pale of His presence ("All things were created through him and for him"—Col. 1:16), nothing is irrelevant to it, nothing is without significance in it.

—From *Abba's Child* by Brennan Manning

❧ The fisherman indeed deprives his prey of life, but our Fisher frees all that He takes alive from death's painful bonds, and therefore "did he shew himself upon earth, and conversed with [people]," bringing [those] His life, conveying teaching by means of the visible [humanity], and giving to reasonable beings the law of a suitable life and conversation. This law He has confirmed by miracles, and by the death of the flesh has destroyed death. By raising the flesh He has given the promise of resurrection to us all, after giving the resurrection of His own precious body as a worthy pledge of ours. So loved He [others] even when they hated Him that the mystery of the economy fails to obtain credence with some on account of the very bitterness of His sufferings, and it is enough to show the depths of His loving kindness that He is even yet day by day calling to [those] who do not believe. And He does so not as though He were in need of the service of [humanity],—for of what is the Creator of the universe in want?—but because He thirsts for the salvation of every [person]. Grasp then, my excellent

friend, His gift: sing praises to the Giver, and procure for us a very great and right goodly feast.
—From "Letter to Uranius, Governor of Cyprus" by Theodoret

❧ It matters not whether you believe in life after death or resurrection or pie in the sky when you die. God's designs do not depend upon your assent. Rather, you can depend upon God's ability to bring to pass those things regarding which God has spoken. The awesome promises of God depend upon God and not whether you can or cannot believe God's promises.
—Norman Shawchuck

❧ All spiritual disciplines are to help you trust this personal experience of *yourself*, which is, not surprisingly, also an experience of God. People are usually amazed that the two experiences coincide: when we know God, we seem to know and accept our own humanity; when we meet ourselves at profound levels of recognition, we also meet God. We don't have any real access to who we are except through God, and we don't have any real access to God except through forgiving and rejoicing in our own humanity.
—From *Everything Belongs* by Richard Rohr

❧ When the Word became human, Jesus Christ lived the same relationship in a human mode and it is in this relationship that we are called to share. Like the Word, like Jesus in the flesh, we are invited to live our life here on earth as a journey *toward God*.

Throughout the Gospels there are two salient aspects of the identity of Jesus. He is from the [Creator], sent by God to accomplish a task. Secondly, the human journey of Jesus is one that leads back toward God. It is this movement back toward God that is opened to believers of all generations. In following Jesus, we are shown the way that leads toward the [Creator]. Our life is not aimless; it has a destination. We have not been left to wander in the desert; the Shepherd has come to seek what is lost and bring us home.

—From *Toward God* by Michael Casey

❧ For those who profess and call themselves Christians, the lens through which everything else is interpreted is a person: Jesus Christ and his death and resurrection. Just as the lover never plumbs the mystery of the beloved, so we do not exhaust the mystery of Jesus. This, at first, seems a strange claim. But it is no less extraordinary that contemporary "messiahs, saviors, and gurus" possess the consciousness of modern men and women. . . . A walk on a Saturday evening through the streets of a busy city reveals what models, exemplars, paradigms are operating in the lives of the people.

We cannot do without a paradigm to help us live. As a believer, I keep bumping into Jesus. I wander away, and there he is, perhaps in the eyes of someone on the street. There is no escape for me. Nor do I want there to be.

—From *Soul Making* by Alan W. Jones

❧ It is being included in the eternal life of God that heals all wounds and allows us to stop demanding satisfaction. What really matters, of a personal nature, once it is clear that *you are included*? You have been *chosen*. *God* chooses you. This is the message of the kingdom.

—From *The Divine Conspiracy* by Dallas Willard

❧ There are times, though, when the impression of presence is not there, when it seems therefore God is not there. We go through something we didn't think God would allow, a testing of the heart, the kind of thing we pray against, "And lead us not into temptation, but deliver us from evil." Then it can seem we have encountered another side of God, a side turned away from us like the other side of the moon. If we hold to

God nonetheless, we come to realize it is not another side of God we are experiencing so much as the essential ordeal of a journey with God. Every journey has its ordeal, according to storytelling, an ordeal by fire, by water, by sheer endurance, and a journey with God has its ordeal too, the ordeal of the human heart, the trial where the secrets of the heart are revealed. If I come upon that ordeal, I may find that my heart is divided, that it is not entirely with God. Still, I do not thereby fail the test. For I can bring my divided heart to God to be made whole. I can bring all my heart to God, although it is a heart in pieces, a broken heart.

—From *Love's Mind* by John S. Dunne

24: *From Fear to Courage*

Affirmation
Then the LORD turned to him and said, "Go in this might of yours and deliver Israel from the hand of Midian; I hereby commission you" (Judg. 6:14).

Petition
He responded, "But sir, how can I deliver Israel? My clan is the weakest in Manasseh, and I am the least in my family" (Judg. 6:15).

Sacred Reading: anthology or other selected reading

Daily Scripture Readings

Sunday	A.	Acts 2:14, 36-41; Psalm 116:1-4, 12-19; 1 Peter 1:17-23; Luke 24:13-35
	B.	Acts 3:12-19; Psalm 4; 1 John 3:1-7; Luke 24:36-48
	C.	Acts 9:1-6; Psalm 30; Revelation 5:11-14; John 21:1-19
Monday		John 20:19-23
Tuesday		Deuteronomy 31:7-8
Wednesday		Genesis 15:1-6
Thursday		Matthew 10:26-31
Friday		Luke 5:1-11
Saturday		Philippians 1:12-14

Prayer: thanksgiving, petition, intercession, praise, and offering

Reflection: silent (listening to God), written (journaling)

God's Promise
The LORD said to him, "I will be with you.". . . The LORD said . . . ,"Peace be to you; do not fear, you shall not die" (Judg. 6:16, 23).

My Response
So Gideon took ten of his servants, and did as the Lord had told him; but because he was too afraid of his family and the townspeople to do it by day, he did it by night (Judg. 6:27).

Readings for Reflection

❧ To feel fear is not unusual and sometimes it is a necessary and life-saving experience. Fear alerts us to the dangers that could harm us or even take our lives. However, when our fears dictate all our actions, we can become paralyzed and incapable of thinking clearly or living faithfully.

The disciples, victims of their fears, were behind closed and locked doors when Jesus appeared to them. Once the reality of his living presence was clear, their fears gave way to courage. Ever since Jesus appeared to the disciples, Christians have discovered that there is no need for fear when one is in the presence of God. To walk with God not only rebukes our fears and sends them away but also increases our courage.

To walk with God is to be reassured of direction, guidance, and strength for our daily journey. What do we have to fear when we are in God's presence and care? Nothing at all! This does not mean that we will be spared discouragement, disease, or death itself. *It does mean that we will never be alone.* It means that we will be given strength to meet the demands of our daily lives. It means that we will receive wisdom to judge wisely and well in the directions we must take. It means that we will know the joy and tranquility of living in the presence of God in every circumstance of life. From fear to courage is the natural journey of all that walk with God.
—Rueben P. Job

❧ Fear kills a mind and soul by slowly obliterating the visions we hold for our lives. That we should not fall prey to fear is a constant theme in the scriptures. God does not want us to succumb to the chilling and killing aspects of fear; God encourages people not to be afraid of the circumstances in which they find themselves. It seems that one of God's favorite themes is "Do not be afraid" or "Do not fear." Perhaps God repeats this theme so often because we so often fear circumstances that confront us in our lives and ministries.

God is not suggesting that we will not confront fearful realities in our lives. God is simply promising not to abandon us to fearful circumstance but to go with us through the dark night of fear, danger, and uncertainty.

Fear, left to eat away at us, finally brings us to a "little-death." We must not deny our fear or avoid dealing with the fearful moment. In scripture God never suggests an escapist attitude as an antidote for fear. The many "do not be afraid" promises in scripture do not suggest that we shun the fearful prospects in which we find ourselves, but God consistently promises to be with us in the dark and ominous moment.

—Norman Shawchuck

❧ Real spirituality dawns when our life with God becomes as real as the problems and joys we experience each day. Until then we live in two different worlds—one, a seemingly real, practical and demanding world; the other, a wistful, so-called "spiritual" world. In our daily activities, we may see ourselves enmeshed in the world, perhaps burdened. However, in our prayer we walk in the mystery of God, we dwell in peace, and we wish we could simply remain there.

This separation cannot remain if all our life is to be filled with real meaning, peace, and awe, no matter how violent or stormy our days may become. When we are *truly prayerful* we join both worlds. As we become naturally aware of God throughout the day,

we journey in *both* worlds simultaneously. That is truly the spiritual life.
—From *Everyday Simplicity* by Robert J. Wicks

❧ The greatest gift I have ever received from Jesus Christ has been the Abba experience. "No one knows the Son except the Father, just as no one knows the Father except the Son and those to whom the Son chooses to reveal him" (Matt. 11:27). My dignity as Abba's child is my most coherent sense of self. When I seek to fashion a self-image from the adulation of others and the inner voice whispers, "You've arrived; you're a player in the Kingdom enterprise," there is no truth in that self-concept. When I sink into despondency and the inner voice whispers, "You are no good, a fraud, a hypocrite and a dilettante," there is no truth in any image shaped from that message.
—From *Abba's Child* by Brennan Manning

❧ Two years ago I faced the crisis of cancer. The dreaded disease, which had already taken the life of two close relatives and invaded two others, now attacked me. In stark moments of confrontation with the truth, we can never predict our own response. At first I fell into a black hole, defeated. Then I swam in a sea of surrounding realities: my connectedness to others, my faith in the immensity of life, a strength whose source I simply accepted. In time my feelings roamed the spectrum of fear and despair. My body endangered by a mortal enemy. My life thrown into turmoil and my future made uncertain. My total helplessness in the face of a silent, aggressive foe.

My recovery was quick, my prognosis good, my basic attitudes healthy. I was immersed in understanding and love. My pain was borne by others and in that sharing there was comfort and hope. Before long I was engaged in all my normal activities. But "normal" has become a meaningless word. Health has become a relative experience. Time is etched with urgency. Life, which I too am prone to take for granted, has assumed a precious value. People and the time spent with them are treasures, not to be calculated, and not to be abused.

—From *Every Bush Is Burning* by Joan Puls

❧ We are desperately afraid of having no power. We fear loneliness, poverty and boredom. We fear failure terribly.

Nonviolence, nonpleasure, nonaggression are also part of our American shadow. These are the things that we avoid to create our character armor. We lust after the kind of aggression that allows us to be dominant, to be powerful. We settle for a certain kind of pleasure that really isn't joyous. Sometimes pleasure, as a liminoid [secularized sacred] experience, is the avoidance of joy. It is to entertain one part of our body, perhaps, but at the price of the inner glow and juice of our whole being. Poverty is the ultimate shadow for many of us. We cannot imagine being happy without our money. We would be petrified to be without our many options. We've substituted freedom of choice for the freedom of the soul which alone gives spiritual joy.

—From *Everything Belongs* by Richard Rohr

❧ We need to look for what we dismiss and what we disdain. Look at what we've spent our whole life avoiding. We don't want to look unsuccessful. That's our shadow. If we fear looking weak, that is our shadow. I can see why my father, Francis, intentionally countered the way the West was moving. He moved entirely into the shadow self and said, "Here is where I will rejoice." I will delight in nonpower, nonaggression, nondomination, nonpleasure, nonwealth and nonsuccess. He lived so close to the bottom of things that he could never fall very far. Now that is freedom!

—From *Everything Belongs* by Richard Rohr

❧ They did not nail him then, but simply bound him. And he, placing his hands behind him, and being bound like a distinguished ram [taken] out of a great flock for sacrifice, and prepared to be an acceptable burnt-offering unto God, looked up to heaven, and said, "O Lord God Almighty, the Father of thy beloved and blessed Son Jesus Christ, by whom we have received the knowledge of Thee, the God of angels and powers, and of every creature, and of the whole race of the righteous who live before Thee, I give Thee thanks that Thou hast counted me worthy of this day and this hour, that I should have a part in the number of Thy martyrs, in the cup of thy Christ, to the resurrection of eternal life, both of soul and body, through the incorruption [imparted] by the Holy Ghost. Among whom may I be accepted this day before Thee as a fat and acceptable sacrifice, according as Thou, the ever-truthful God, hast fore-ordained, hast revealed beforehand to me, and now hast fulfilled. Wherefore also I praise Thee for all things, I bless Thee, I glorify Thee, along with the everlasting and heavenly Jesus Christ, Thy beloved Son, with whom, to Thee, and the Holy Ghost, be glory both now and to all coming ages. Amen."

—From "The Prayer of Polycarp"

25: Love Makes the Difference

Affirmation
At the word of God the heavens and earth were born; and by God's word they forever remain. I pledge to live this day according to the words of promise I now confess to you.

Petition
O, my God! Loving God! In this hour of prayer come to me. Speak words of life and love into the depths of my being. I love you, my God. Truly I love you!

Sacred Reading: anthology or other selected reading

Daily Scripture Readings

Sunday	A.	Acts 2:42-47; Psalm 23; 1 Peter 2:19-25; John 10:1-10
	B.	Acts 4:5-12; Psalm 23; 1 John 3:16-24; John 10:11-18
	C.	Acts 9:36-43; Psalm 23; Revelation 7:9-17; John 10:22-30
Monday		John 21:15-17
Tuesday		Deuteronomy 6:1-9
Wednesday		John 11:28-37
Thursday		John 15:9-11
Friday		Colossians 3:12-14
Saturday		Galatians 5:22-26

Prayer: thanksgiving, petition, intercession, praise, and offering

Reflection: silent (listening to God), written (journaling)

God's Promise
My love for you knows no limit. Out of my love for you, you were born. And out of my love for you, my

eye is upon you every hour. For, you see, you are my beloved in whom I am well pleased.

My Response
I do love you, my Lord, but not faithfully enough. I confess that my love runs hot and cold. My God, help me to understand this mystery about myself. Why must my relationship with you be a come-and-go affair?

Readings for Reflection

❧ As I drove up the driveway, our children raced out the front door and met me at the car. Before I could get my suitcase out of the car, they were telling me about Puddles, the dog that had followed them home from the little store a few blocks away. We had talked nearly every day about the dog we were going to get when we were able to move into the country. Everyone wanted a big dog like a Dalmatian or a black Labrador. But as I got out of the car I noticed a dog that was small and scraggly, of mixed origin, very soon to be a mother, and yet very personable. The chorus of affirmation for the dog from our children was compelling. But I gave no clear answer to their question, "Can we keep Puddles?" I did not want to adopt a dog like this, and I knew I had to move quickly to make sure we did not have a dog and a litter of puppies on our hands.

I suggested that after our evening meal and our chores were completed we would talk about what to do with the dog. Later, when we were all settled in the family room, and with the dog in the garage, I asked each of the children to tell me why he or she thought we should keep Puddles when we could get a beautiful and large dog. Each of them had a good reason. She needed a home. We would enjoy the puppies. She would be a watchdog. Last I turned to our eight-year-old son and asked him what we should do with the dog and why. His eyes filled with tears and he said, "We should keep her." I asked him for his reason why we should keep this scraggly dog. He responded through his tears, "Because she loves me." We kept Puddles. She was with us while our children grew up and when they called home from college and career, their first question was always, "How is Puddles?" She lived with us seventeen years because one little boy loved her enough to save her.

Jesus knew that only love was strong enough to keep the disciples faithful in the days ahead. His repeated questions to Peter were meant to clarify for Peter what the real love of his life was. Only love is strong enough to keep us faithful, and the question to us from the One who loves us without condition or qualification is first of all about our love. For God knows what we know: Only love is strong enough to keep us faithful . . . and joyful. May our love for God continue to grow in the presence of God's love for us.
—Rueben P. Job

❧ Giving needs not be confined to money or material gifts, but I would like more people to give their hands to serve and their hearts to love—to recognise the poor in their own homes, towns and countries, and to reach out to them in love and compassion.
—From *My Life for the Poor* by Mother Teresa

❧ I'll never forget during the Bangladesh suffering: we had ten million people in and around Calcutta.

I asked the government of India to allow a number of other congregations to come to our aid, to help us, because we were working the whole time.

They allowed them to come: about fifteen or sixteen different sisters came to help us, and each one, on leaving Calcutta, said the same thing, "I have received much more than I have given and I can never be the same person again; because I have touched Christ, I have understood what love is. What it is to love and to be loved!"
—From *My Life for the Poor* by Mother Teresa

❧ And in this [God] showed me something small, no bigger than a hazelnut, lying in the palm of my hand, as it seemed to me, and it was as round as a ball. I looked at it with the eye of my understanding and thought: What can this be? I was amazed that it could last, for I thought that because of its littleness it would suddenly have fallen into nothing. And I was answered in my understanding: It lasts and always will, because God loves it; and thus everything has being through the love of God.

In this little thing I saw three properties. The first is that God made it, the second is that God loves it, the third is that God preserves it. But what did I see in it? It is that God is the Creator and the protector and the lover. For until I am substantially united to [God], I can never have perfect rest or true happiness, until, that is, I am so attached to [God] that there can be no created thing between my God and me.

—From *Showings* by Julian of Norwich

❧ How do we get in touch with our chosenness when we are surrounded by rejections? I have already said that this involves a real spiritual struggle. Are there any guidelines in this struggle? Let me try to formulate a few.

First of all, you have to keep unmasking the world about you for what it is: manipulative, controlling, power-hungry and, in the long run, destructive. The world tells you many lies about who you are, and you simply have to be realistic enough to remind yourself of this. Every time you feel hurt, offended or rejected, you have to dare to say to yourself: "These feelings, strong as they may be, are not telling me the truth about myself. The truth, even though I cannot feel it right now, is that I am the chosen child of God, precious in God's eyes, called the Beloved from all eternity and held safe in an everlasting embrace."

Secondly, you have to keep looking for people and places where your truth is spoken and where you are reminded of your deepest identity as the chosen one.

Yes, we must dare to opt consciously for our chosenness and not allow our emotions, feelings or passions to seduce us into self-rejection. The synagogues, the churches, the many communities of faith, the different support groups helping us with our addictions, family, friends, teachers and students: all of these can become reminders of our truth. The limited, sometimes broken, love of those who share our humanity can often point us to the truth of who we are: precious in God's eyes. This truth is not simply an inner truth that emerges from our center. It is also a truth that is revealed to us by the One who has chosen us. That is why we have to keep listening to the many men and women in history who, through their lives and their words, call us back to it.

Thirdly, you have to celebrate your chosenness constantly. This means saying "thank you" to God for having chosen you, and "thank you" to all who remind you of your chosenness. Gratitude is the most fruitful way of deepening your consciousness that you are not an "accident," but a divine choice. It is important to realize how often we have had chances to be grateful and have not used them. When someone is kind to us, when an event turns out well, when a problem is solved, a relationship restored, a wound healed, there are very concrete reasons to offer thanks: be it with words, with flowers, with a letter, a card, a phone call or just a gesture of affection.
—From *Life of the Beloved* by Henri J. M. Nouwen

❧ Does it not happen all too often that if the victims of our love dared to speak they would plead: "Oh, please love me less but leave me free, I'm a prisoner of your love; because you love me you want to determine all my life, you want to shape all my happiness. If only you did not love me, I could be myself!" Does that not happen all too often between parents and children, friends, and husbands and wives? How costly our love is to others and how cheap it is for us, and yet Christ's command is that we should love one another as he loves us; to give his life was his way of loving: we could begin with much less than giving our lives, but we should begin with the commandment Christ gives to the selfish, the most selfish of us—"Do unto others what you wish them to do to you." You want to be happy; do so, but with justice. Give to your neighbor exactly as much as you claim for yourself. You want happiness—give an equal measure of happiness; you want freedom—give freedom in exactly the same measure. You want food, give food; you want love, unselfish and thoughtful—give unselfish and thoughtful love.

—From *Meditations on a Theme* by Metropolitan Anthony of Sourozh

❧ Fairy tales and myths have often been used as vehicles to teach a truth that is too deep for ordinary words. Our invitation to become one with God is too deep for ordinary words. How do we talk about a call to be like God? The early Christians were much more concerned about being divinized than about keeping laws. Sadly, somewhere along our historical journey we got preoccupied with law and doing things that would keep us out of hell. We lost sight of our original union with God and the continuing call to be like God. In fact, we became so busy keeping out of hell that we forgot we were on the way to heaven. We started loving God for the gifts we would receive or the punishment we would avoid. But is that truly love? What about the wonder and possibility of being simply and utterly in love, the only reason being that once upon a time before a burning bush the One Who Is said, "I Am who Am!" The bush still burns. What about our love? How bright is the flame?

—From *A Tree Full of Angels* by Macrina Wiederkehr

❧ It's not enough not to do evil; you must do good.
I am God and have defined myself as Love.

You are my children and have to become Love.
Love is perfection for me and for you.
Love is my life and must become your life.
Love is my joy and must become your joy.
Love conquers all, achieves all, resolves all.
Try it, and you'll see.
When you're sad, do a loving deed and your sadness will pass.
When you're lonely, try to communicate with me or with your fellow-beings and loneliness will vanish.
When you want to experience the taste of my presence within you, do a charitable action and you will feel me.
When you feel you are dying, love; life will pulsate through you.
Love lights up all, heals all, makes sense of all.
Love is Paradise.
Who loves is in joy; who loves not is in sorrow.
Love is truth; who loves is veracious.
Love is eternal life.
The joy of the saints is to live for love.
The fulfilment of human nature is to die for love.
Where charity and love reign, there is God.
I your God have defined myself as Love.
I am Love.
—From *And God Saw That It Was Good* by Carlo Carretto

❧ We may see that to live as Jesus did is to experience what it means to be beloved sons and daughters of God. The more we know our belovedness, the more freely we may live by the measure of Jesus' own example in the power of loving humility and transforming mercy. Here lie the spiritual roots of forgiveness and reconciliation. But the possibility of forgiveness and reconciliation can be as difficult to embrace as the notion of our belovedness.
—From *The Way of Forgiveness, Participant's Book* by Marjorie J. Thompson

❧ At a baptismal service recently, I was deeply impressed when the pastor did not dip his hand into a baptismal font already filled with water. Instead he took a pitcher, lifted his arm above his head, and *poured* the water into the font, creating a small waterfall. As he poured, he gave us scriptural verses on the water of life as a direct, loving energy from God that blesses and heals and flows from within us, through us, beyond us.

We begin to see our daily acts of love as flowing like a river from our center, and poured out on the dry and needy lands around us. Our actions become not willpower but *released gestures of pouring*, flowing.

When the woman of Bethany came to Jesus and poured precious ointment on his head, it was a *released* gesture of generous love. "She has done a beautiful thing to me," said Jesus to those who were scandalized at such an act.

To do a "beautiful thing" to God in released, responsive love is intended to be the *only* source of the Christian's words and actions. As one of my students once said to me, "The Christian is released from per-fectionism to being a lover of life."

—From *Release* by Flora Slosson Wuellner

26: Taken Where You Do Not Want to Go

Affirmation
Jesus calls me, I must follow, Follow him today;
When His tender voice is pleading How can I delay?
Follow, I will follow Thee,
     my Lord, Follow ev'ry passing day.
My tomorrows are all known to Thee,
     Thou wilt lead me all the way
          (© 1935 Howard L. Brown).

Petition
But you, O LORD, do not be far away!
     O my help, come quickly to my aid!
Deliver my soul from the sword,
     my life from the power of the dog!
     Save me from the mouth of the lion!
From the horns of the wild oxen you have rescued me
          (Ps. 22:19-21).

Sacred Reading: anthology or other selected reading

Daily Scripture Readings

Sunday	A.	Acts 7:55-60; Psalm 31:1-5, 15-16; 1 Peter 2:2-10; John 14:1-14
	B.	Acts 8:26-40; Psalm 22:25-31; 1 John 4:7-21; John 15:1-8
	C.	Acts 11:1-18; Psalm 148; Revelation 21:1-6; John 13:31-35
Monday		John 21:18-19
Tuesday		Acts 9:1-9
Wednesday		Acts 9:10-19
Thursday		2 Corinthians 11:16-32
Friday		Acts 16:6-10
Saturday		Acts 16:16-34

Prayer: thanksgiving, petition, intercession, praise, and offering

Reflection: silent (listening to God), written (journaling)

God's Promise
The LORD will keep you from all evil;
    he will keep your life.
The LORD will keep
    your going out and your coming in
    from this time on and forevermore (Ps. 121:7-8).

My Response
The waters closed in over me;
    the deep surrounded me;
weeds were wrapped around my head
    at the roots of the mountains.
I went down to the land
    whose bars closed upon me forever;
yet you brought up my life from the Pit,
    O LORD my God (Jon. 2:5-6).

Readings for Reflection

❧ To follow Jesus Christ, who was betrayed, wept, bled, and died before he rose again, is to be at high risk of being taken where we had not intended to go. Eugene Peterson pinpoints the trouble with praying: We are often asked to respond in ways that we never intended when we first began to pray.

It matters little where or in what century we are called to live out our Christian life. The witness of those who have gone before informs my own experience, telling me that we are often taken to places where we receive unwarranted accolades and to other places where we receive unwarranted suffering and pain. A disciple, one who chooses to be student and follower of Jesus, is not a "self-made person" and is not on a personally designed journey.

The key word in this theme is *taken*. Just as Jesus was taken into the wilderness after his baptism, so we are taken into the experiences of discipleship that we do not necessarily choose for ourselves. We choose to follow Jesus and then Jesus chooses where we will go. It is that simple.

The saving truth here is not that we are taken where we do not want to go; rather the saving truth is that we are not alone. There is One who leads us and goes with us. Jesus arose from baptism and "the Spirit immediately drove him out into the wilderness" (Mark 1:12). But even there the angels (messengers of God) were with him and tended to his needs. While we may not choose the place to go, *we can choose* to remain with the One who sends us and there find comfort, companionship, grace, peace, and joy.

—Rueben P. Job

   Nothing surpasses the holiness of those who have learned perfect acceptance of everything that is.

In the game of cards called life one plays the hand one is dealt to the best of one's ability.

Those who insist on playing, not the hand they were given, but the one they insist they should have been dealt—these are life's failures.

We are not asked if we will play. That is not an option. Play we must. The option is how.

—From *Taking Flight* by Anthony de Mello

   I have never felt ashamed to look at the cross until one day when a young woman came with her child in her hands.

She said to me she had gone to two or three different convents asking for a little bit of milk for her child.

She was answered, "You are lazy. Go and work!" and so on.

By the time she came to our house, when I took the child it died in my hands. I felt ashamed to look at

the cross because Jesus has given us so much and we could not give even a glass of milk to this little child.
—From *My Life for the Poor* by Mother Teresa

❧ The president of Mexico sent for me. I told him that he had to become holy as a president: not a Missionary of Charity, but as a president.

He looked at me a bit surprised, but it is like that: we have to become holy, each of us, in the place where God has put us.
—From *My Life for the Poor* by Mother Teresa

❧ Those who have gone before us have left a clear witness: We may seek God or we may seek ease, but we cannot seek both. The road we travel is anything but easy. It is true that God loves us and has a wonderful plan for our lives, but it is equally true that the plan is often fraught with tension and uncertainty, and with emotional, spiritual, and physical pain.
—From *Seeking the Face of God* by Gary Thomas

❧ It is, I believe, this discovery of our own radical powerlessness for good and potential for evil that causes us to be identified with the crucified Christ. The details vary for each individual: they may concern the governance of one's own life, bringing up one's family or one's work for the Church. Instead of being filled with the power of the Spirit we find ourselves empty and resourceless, victims of our own weakness and, quite possibly, the objects of others' disapproval. Generally one's first solution is to work harder, trying to demonstrate competence. The situation deteriorates further. What we need to do is take the powerlessness as a basic premise, and use this as a fulcrum to lift our hearts in prayer toward God.
—From *Toward God* by Michael Casey

❧ Human beings are ambivalent toward holiness. We are drawn toward those qualities exemplified by a St.

Francis or by Mother Teresa, or by communities who witness to the gospel under severe persecution. Yet we find such qualities disturbing, too far removed from the way we must live our daily lives. Something deep within our existence creates a restlessness for God, yet we live and move and work in a culture of technology, efficiency, and the tyranny of the literal. The hunger for holiness coexists uneasily with the practical atheism of our way of life. Still, the deepest language of the Christian biblical tradition claims that the created world itself already reflects the goodness of God but also groans in travail for sanctification and recreation. The time and place where these tensions intersect is the gathered church at worship.

—From "Sanctifying Time, Place *and* People" by Don E. Saliers in *The Weavings Reader*

❧ Who would not wish to follow Christ to supreme happiness, perfect peace, and lasting security? We shall do well to follow him there, but we need to know the way. The Lord Jesus had not yet risen from the dead when he gave this invitation. His passion was still before him; he had still to endure the cross, to face outrages, reproaches, scourging; to be pierced by thorns, wounded, insulted, taunted, and put to death. The road seems rough, you draw back, you do not want to follow Christ. Follow him just the same. The road we made for ourselves is rough, but Christ has leveled it by passing over it himself.

Who does not desire to be exalted? Everyone enjoys a high position. But self-abasement is the step that leads to it. Why take strides that are too big for you—do you want to fall instead of going up? Begin with this step and you will find yourself climbing. The two disciples who said: *Lord, command that one of us shall sit at your right hand in your kingdom and the other at your left* had no wish to think about this step of self-abasement. They wanted to reach the top without noticing the step that led there. The Lord showed them the step, however, by his reply: *Can you drink the cup that I am to drink?* You who aim at the highest exaltation, can you drink the cup of humiliation? He did not simply give the general command: *Let him renounce himself and follow me* but added: *Let him take up his cross and follow me.*

—From "Sermon 96" by Saint Augustine in *Journey with the Fathers, Year A*

❖ Thinking all is lost after the crucifixion, some of the disciples go fishing on the Sea of Tiberius—a dismal, depressing fishing expedition. Hot, naked, and exhausted, the disciples try valiantly to return to the way things were before they met Jesus. Suddenly a voice from the shore (big rock thrown here): "Catchin' anything?" "Nah," they shout back, more depressed than ever. "Then try the other side of the boat!" the voice yells again. Peter stands up to see who this wise guy is. Wait—no, it can't be—but, yes, it is: the Lord! Suddenly Peter can't move fast enough. He leaps into the water, and swims to shore, leaving the others to haul in a miraculous catch. His faith grows three sizes in a matter of minutes. The boundaries of what he thinks God can do explode, and his love and gratitude for what God is doing in Jesus Christ, the Lord of Life, is simply too large to fit in the boat any more.

—From *The Godbearing Life* by Kenda Creasy Dean and Ron Foster

27: Receiving Direction

Affirmation
Truly, one who touches you touches the apple of my eye. See now, I am going to raise my hand against them, and they shall become plunder for their own slaves. Then you will know that the LORD of hosts has sent me (Zech. 2:8-9).

Petition
Why do you look on the treacherous,
    and are silent when the wicked swallow
    those more righteous than they?
        (Hab. 1:13).

Sacred Reading: anthology or other selected reading

Daily Scripture Readings

Sunday	A.	Acts 17:22-31; Psalm 66:8-20; 1 Peter 3:13-22; John 14:15-21
	B.	Acts 10:44-48; Psalm 98; 1 John 5:1-6; John 15:9-17
	C.	Acts 16:9-15; Psalm 67; Revelation 21:10, 22–22:5; John 14:23-29
Monday		Matthew 28:18-20
Tuesday		Psalm 32:1-11
Wednesday		Luke 10:1-12
Thursday		Acts 9:1-9
Friday		Acts 10:1-16
Saturday		Acts 10:17-33

Prayer: thanksgiving, petition, intercession, praise, and offering

Reflection: silent (listening to God), written (journaling)

God's Promise
You call me Teacher and Lord—and you are right, for
that is what I am. . . . For I have set you an example,
that you also should do as I have done to you. . . . If
you know these things, you are blessed if you do them
(John 13:13, 15, 17).

My Response
But as for me, I will look to the LORD,
     I will wait for the God of my salvation;
     my God will hear me (Mic. 7:7).

Readings for Reflection

❧ According to the final verses of the Gospel of Matthew, Jesus met the disciples to give them direction and
the promise of his presence. The Bible is filled with
stories of people who received direction from God.
Through the centuries, faithful disciples have discovered some essential qualities for the life and stance that
permits us to receive God's direction.

Practicing a preference for God and God's will is
the place to begin. That means putting God ahead of
all else in our list of priorities. This is not only the way
to receive direction but also the way to a joyful and
faithful walk with God every day. Preference for God
profoundly affects our lives. We not only receive direction but find our lives transformed as we learn to turn
to God and seek to walk with God.

This kind of companionship with God leads to a
life of trust and confidence in God that permits us to
receive and respond to God's whisper of direction. Do
you want to live increasingly in God's presence,
receive God's direction, and walk in God's presence?
Begin practicing a preference for God and you will
discover a growing capacity to receive and respond to
God's direction of your life.
—Rueben P. Job

🙵 Once I asked my confessor for advice about my vocation. I asked, "How can I know if God is calling me and for what he is calling me?"

He answered, "You will know by your happiness. If you are happy with the idea that God calls you to serve him and your neighbor, this will be the proof of your vocation. Profound joy of the heart is like a magnet that indicates the path of life. One has to follow it, even though one enters into a way full of difficulties."

—From *My Life for the Poor* by Mother Teresa

🙵 One of Jesus' favorite visual aids is a child. Every time the disciples get into head games, he puts a child in front of them. He says the only people who can recognize and be ready for what he's talking about are the ones who come with the mind and heart of a child. It's the same reality as the beginner's mind. The older we get, the more we've been betrayed and hurt and disappointed, the more barriers we put up to beginner's mind. It's so hard to go back, to be vulnerable, to say to your soul, "I don't know anything."

—From *Everything Belongs* by Richard Rohr

🙵 Deep within us all there is an amazing inner sanctuary of the soul, a holy place, a Divine Center, a speaking Voice, to which we may continually return. Eternity is at our hearts, pressing upon our time-torn lives, warming us with intimations of an astounding destiny, calling us home unto Itself. . . . It is a Light Within that illumines the face of God and casts new shadows and new glories upon the human face. It is a seed stirring to life if we do not choke it. . . . Here is the Slumbering Christ, stirring to be awakened, to become the soul we clothe in earthly form and action. And He is within us all.

—From *A Testament of Devotion* by Thomas R. Kelly

❧ A key difference between mystics and all others is that their spiritual eyes have been opened, and they have "seen." From the chaos of their early inner confusion, mystics awaken to an illumined posture of Being. They are in a state of Being, rather than—like most others—seeking to become. Mystics are our poets and artists, our intuitional, creative thinkers, our inventors and saints.

—From *Ordinary People as Monks and Mystics* by Marsha Sinetar

❧ The most secret, sacred wish that lies deep down at the bottom of your heart, the wonderful thing that you hardly dare to look at, or to think about—the thing that you would rather die than have anyone else know of, because it seems to be so far beyond anything that you are, or have at the present time, that you fear that you would be cruelly ridiculed if the mere thought of it were known—that is just the very thing that God is wishing you to do or to be for Him. And the birth of that marvelous wish in your soul—the dawning of that secret dream—was the Voice of God . . . telling you to arise and come up higher because He had need of you.

—From *Power Through Constructive Thinking* by Emmet Fox

❧ Guidance is about hearing the inner voice in us that keeps us closely connected with God's ways, giving us direction for our lives. It's not that our lives are all mapped out for us by God. The path is rarely a clear, visible, neatly defined one. No, rather Divine Wisdom helps us to discover, each step of the way, how we are to be a loving person in our world with our chipped, flawed condition.

—From *The Cup of Our Life* by Joyce Rupp

❧ I feel an urgency at this stage in my life to name the human expressions and vivid manifestations of our life in the Spirit. I believe that nothing human is foreign to the Spirit, that the Spirit embraces all. Our mundane experiences contain all the stuff of holiness and of human growth in grace. Our world is rife with messages and signatures of the Spirit. Our encounters with one another are potential sites of the awakening and energizing that characterize the Spirit. But so much goes unnoticed. We fail so often to recognize the light that shines through the tiny chinks and the dusty panes of our daily lives. We are too busy to name the event that is blessed in its ordinariness, holy in its uniqueness, and grace-filled in its underlying challenge.

—From *Every Bush Is Burning* by Joan Puls

❧ Discernment for the Christian community begins with the individual Christian. Do I want to know God's will more than anything else? This question is the entry way into discernment. And it can be answered with affirmation only by those who love God and have learned to trust God. If we have any higher priority in our search for God's guidance, we will not be able to trust our discernment. I must spend enough time in prayer and faithful listening to the voice of God to be brought to that moment of trust and surrender when I can give up my preconceived ideas and become open to God's idea. My first concern is not my desired result. My first concern is always God and the fidelity of our relationship, and then the result of my discernment efforts will come quite naturally. We know that God is completely faithful, and we must be alert, prayerful, open, and ready to respond in obedience if we are to be led toward greater faithfulness on our part.

—From *A Guide to Spiritual Discernment* by Rueben P. Job

❧ It is enough to affirm Jesus' living presence at work in our lives, to call on the power of the Risen One, to pray in Jesus' name, to ask the living Jesus to enfold our lives with his transcendent life. It is enough to picture or to think of Jesus looking directly at us and speaking our name as those who are personally loved and loved forever. It is enough to grow in the trust that enables us to tell "him the whole truth."

—From *Feed My Shepherds* by Flora Slosson Wuellner

28: *Waiting to Receive Instructions*

Affirmation
For unto us a Child is born,
Unto us a Son is given;
And the government will be upon His shoulder.
And His name will be called
Wonderful, Counselor, Mighty God,
Everlasting Father, Prince of Peace.
Of the increase of His government and peace
There will be no end (Isa. 9:6-7, NKJV).

Petition
In the path of your judgments,
    O LORD, we wait for you;
your name and your renown
        are the soul's desire.
My soul yearns for you in the night,
        my spirit within me earnestly seeks you.
For when your judgments are in the earth,
        the inhabitants of the world
            learn righteousness (Isa. 26:8-9).

Sacred Reading: anthology or other selected reading

Daily Scripture Readings

Sunday	A.	Acts 1:6-14; Psalm 68:1-10, 32-35; 1 Peter 4:12-14, 5:6-11; John 17:1-11
	B.	Acts 1:15-17, 21-26; Psalm 1; 1 John 5:9-13; John 17:6-19
	C.	Acts 16:16-34; Psalm 97; Revelation 22:12-14, 16-17, 20-21; John 17:20-26
Monday		Acts 1:1-5
Tuesday		Psalm 25:1-10
Wednesday		John 16:12-15
Thursday		2 Timothy 3:10-17

Friday   Luke 8:40-42
Saturday   Psalm 40:1-8

Prayer: thanksgiving, petition, intercession, praise, and offering

Reflection: silent (listening to God), written (journaling)

God's Promise
Come now, let us argue it out, says the LORD:
though your sins are like scarlet,
    they shall be like snow;
though they are red like crimson,
    they shall become like wool.
If you are willing and obedient,
    you shall eat the good of the land;
but if you refuse and rebel,
    you shall be devoured by the sword;
    for the mouth of the LORD has spoken
        (Isa. 1:18-20).

My Response
It will be said on that day,
Lo, this is our God; we have waited for him, so that he
    might save us.
This is the LORD for whom we have waited;
let us be glad and rejoice in his salvation (Isa. 25:9).

Readings for Reflection

❧ Most of us do not wait well. A checkout line at the grocery store, a registration line at school, a doctor's appointment, or holiday traffic can quickly make us impatient, uneasy, and irritable. We want things at once and do not like to wait. Further, our culture thrives on instant response from fast food to computers—we want everything fast. So waiting is often a hard lesson for us to learn. My young grandchildren planted watermelon seeds with the dream of eating their own red, juicy watermelon. Despite frequent reminders that the melons would take eighty days to ripen, the children could not resist picking a couple of melons long before they matured. They were disappointed when the cut melons delivered far less than the taste treat they had dreamed about. As we grow older, we sometimes find waiting easier, but we still want God to respond to our requests with speed and accuracy.

However, deep in our hearts we know that many things cannot be hurried without endangering the results for which we wait. Friendship, character, personal transformation, pregnancy, ripened fruit, and sprouting seeds all take time. Each has its own schedule. While we may encourage a peach to ripen, it still requires a certain number of days on the tree and in the sun. Trying to hasten the process can lead to less than desirable results.

Jesus asked the disciples to wait in Jerusalem until they received the promised power to meet all that lay ahead of them as well as an advocate to teach them all that they needed to know. It must have been hard to wait. They were under suspicion by the authorities; they wanted to get on with their lives; and how did they know that waiting would make any difference? The disciples were obedient to the command of Jesus, though, and their obedience was rewarded with power and with a companion.

That power and that companion have been with Christians ever since. We claim the power of the Holy Spirit today to strengthen us for living fully, faithfully, and joyfully. We claim the companionship of Jesus Christ to guide, instruct, and sustain us day by day. Sometimes we wait for that power to become active or for that kind of companionship to blossom in our relationship with God in Christ. As we learn to earnestly seek and patiently wait—in God's perfect timing—the gifts are given. Then we know it was worth the wait.
—Rueben P. Job

❧ Mystics are the ones who hunger and thirst after righteousness, as the Bible puts it, the ones who yearn for continued or increased union with the other reality they themselves feel is the *real* reality—the reality which heals and makes all things new again. Their yearning is their most distinctive mark and has been called by some a "deep and burning wound," because it propels them toward the transcendent nature of life much as a lover is drawn toward the object of his love.

—From *Ordinary People as Monks and Mystics* by Marsha Sinetar

❧ Here, then, is another reason why apostles withdraw to make a retreat: they need to be charged with the Holy Spirit. The Holy Spirit is given to those who watch and pray and wait patiently, those who have the courage to get away from everything and come to grips with themselves and with God in solitude and silence. No wonder every one of the great prophets, indeed Jesus himself, retired to the desert for prolonged periods of silence, praying, fasting, wrestling with the forces of evil. The desert is the furnace where the apostle and the prophet are forged. The desert, not the marketplace. The marketplace is where apostles function. The desert is where they are formed and seasoned and receive their commission and their message for the world, "their" gospel.

—From *Contact with God* by Anthony de Mello

❧ Willingness is the opposite of willfulness, being full of our own will and ways and the satisfaction in being self-made or self-controlled persons. Willingness to be aware and willingness in general are prerequisites for spiritual direction. Willingness is a chosen position of vulnerability that recognizes we are ordinary beings in need of God's love, companionship, and guidance. It includes our acknowledgment that we are not all we would like to be or all that God hopes for us and points toward our desire to hear and follow the Spirit's invitations even when it means giving up our ways in favor of what we perceive as God's ways.

When we are even a little bit honest, we recognize that our measure of willingness varies depending on what is being asked of us and by whom. Some of God's opportunities seem to offer pleasurable outcomes. Surrender to these requests is easy. But there are times when the Spirit invites or simply takes us into unfamiliar territory either inwardly or outwardly. Then we may feel decidedly uneasy about following. God's love and intentions are larger and farther reaching than we realized. They extend beyond the kind of people we are used to and the kinds of problems, possibilities, and joys that are familiar to us.

—From *Holy Invitations* by Jeannette A. Bakke

❧ As we mature in faith, our willingness is tested, expanded, and refined. We become more conscious of our limitations and turn to God. The necessity of God's grace becomes clearer as we become more attuned and accurate in our recognition of our dependence on God and less sure of anything that causes us to describe ourselves self-righteously. At times, when confronted by the less-than-ideal behavior of others, we may recognize that we are capable of similar actions and give thanks to God for helping us avoid unwelcome pitfalls. Scripture instructs us to be holy as God is holy, yet we increasingly realize the impossibility of holy behavior unless it is brought about by the Spirit's empowerment and our willing responsiveness and cooperation. Many people use spiritual direction as a window through which to notice and attend to their own expectations and expressions of willingness and willfulness.

—From *Holy Invitations* by Jeannette A. Bakke

❧ Benedict chose to simplify his life in order to be more available to God, to listen and to learn the way of

Truth. Others with a similar yearning soon joined him, and guidelines for their life together became necessary; hence the Rule, for simplicity is not easy. There is risk involved in refusing to live by cultural norms, as well as struggle in trusting God for daily needs. Most of us will not be called to monastic life; our challenge is to find ways to let go intentionally of our dependency on things, status, and expectations. Only then can we make space for God's word.

—From *Heart Whispers* by Elizabeth J. Canham

⁂ Though we can teach methods for listening and cultivate them in our own lives, hearing and recognizing God's voice ultimately is a spiritual gift, not an achievement that one can master. Methods such as the *lectio* or the Jesuit pattern are like scales on the piano that are helpful for beginners and good reminders for the proficient. They help the mind find receptive patterns. But prayerfulness, begging for the Spirit to teach, is the attitude that makes listening possible.

—From *Spiritual Awakening* by John Ackerman

⁂ God is the one who teaches to listen and to pray. We must pray for the gift and pray for the gift to be taught. They say that mature writers have "found their voice." I think we need to "find our ear"—our best way of recognizing God's voice, knowing that, once we have found our ear, God may decide to speak in a different language.

Some people simply cannot listen to God in scripture. Some find God most readily in music or in the outdoors. Contemplation in the Jesuit understanding is paying attention to the reality of God, whether God be in scripture, music, the other person, or in nature. Whenever we get beyond our own small preoccupations, whenever we have some degree of self-transcendence, whenever we are aware of the reality of God, contemplation has begun. If you are absolutely unable to find God in your Bible, go outside, listen to music, do whatever you do that puts you in touch with Something More.

—From *Spiritual Awakening* by John Ackerman

❧ By all means remember to pray earnestly for me. I would not have you yield such deference to the office fraught with perils which I bear, as to refrain from giving the assistance which I know myself to need. Prayer was made by the household of Christ for Peter and for Paul. I rejoice that you are in His household; and I need, incomparably more than Peter and Paul did, the help of the prayers of the brethren. Emulate each other in prayer with holy rivalry, with one heart, for you wrestle not against each other, but against the devil, who is the common enemy of all the saints. "By fasting, by vigils, and all mortification of the body, prayer is greatly helped." Let each one do what she can; what one cannot herself do, she does by another who can do it, if she loves in another that which personal inability alone hinders her from doing; wherefore let her who can do less not keep back the one who can do more, and let her who can do more not urge unduly her who can do less. For your conscience is responsible to God; to each other owe nothing but mutual love. May the Lord, who is able to do above what we ask or think, give ear to your prayers.

—From "Letter 130—to Proba" by Saint Augustine

The Day of Pentecost

Next to Easter, Pentecost is the most important day in the Christian calendar. Without Pentecost, the incarnation of God in Christ would be just a story told through the centuries. At Pentecost, that story was internalized and became personal; God in Christ became incarnate in ordinary disciples. Wind and fire shook, transformed, and filled those very human and ordinary believers with the divine Spirit of God, thus giving birth to the church. The faithful continue to receive this gift of God-dwelling-within to provide direction, courage, comfort, hope, companionship, and peace.

Through the Holy Spirit at Pentecost God in Christ became available to every believer. Christians now had firsthand experience with God in Christ. From Pentecost on, the good news was not held only by a select few who had been with Jesus, felt his hand upon their lives, and sought to follow him throughout his earthly days. Now everyone could experience that touch of the Savior's hand; everyone could know the healing and saving presence of Jesus Christ. No Christian need ever walk alone, for now God was present with every believer who chose to accept this holy presence.

Pentecost was no ordinary experience, but it happened to and within ordinary people as God's Holy Spirit appeared among and within them. Ordinary men and women became full of faith and fearless. Fearful men and women became courageous witnesses to God's mighty and saving acts. Weak and timid disciples became strong and powerful witnesses to the Good News of God's saving acts in the world. Each disciple received comfort, assurance, and hope as each was companioned by God through the power and presence of the Holy Spirit. From that day until this, those who repent and are baptized receive the gift of the Holy Spirit, God with us always and in every circumstance of life (Acts 2:38).

29: Power from Beyond Ourselves

Affirmation
And that all this assembly may know that the LORD
does not save by sword and spear; for the battle is the
LORD's and he will give you into our hand" (1 Sam.
17:47).

Petition
Do not forsake me, O LORD;
    O my God, do not be far from me;
make haste to help me,
    O LORD, my salvation (Ps. 38:21-22).

Sacred Reading: anthology or other selected reading

Daily Scripture Readings

Sunday	A.	Acts 2:1-21; Ps. 104:24-34, 35; 1 Corinthians 12:3-13; John 20:19-23
	B.	Ezekiel 37:1-14; Acts 2:1-21; Psalm 104:24-34, 35; John 15:26-27; 16:4-15
	C.	Acts 2:1-21; Psalm 104:24-34, 35; Romans 8:14-17; John 14:8-17
Monday		Acts 2:1-4
Tuesday		John 14:25-31
Wednesday		2 Corinthians 12:1-10
Thursday		Luke 24:44-49
Friday		Ephesians 3:20-21
Saturday		1 Corinthians 12:1-11

Prayer: thanksgiving, petition, intercession, praise,
and offering

Reflection: silent (listening to God), written (journaling)

God's Promise
But you will receive power when the Holy Spirit has come upon you; and you will be my witnesses in Jerusalem, in all Judea and Samaria, and to the ends of the earth (Acts 1:8).

My Response
With great power the apostles gave their testimony to the resurrection of the Lord Jesus, and great grace was upon them all (Acts 4:33).

Readings for Reflection

❧ Most of us have lived long enough to have thought or said, "I could never do that!" It is a common response of ordinary people like us to a task that seems to demand extraordinary wisdom, strength, or faith. However, the Bible is filled with stories of those who told God they could not lead, witness, or perform the task they were asked to do. Of course they were right! They could not do the difficult—or even the simple and easy—on their own. The biblical stories from Abraham to the first-century Christians point out that only with power from beyond themselves could the faithful fulfill their calling.

What are you planning to do that you cannot possibly achieve without help from beyond yourself? What do you feel God is calling you to be and do that is impossible without God's intervention in your life? These questions move us quickly to the realization that we often live our lives on the easy path of the least faith and effort. To observe the church is to see that we are not alone in choosing the easy path. Yet we know there is a better way and a higher calling for us as individuals, as congregations, and as denominations.

The early disciples were told to wait upon God until the power came. They waited and the power did come. The book of Acts is a brief record of how the early church carried on its life and ministry with power from beyond itself. The record of individuals and Christian movements that have transformed the world within and around them is testimony to their capacity to receive power from beyond themselves to fulfill their calling. This power was given to ordinary people who were called to live in an extraordinary way. Could that be your calling today?

—Rueben P. Job

❧ In all your experience of Christ, it is wisest for you to stay away from any set form, or pattern, or *way*. Instead, *be wholly given up to the leading* of *the Holy Spirit*. By following your spirit, every encounter you have with the Lord is one that is *perfect* . . . no matter what the encounter is like.

—From *Experiencing the Depths of Jesus Christ* by Jeanne Guyon

❧ A student once asked me to pray for him so that he might receive the power of the Holy Spirit in his life. I complied; laying my hands on his head, I began to pray. Suddenly in the midst of the prayer he erupted, "Stop, I'm not ready for this yet!" Even though I was doing as *he* had asked, the ambivalence toward the Holy entering one's life is too powerful to be taken lightly. He was right; he wasn't ready.

—From *The Transforming Moment* by James E. Loder

❧ Many priests today are said to be abandoning prayer. One simple reason for this is that they have never experienced the power that prayer brings. Those who have once experienced that prayer is power will never again abandon prayer for the rest of their lives. Mahatma Gandhi put it well: "I am telling you my own experience," he said, "and that of my colleagues: we could go for days on end without food; we could not live a single minute without prayer." Or, as he said another time, "Given the type of life I am leading, if I ceased to pray I should go mad!" If we ask God for so

little it may well be because we feel the need for him so little. We are leading complacent, secure, well-protected, mediocre lives. We aren't living dangerously enough; we aren't living the way Jesus wanted us to live when he proclaimed the good news. The less we pray the less we are likely to live the risky, challenging life that the Gospels urge us to; the less of a challenge there is in our life, and the less we are likely to pray.
—From *Contact with God* by Anthony de Mello

❧ Not only is the presence of God in Jesus Christ to be experienced occasionally, the indwelling Christ is to become the shaping power of our lives. This is the dynamic of our spiritual formation.
—From *Alive in Christ* by Maxie Dunnam

❧ God is greater than my senses, greater than my thoughts, greater than my heart. I do believe that he touches me in places that are unknown even to myself. I seldom can point directly to these places; but when I feel this inner pull to return again to that hidden hour of prayer, I realize that something is happening that is so deep that it becomes like the riverbed through which the waters can safety flow and find their way to the open sea.
—From *¡Gracias!* by Henri J. M. Nouwen

❧ The practical question is: Do I adequately acknowledge the Spirit's role in the good actions I perform every day, or do I attribute them only to my own initiative and hard work? The scriptural model insists that if the action was good, the Spirit was present from the beginning to the end. Since I am a teacher of theology it is most important for me to acknowledge God's role in this area. Do I see the desire in me to teach well for the love of God and others as coming from the Spirit? Do I recognize that the strength and insight to carry out the good desire well are also infused by the Spirit? At the end of the day, do I adequately acknowledge God's role

in my successes and give [God] appropriate thanks? In addition to my teaching, I must do the same review for my counseling, my committee work at the university, my writing, my prayer, my helping others in any way throughout the day. I have allowed grace to be present and operative in myself to the extent that I have tried to do my daily service for the love of God and others. To this extent the Spirit of life in Christ Jesus our Lord has been dominant over the pressures on me not to serve with love. To the extent that I have not served in love, I humbly admit my faults and ask for a greater increase of grace to transform these areas. My reward for living in the Spirit is the habitual peace and joy I experience.
—From *In His Spirit* by Richard J. Hauser

ఆ We can never forecast the path God's energy of rescue will take. It is never any use saying to God, "I am getting desperate! Please answer my prayer by the next mail and please send a blank check." God will answer but not necessarily like that; more probably God will transform and use the unlikely looking material already in hand—the loaves and the tiny fishes—looking up to Heaven and blessing it and making it do after all. A priest was once asked if many miracles happened at Lourdes. He said, "Yes many; but the greatest are not miracles of healing but the spiritual miracles, the transformation of those who pray desperately for cure of this or that and come back, not physically cured, but filled with peace and joy, surrendered to the Will of God, conformed to the Cross."
—From *The Light of Christ* by Evelyn Underhill

ఆ The indwelling Spirit of God is never a source of trouble and scruple, but a stabilizing power, a constant. *If I ascend to heaven, you are there; if I make my bed in Sheol, you are there*—when I am exultant and when I am depressed. *Darkness is as light* to you. The friendship of God is like that, and God asks the same faithfulness of us in return. It takes a brave and loving soul

to understand and respond to this sturdy faithfulness of God, for there is nothing sentimental about it.
—From *The Fruits of the Spirit* by Evelyn Underhill

❧ Even when God intervenes mightily, such as melting a tumor within minutes or pouring miraculous spiritual comfort on breathtaking pain, healing is still a process, one that continues as long as you are alive to God's presence. You can expect an awareness of God's presence to break into your life many times. God continually invites you to yet another step toward wholeness.
—From *Ashes Transformed* by Tilda Norberg

❧ Our journey toward abundant living is like walking a spiritual labyrinth repeatedly, from an ever deepening inner space. We walk toward the center to be transformed by God's love; then we walk outward to transform our small space in the world by reflecting God's love. There is no intention to trick us or get us lost along the journey. But there is mystery. Always mystery. And awe. And amazing grace.
—From *Abundance* by Marilyn Brown Oden

The Season after Pentecost/Ordinary Time

The period after Pentecost is known by a variety of names: Kingdomtide, Whitsuntide, the Season after Pentecost, and more recently, especially by Roman Catholics, Ordinary Time. However, there is nothing *ordinary* about this period of the Christian calendar. There continues to be a distinct emphasis upon telling the redemption story in all its fullness as the church gathers to remember how God has come, is coming, and will come again to redeem humankind and all creation (Rom. 8:19-23).

The church especially remembers in worship and deeds the truth that God dwells within the body of Christ and within the believer. Through the Holy Spirit, God companions, directs, and gives power, wisdom, courage, and faith to believers and the church for living obediently. Therefore, the church—gathered and dispersed—not only represents God but also in a real way embodies God in the world. Christians seek to bring justice, peace, and love to every situation because we embody the very God we worship.

No day can be ordinary when God dwells within. Every day is seen as blessed and holy, filled with opportunity and grace for all who put their trust in God.

Trinity Sunday: First Sunday after Pentecost

The first Sunday after Pentecost has been observed as Trinity Sunday since 1000 C.E. Unlike other special or feast days, Trinity Sunday relates to a theological doctrine rather than a historical event. It was and continues to be the time when attention is focused on the doctrine of God as three persons in one. While Christians from the time of the first Pentecost experienced God as Father, Son, and Holy Spirit, this doctrine was not formalized until the fourth century as the church sought to explain its experience of God.

Jesus frequently proclaimed that he was in the Father and the Father was in him and that he would send the "Advocate," or Holy Spirit, to the disciples to continue to guide and companion them (John 10:38, 14:11, 26). Jesus not only promised that God would live in community with the disciples but also declared the reality of a divine community. Trinity Sunday highlights the deep mystery of God in three persons living in divine community and invites the church to reflect that divine community in the contemporary world.

30: *God Lives in Community*

Affirmation

> I bind unto myself today the strong name of
> the Trinity,
> by invocation of the same, the Three in One,
> and One in Three.
> I bind this day to me forever by power of faith
> Christ's incarnation,
> his baptism in the Jordan River, his death on
> the cross for my salvation;
> his bursting from the spiced tomb, his riding up
> the heavenly way,
> his coming at the day of doom I bind unto
> myself today.*

Petition

> Christ be with me, Christ within me, Christ
> behind me, Christ before me,
> Christ beside me, Christ to win me; Christ to
> comfort and restore me;
> Christ beneath me, Christ above me, Christ in
> quiet, Christ in danger, Christ in hearts of
> all that love me, Christ in mouth of friend
> and stranger.*

Sacred Reading: anthology or other selected reading

Daily Scripture Readings

> Sunday   A. Genesis 1:1–2:4; Psalm 8;
> 2 Corinthians 13:11-13;
> Matthew 28:16-20

---

* *Affirmation, Petition,* and *My Response* are from "I Bind unto Myself Today" attr. to Saint Patrick, c. 430; paraphrased by Cecil Frances Alexander, 1889.

	B. Isaiah 6:1-8; Psalm 29;
	Romans 8:12-17; John 3:1-17
	C. Proverbs 8:1-4, 22-31;
	Psalm 8; Romans 5:1-5;
	John 16:12-15
Monday	John 17:11-24
Tuesday	Matthew 18:15-20
Wednesday	John 10:22-30
Thursday	Romans 12:3-5
Friday	Ephesians 2:11-21
Saturday	Galatians 3:23-29

Prayer: thanksgiving, petition, intercession, praise, and offering

Reflection: silent (listening to God), written (journaling)

God's Promise
I will come and dwell in your midst, says the LORD. Many nations shall join themselves to the LORD on that day, and shall be my people; and I will dwell in your midst (Zech. 2:10-11).

My Response
>   I bind unto myself today the power of God
>   to hold and lead,
>   his eye to watch, his might to stay, his ear
>   to hearken to my need,
>   The wisdom of my God to teach, his hand
>   to guide, his shield to ward,
>   the Word of God to give me speech, His
>   heavenly host to be my guard.*

Readings for Reflection

❧ Jesus lived his life in community. From his childhood with Mary and Joseph to his calling and traveling with the disciples to his declaration that he and the Father were one, Jesus lived in community. A community of faith nurtured him, supported him, and informed him ("Who do the crowds say that I am?" [Luke 9:18]). It is unthinkable that we would try to live a faithful life without the gifts offered in a faithful community of Jesus. Jesus was known for valuing solitude since he retired to rest and pray, but living in community also marked his life.

Jesus makes a dramatic and revolutionary promise when he says, "Where two or three are gathered in my name, I am there among them" (Matt. 18:20). This is a welcome promise to those who may wonder if God is present in their lives or their affairs. This is a hopeful promise for those who sometimes feel alone and forsaken. This is an enormous assurance for those who face the unknown and need companionship and community.

We can be sure that Jesus keeps his promise and that when we gather in his name, he will be with us. We are often blessed by being in community. We receive encouragement, guidance, comfort, and hope by participating in a community. We often find our faith strengthened in community. These gifts of community are available to us all, and we receive them more readily when we remember that Jesus meets us there.
—Rueben P. Job

☙ O God, I have tasted [your] goodness, and it has both satisfied me and made me thirsty for more. I am painfully conscious of my need of further grace. I am ashamed of my lack of desire. O God, the Triune God, I want to want [you]; I long to be filled with longing; I thirst to be made more thirsty still. Show me [your] glory, I pray, so that I may know [you] indeed. Begin in mercy a new work of love within me. Say to my soul, "Rise up, my love, my fair one, and come away." Then give me grace to rise and follow [you] up from this misty lowland where I have wandered so long.
In Jesus' Name. Amen
—From *The Pursuit of God* by A. W. Tozer

⋅ The basis of the Christian community is not the family tie, or social or economic equality, or shared oppression or complaint, or mutual attraction, . . . but the divine call. The Christian community is not the result of human efforts. God has made us into his people by calling us out of "Egypt" to the "New Land," out of the desert to fertile ground, out of slavery to freedom, out of our sin to salvation, out of captivity to liberation. All these words and images give expression to the fact that the initiative belongs to God and that he is the source of our new life together.
—From *Reaching Out* by Henri J. M. Nouwen

⋅ In the Christian community thankfulness is just what it is anywhere else in the Christian life. Only he who gives thanks for little things receives the big things. We prevent God from giving us the great spiritual gifts He has in store for us, because we do not give thanks for daily gifts. We think we dare not be satisfied with the small measure of spiritual knowledge, experience, and love that has been given to us, and that we must constantly be looking forward eagerly for the highest good. Then we deplore the fact that we lack the deep certainty, the strong faith, and the rich experience that God has given to others, and we consider this lament to be pious. We pray for the big things and forget to give thanks for the ordinary, small (and yet really not small) gifts. How can God entrust great things to one who will not thankfully receive from Him the little things?
—From *Life Together* by Dietrich Bonhoeffer

⋅ If we do not give thanks daily for the Christian fellowship in which we have been placed, even where there is no great experience, no discoverable riches, but much weakness, small faith, and difficulty; if on the contrary, we only keep complaining to God that everything is so paltry and petty, so far from what we expected, then we hinder God from letting our

fellowship grow according to the measure and riches which are there for us all in Jesus Christ.
—From *Life Together* by Dietrich Bonhoeffer

❧ The advantage of believing in the reality of the Trinity is not that we get an A from God for giving "the right answer." Remember, to believe something is to act as if it is so. To believe that two plus two equals four is to behave accordingly when trying to find out how many dollars or apples are in the house. The advantage of believing it is not that we can pass tests in arithmetic; it is that we can deal much more successfully with reality. Just try dealing with it as if two plus two equaled six.

Hence, the advantage of *believing* in the Trinity is that we then live as if the Trinity is real: as if the cosmos environing us actually is, beyond all else, a self-sufficing community of unspeakably magnificent personal beings of boundless love, knowledge, and power. And, thus believing, our lives naturally integrate themselves, through our actions, into the reality of such a universe, just as with two plus two equals four. In faith we rest ourselves upon the reality of the Trinity in action—and it graciously meets us. For it is there. And our lives are then enmeshed in the true world of God.
—From *The Divine Conspiracy* by Dallas Willard

❧ Glory of the Trinity
Beauty of divinity
Gracing humanity

God of all mystery
Improbable history
Unity. Community

Holy simplicity
Present in Nativity
Celebrate the Trinity
—Jeannette A. Bakke

❧ Clearly, in the serious contemplation of our place in the human community lies the quality of our contemplation. To be a real contemplative we must every day take others into the narrow little confines of our lives—and listen to their call to us to be about something greater than ourselves.

—From *Illuminated Life* by Joan Chittister

❧ Something happens to us when we consult one another in Christian community. In sharing our thoughts with others, surprising insights often emerge—opening our eyes to what we have not seen and our ears to what we have not heard. This can transform and liberate us beyond our own narrow expectations. Both the one experiencing a call and those helping that person may express God's wisdom and grace in the process. "I will give you shepherds after my own heart, who will feed you with knowledge and understanding" (Jer. 3:15).

Although God calls each of us personally, as individuals we see only partially. Individual perception, reasoning, and understanding are always limited. Even a person who feels absolutely certain that a specific revelation comes from God may be mistaken as to how it is to be applied. Because God often reveals part of the picture to one person and another part to another person, it is prudent to consult one another to discern God's counsel, guidance, and direction, even if there is no apparent reason to do so. While circumstances sometimes require us to act without consulting others, the danger of arrogance and error in proceeding on our own can be great.

—From *Listening Hearts* by Suzanne G. Farnham et al.

❧ A wise swimmer does not cross a difficult channel without a boat close behind, with those aboard watching for signs of danger or weariness and providing words of encouragement along the way. Nor does a prudent climber scale a mountain alone, without

companions to hold the rope and help along the way.
—From *Listening Hearts* by Suzanne G. Farnham et al.

❧ The Christian is a citizen of the church universal. While we delight in the uniqueness of each individual, our deepest joy is to be part of the community that Christ embraces as his own body. Invited to his marriage feast yet to be, we partake of his body and blood. And at these sacred moments, it is enough just to stand around, passing the peace for which the world yearns, being the church adorned as a bride awaiting her divine Lover.
—From *The Art of Spiritual Direction* by W. Paul Jones

❧ Without the discipline of community, solitude degenerates into self-absorption and isolation; without the discipline of solitude, community degenerates into codependency and enmeshment. . . . The community of faith is where we learn the language of love. And the church uses two kinds of language—the verbal language of liturgy, scripture, and sermon, and the body language of sacraments, gestures, and social outreach. . . . Being a part of a life-giving faith community is like a healthy foot getting directional signals from the rest of the body. A life-giving church is one where human brokenness is lifted up like bread and wine to be held, and touched, and blessed—to heal the world.
—From *Journeymen* by Kent Ira Groff

❧ The source of all such coming together is surely Jesus himself. Community is ever his gift. It was this way from the start. He formed the table fellowship. He sent his followers out not alone but in the company of one another. When he came upon them after the Resurrection, he joined two on the road, encouraged a frightened crew huddled behind locked doors, fed a hungry band of them at dawn on the shores of Galilee. He initially had drawn persons together, and he continued to shape them as a body. When the Holy Spirit burned forth Pentecost, it settled not on one but on a whole assembly. . . .

In Christ Jesus we are formed into one people stretching through the ages of time. And in this sense, the community he creates is not only a gift. It is holy. That is, its source is not in us. It emanates from him. Community sweeps forth and claims us from the realms of grace.

—From *Discovering Community* by Stephen V. Doughty

Second Sunday after Pentecost (Begin Ordinary Time)
Sunday between May 29 and June 4
(If the Sunday between May 24 and 28 follows Trinity Sunday, use
Week 14, then return to the regular sequence.)

31: A Driving Passion

Affirmation
I bless the LORD who gives me counsel;
  in the night also my heart instructs me.
I keep the LORD always before me;
  because he is at my right hand, I shall not be
    moved.

Therefore my heart is glad, and my soul rejoices;
  my body also rests secure (Ps. 16:7-9).

Petition
O God, do not be far from me;
  O my God, make haste to help me! (Ps. 71:12).

Sacred Reading: anthology or other selected reading

Daily Scripture Readings

Sunday	A.	Genesis 6:9-22; 7:24; 8:14-19; Psalm 46; Romans 1:16-17; 3:22-28; Matthew 7:21-29
	B.	1 Samuel 3:1-10; Psalm 139:1-6, 13-18; 2 Corinthians 4:5-12; Mark 2:23–3:6
	C.	1 Kings 18:20-21, 30-39; Psalm 96; Galatians 1:1-12; Luke 7:1-10
Monday		Acts 2:14-21
Tuesday		Acts 4:1-12
Wednesday		Acts 4:13-22
Thursday		Acts 4:23-31
Friday		Acts 4:32-37
Saturday		1 Thessalonians 1:1-10

Prayer: thanksgiving, petition, intercession, praise, and offering

Reflection: silent (listening to God), written (journaling)

God's Promise

Get up and stand on your feet; for I have appeared to you for this purpose, to appoint you to serve and testify to the things in which you have seen me and to those in which I will appear to you. I will rescue you from your people and from the Gentiles—to whom I am sending you to open their eyes so that they may turn from darkness to light and from the power of Satan to God, so that they may receive forgiveness of sins and a place among those who are sanctified by faith in me (Acts 26:16-18).

My Response

And now, as a captive to the Spirit, . . . I do not count my life of any value to myself, if only I may finish my course and the ministry that I received from the Lord Jesus, to testify to the good news of God's grace (Acts 20:22-24).

Readings for Reflection

❧ We have seen it in athletes and politicians and now and then in religious leaders such as Mother Teresa, Martin Luther King, Billy Graham, and Dorothy Day. A driving passion is a joy to behold when it is given to a noble and righteous cause. It is unlikely that a noble or righteous cause will succeed without the driving passion of those who share the ideals of the mission.

However, it is not only the well-known athletes, politicians, religious leaders, and celebrities who need or demonstrate a driving passion. We can thank God that every day countless men and women give themselves fully to bringing a vision of the world inspired by Jesus Christ to reality. These men and women place God at the center of their lives and place God's will at the top of their priority list. Most often these heroic servants of Christ are not recognized and are invisible behind the scenes doing what they do best—loving God and neighbor with a pure love expressed in their actions every day of their lives.

A driving passion can be destructive to the person driven and to those in the way of that passion unless it is grounded in Jesus Christ. We can each fall prey and victim to a driving passion for the wrong purpose or goal. Our only safety net is a life given completely and without reservation to God in Christ. When we can say that it is indeed Christ who lives and rules within us, we can be free of worry about the results of our driving passion. That passion will be directed, as was the passion of Jesus, only for good and noble ends. What is the driving passion of your life? Where will it lead you if you follow it for the rest of your life?
—Rueben P. Job

❧ When we stand ready to suffer for our faith, we are standing where Jesus stood—and where he stands even now. He stands with one foot in heaven and the other upon earth, his hands and side scarred by nails and spear. He stands at the very heart of human history, human suffering, human death, anguish, and tragedy.

But he stands there like a rock! He stands there having endured everything—every human suffering in thought and body. And he says to us, "This is where you must stand, not in a dreamland of faith that deceives you into thinking you can float into heaven on a billowy cloud. No, if ever you are to enter heaven, you will do so at the cost of serving God at the vortex of human suffering and tragedy, and your only earthly reward will be that people curse you for it."

In offering this to you, Jesus is merely suggesting what he already has endured. Saint Paul points to the this truth when he suggests that we "run with perseverance the race that is set before us, looking to Jesus the pioneer and perfecter of our faith, who for the sake of the joy that was set before him endured the cross, disregarding its shame, and has taken his seat at the right hand of the throne of God" (Heb. 12:1-2).

So it is! If we follow Jesus closely enough we may experience all that he endured. Do you remember the poignant question he put to his disciples, "Are you prepared to drink of the cup from which I shall drink?" "Yes," the giddy disciples responded. And so they did.

This must be our answer also. Then when suffering and sacrifice are required of us, we must respond like Isaiah. "Whom shall I send?" inquired the Lord, "Here!" called Isaiah, "Here I am, send me." Like a sheep among wolves. Like the Son of God among broken humanity, send me, O Lord, send me!
—Norman Shawchuck

❧   I ask you, Lord Jesus,
    to develop in me, your lover,
    an immeasurable urge towards you,
    an affection that is unbounded,
    longing that is unrestrained,
    fervour that throws discretion to the winds!
    The more worthwhile our love for you,
        all the more pressing does it become.
    Reason cannot hold it in check,
        fear does not make it tremble,
        wise judgement does not temper it.
    —From *The Fire of Love* by Richard Rolle

❧   Stand firm, as does an anvil which is beaten. It is the part of a noble athlete to be wounded, and yet to conquer. And especially, we ought to bear all things for the sake of God, that [God] also may bear with us, and bring us into the kingdom. Add more and more to [your] diligence; run [your] race with increasing energy; weigh carefully the times. While [you are] here, be a conqueror; for here is the course, and there are the crowns. Look for Christ, the Son of God; who was before time, yet appeared in time; who was invisible by nature, yet visible in the flesh; who was impalpable, and could not be touched, as being without a body, but for our sakes became such, might be touched and handled in the body; who was impassible as God, but became passible for our sakes as [a human]; and who in every kind of way suffered for our sakes.

—From "Epistle to Polycarp" by Saint Ignatius

❧ Every time the Gospels mention that Jesus was moved with the deepest emotions or felt sorry for people, it led to his doing something—physical or inner healing, deliverance or exorcism, feeding the hungry crowds or praying for others. The Good Samaritan was commended precisely because he acted. The priest and Levite, paragons of Jewish virtue, flunked the test because they didn't do anything. "Which of these three, in your opinion, was neighbor to the man who fell in with the robbers?" The answer came, "The one who treated him with compassion." Jesus said to them, "Then go and do the same."

—From *Reflections for Ragamuffins* by Brennan Manning

❧ When we are hungry to experience God's loving presence near us and believe we are searching for God, it is important to ask ourselves whether we are truly seeking God or pursuing spiritual experience. We do get lonesome for God and can feel isolated and confused. But sometimes our search is not as much for God as it is for spiritual adventure. Perhaps we are bored. We might like to see ourselves as important spiritual persons and think a particular kind of spiritual experience is one of the criteria necessary for others to view us in this way. Perhaps we would like God to heal someone through our prayer or bring about instantaneous, major life changes in us or in someone else with whom we have been praying more as a kind of witness to our supposed godliness than as an overflowing of God's compassion.

—From *Holy Invitations* by Jeannette A. Bakke

❧ Jesus says, "If anyone wants to be a follower of mine, let him . . . take up his cross and follow me" (Matt. 16:24). He does not say, "Make a cross" or "Look for a cross." Each of us has a cross to carry. There is no need to make one or look for one. The cross we have is hard enough for us! But are we willing to take it up, to accept it as our cross?

Maybe we can't study, maybe we are handicapped, maybe we suffer from depression, maybe we experience conflict in our families, maybe we are victims of violence or abuse. We didn't choose any of it, but these things are our crosses. We can ignore them, reject them, refuse them or hate them. But we can also take up these crosses and follow Jesus with them.
—From *Bread for the Journey* by Henri J. M. Nouwen

❧ In absolutely every situation my only desire is to fulfill the divine will. But alas, I have so little love for Jesus that I dare not call him my Beloved. Yet I want—I long—to love him more than anything on earth or in heaven. My heart and my life are his alone.
—From *Spiritual Autobiography of Charles de Foucauld* as reprinted in *Charles de Foucauld: Writings Selected with an Introduction by Robert Ellsberg*

❧ The spiritual path of Charles de Foucauld was modeled on the hidden life of Jesus of Nazareth, a way of constant abandonment to the love of God, whether in the silence of desert spaces or in the midst of others. There is no doubt that in embarking on this path Foucauld prepared himself to give everything and that he carefully calculated the cost.
—Robert Ellsberg in *Charles de Foucauld: Writings Selected with an Introduction by Robert Ellsberg*

Third Sunday after Pentecost (Ordinary Time)
Sunday between June 5 and June 11
(If after Trinity Sunday; otherwise turn to next Sunday.)

32: Choosing Faithful Leaders

Affirmation

Now the angel of the LORD came and sat under the oak
. . . as Gideon was beating out wheat in the wine press,
to hide it from the Midianites. The angel of the LORD
appeared to him and said to him, "The LORD is with
you, you mighty warrior" (Judg. 6:11-12).

Petition

"But sir, if the LORD is with us, why then has all this
happened to us? And where are all his wonderful
deeds that our ancestors recounted to us, saying, 'Did
not the LORD bring us up from Egypt?' But now the
LORD has cast us off" (Judg. 6:13).

Sacred Reading: anthology or other selected reading

Daily Scripture Readings

Sunday	A.	Genesis 12:1-9; Psalm 33:1-12; Romans 4:13-25; Matthew 9:9-13, 18-26
	B.	1 Samuel 8:4-11, 16-20; Psalm 138; 2 Corinthians 4:13–5:1; Mark 3:20-35
	C.	1 Kings 17:8-16; Psalm 146; Galatians 1:11-24; Luke 7:11-17
Monday		Acts 1:21-26
Tuesday		1 Samuel 16:1-13
Wednesday		Matthew 4:18-22
Thursday		Acts 6:1-6
Friday		Exodus 18:13-27
Saturday		Acts 16:11-15

Prayer: thanksgiving, petition, intercession, praise,
and offering

Reflection: silent (listening to God), written (journaling)

God's Promise
I now do according to your word. Indeed I give you a wise and discerning mind; no one like you has been before you and no one like you shall arise after you (1 Kings 3:12).

My Response
O LORD, God of Israel, there is no God like you in heaven above or on earth beneath, keeping covenant and steadfast love for your servants who walk before you with all their heart. . . . Therefore, O LORD, God of Israel, keep for your servant my father David that which you promised him, saying, "There shall never fail you a successor before me to sit on the throne of Israel, if only your children look to their way, to walk before me as you have walked before me." Therefore, O God of Israel, let your word be confirmed, which you promised to your servant (1 Kings 8:23, 25-26).

Readings for Reflection

❧ All of us want faithful leaders, and we reject the notion that leaders don't make a difference to the organizations, movements, and groups influencing our lives. We have seen dramatic evidence of the importance of faithful leaders. While we desire faithful leaders, we sometimes make it hard to choose them and even more difficult to keep them. Was the early church better at this than we are? Could the methods used and the qualities sought in those times instruct us in choosing leaders today?

It seems clear that a primary method in the early church was a deliberate search for the will of God. From the choice of David and Gideon to Matthias and Stephen, the method was centered in God and depended upon God. Choosing faithful leaders meant starting with God, continuing with God, concluding with God. Of course, other things were important, but the primary requirement was to know God's choice.

Today the *methods* of choosing political leaders often influence us. Careful polling and building a candidate to meet the polls' suggestions seems to be a popular method. Listening to the people's voice is important, and polling can accomplish that goal. It is more important, though, to listen to the voice of the only One with wisdom for every decision. Prayer and discernment are necessary parts of a faithful process every time we are involved in choosing leaders.
—Rueben P. Job

❧ In America we tend to draw a distinction between secular and religious leaders. However, God never pays much attention to titles of distinction we use to set people apart, perhaps especially regarding leaders.

For you see, God views all leaders equally. There are no distinctions of class with God. God requires civility, honesty, and fidelity of all leaders. God wants humane, honest, capable leaders in all places—from the White House to the Cub Scout den. A leader of a "secular" organization is called by God, and the leader will be accountable to God. All families and organizations are sacred in God's eyes.

Good leaders aren't perfect: David messed up; Moses couldn't speak in public and asked God for a "voice" to speak on his behalf. Leaders will always possess a variety of leadership skills and styles. The question is: Is this man or woman a good leader or an injurious leader?
—Norman Shawchuck

❧ Gabriel begins as he always begins, as God always begins (since this is God's message, not Gabriel's), with the affirmation of God's creation. "Greetings, favored one!" Gabriel proclaims to Mary. "The Lord is with you!" Before she hears anything else, God wants Mary to hear this: She is favored. . . . Although a teenager, Mary need not "find" herself. Her identity is a gift, bestowed upon her by God alone. *Who am I?* Mary may wonder. And God replies, "You are my favored one, beloved and beautiful to me."

In truth, Mary does not stand much chance for an identity *apart* from God. She is too young to have had time to achieve much on which to base her identity. She is too poor to purchase her place in society. Add to this the fact that she is female, which means that even if she did have accomplishments or social stature to her credit, they likely would have gone unrecognized because of her gender. All of this makes Mary a most unlikely candidate for helping God save the world, which is precisely why God enlists her. Nothing about Mary suggests that she can be who she is apart from God's favor of her.

—From *The Godbearing Life* by Kenda Creasy Dean and
   Ron Foster

⧫ Teacher, Guide of helpless Sinners,
       Us receive into thy School,
   Gently lead the young Beginners
       All our Works & Thoughts orerule;
   Every Appetite & Passion,
       Every Sense exalt, refine,
   Order all our Conversation,
       Seal our Souls Forever Thine.

   Choose for Us our whole Condition
       In our Pilgrimage below,
   All that stands in competition
       With thy blessed Will orethrow;
   Tear away the Rival Creature
       Till we fully taste & see
   Good the Gift, but Thou are better,
       Happiness is all in Thee.

   —From *The Unpublished Poetry of Charles
      Wesley*, Vol. 3

It was a snowy Thanksgiving weekend in Duluth, Minnesota, when I became acutely aware of myself as a mediator of the Holy. I was truly aware of my role as priest and knew I functioned as the channel I had prayed so often to become. "Lord make me an instrument of your peace. . . ." On that Friday morning, a family was gathered together because of the holiday. The grandmother's rapidly failing health lent a sense of urgency. On that gray and icy day, with the previous day's cornucopia display still on the chancel steps, we stood just inside the altar rail around the baptismal font to bathe a child's tiny head, melted snow puddling under our booted feet. The water flowed through my fingers, an ordinary element together with the holy words to claim the child for Christ. As she lay, safe in her grandmother's leukemia-weakened arms I spoke the words, "child of God, you have been sealed by the Holy Spirit and marked with the cross of Christ, forever."

The next day I found myself standing on the very same spot. . . . I stood there beside a coffin because a forty-five-year-old man's heart had stopped. In the sermon just finished, I had woven the strands of his life story together with the story of God's unending grace, and drawn together memories shared by family and friends over the past few days. . . . sand flowed through my fingers as I sprinkled the sign of the cross onto the polished wood of the coffin and spoke the words, "earth to earth, ashes to ashes, dust to dust . . ."

When Sunday came it was time for Holy Communion and I stood again in the very same place, just inside the altar rail, robed in white, with silver plate in hand. As streams of people came forward and knelt there, I passed tiny circles of bread, one by one, flesh by flesh, from hand to hand, and spoke the words, "the body of Christ, given for you. . . ."

—From "Ordinary Elements: Sacramental Ministry" by Rebecca A. Ellenson in *Ordinary Ministry: Extraordinary Challenge*

❧ Christopher Lasch suggested that there is a profound difference between celebrities and saints. In a narcissistic, self-pleasing culture, we welcome celebrities because we lack imagination and courage. Traditional heroes make demands on us, but celebrities make no moral claim on us. Glittering stars in our culture merely feed our narcissism, our love of self, our addiction to everything society finds pleasurable. No one ever asks how our constant exposure to the rich and famous is supposed to make us good or wise or faithful. Even if we are trying to live faithful lives, our minds are always being reshaped, just a little, all the time, into the image of what surrounds us. But heroes—saints—stretch our imaginations and stand as imperatives, calling, wooing us into a higher, holier life.
—From *Servants, Misfits, and Martyrs* by James C. Howell

❧ Saints do not possess an extra layer of muscle. They are not taller, and they do not sport superior IQs. They are not richer, and their parents are not more clever than yours or mine. They have no batlike perception that enables them to fly in the dark. They are flesh and blood, just like you and me, no stronger, no more intelligent. And that is the point. They simply offer themselves to God, knowing they are not the elite, fully cognizant that they are inadequate to the task, that their abilities are limited and fallible.
—From *Servants, Misfits, and Martyrs* by James C. Howell

❧ Holiness only appears to be abnormal. The truth is, holiness is normal; to be anything else is to be abnormal. Being a saint is simply being the person God made me to be. Saints at the end of the day are not really strange or odd or misfits. They are simply real, or normal. They actually are what we all are made to be, what we can be.
—From *Servants, Misfits, and Martyrs* by James C. Howell

🔹 The purpose and goal of spiritual discernment is knowing and doing God's will. We can easily become enamored with discernment definitions, strategies for holding meetings, the emotional rush of doing something new, or even the self-adulation for attempting to do something spiritual. The newness of our endeavor may compromise our vision if we fail to see the urgency of knowing and doing God's will. Nothing is more urgent in our lives or in our congregations than yearning to know and do God's will. We must keep our eyes and hearts on our purpose and goal.
—From *Discerning God's Will Together* by Danny E. Morris and Charles M. Olsen

🔹 Sometimes the timing for a selection is conditioned by chaos and even conflict. For John Mark, the road to leadership was a rocky and conflicted one. The timing was dictated by the opportunity for Paul and Barnabas to revisit new churches in Asia Minor in a second missionary journey. They wanted and needed companions and associates but could not agree about one who had failed them on a previous trip. The conflict occasioned some choices, which were verified years later by experience, maturity, and reconciliation.
—From *Selecting Church Leaders* by Charles M. Olsen and Ellen Morseth

🔹 "Stand at the crossroads, and look, and ask for the ancient paths, where the good way lies; and walk in it . . ." (Jer. 6:16). In our crowded and distracted days, one of the ancient paths to deepening communion with God is attentiveness. . . . This vital attentiveness is nourished . . . by love. It is reflected in the attention a young mother and father lavish upon their newborn infant, the finely honed appreciation shared by longtime friends, the alert care of an adult child at the bedside of a frail parent. Love pierces the fog of suspended animation that often surrounds us, and brings us to greater consciousness of God's presence in what we are seeing and hearing. . . .

As we live with increasing attentiveness, the secrets of God's reign reveal themselves to senses illumined by love, and we begin to recognize the face of God in the mirror of our longing to "see the goodness of the Lord in the land of the living"(Ps. 27:13).

—From "Editor's Introduction" by John S. Mogabgab in *Weavings* July/August 2002

Fourth Sunday after Pentecost (Ordinary Time)
Sunday between June 12 and 18
(If after Trinity Sunday; otherwise turn to next Sunday.)

33: Conversion

Affirmation
O LORD my God, I cried to you for help,
     and you have healed me . . .
Sing praises to the LORD, O you his faithful ones,
     and give thanks to his holy name (Ps. 30:2, 4).

Petition
Hear, O LORD, when I cry aloud,
     be gracious to me and answer me!
"Come," my heart says, "seek his face!"
     Your face, LORD, do I seek.
     Do not hide your face from me.

Do not turn your servant away in anger,
     you who have been my help.
Do not cast me off, do not forsake me,
     O God of my salvation! (Ps. 27:7-9).

Sacred Reading: anthology or other selected reading

Daily Scripture Readings

Sunday	A.	Genesis 18:1-15; Psalm 116:1-2, 12-19; Romans 5:1-8; Matthew 9:35–10:8
	B.	1 Samuel 15:34–16:13; Psalm 20; 2 Corinthians 5:6-10, 14-17; Mark 4:26-34
	C.	1 Kings 21:1-10, 15-21; Psalm 5:1-8; Galatians 2:15-21; Luke 7:36–8:3
Monday		Acts 2:37-42
Tuesday		Luke 3:10-14
Wednesday		Hebrews 10:32-39

Thursday	Acts 9:1-9
Friday	1 Timothy 1:12-16
Saturday	1 John 3:4-10

Prayer: thanksgiving, petition, intercession, praise, and offering

Reflection: silent (listening to God), written (journaling)

God's Promise
I will visit you, and fulfill my promise. For surely I know the plans I have for you, says the LORD, plans for your welfare and not for harm, to give you a future with hope (Jer. 29:10-11).

My Response
Blessed be the LORD,
    for he has heard the sound of my pleadings.
The LORD is my strength and my shield;
    in him my heart trusts;
so I am helped, and my heart exults,
    and with my song I give thanks to him (Ps. 28:6-7).

Readings for Reflection

❧ Conversion is going on all the time within us and within the world. The radical change of Christian conversion is also going on within us at all times. While the change of turning toward God may seem like a once-in-a-lifetime experience, it is in reality a continual process. We may think that we have turned fully toward God; then we discover another dimension of God, and we know immediately that more conversion is possible and necessary if we are to move Godward in all of life.

Conversion is a lifelong process of turning more and more fully toward God in all that we are, possess, and do. There may be earthshaking moments when we are being formed in the image of Christ at incredible speed and in remarkable ways. But such moments are not the end; there is more to come as we give ourselves to the transforming power of God.

While conversion requires our decision and action, the grace and strength to be changed—to become more than we are—is the gift of God. Conversion is a partnership project. We cannot transform ourselves, and God does not transform us against our wishes. However, once we invite God's transforming presence into our lives, the necessary power to change comes with the transforming presence.

It is wise not to try to dictate what our conversion will be like. We cannot know what God has in store for us until we begin to live in harmony and companionship with God. As our understanding of and relationship to God grow, we may begin to see where God is leading us in our conversion. On the other hand, we may experience surprises throughout our lives as God seeks to shape us. It is also wise not to assume that our conversion will look like, feel like, or keep pace with any other person's conversion. Since we are unique and God is infinite, our conversion experiences will be unique as well. The important thing is inviting God to be the master potter in our lives. We may not know what the end product will be, but we do know that it will be good when we permit God to be the potter and we agree to be the malleable clay.

—Rueben P. Job

✥ Legend tells of a little girl who had an ugly hump on her back. The girl was so deformed that she was either ridiculed or pitied by everyone. When she died, it turned out that the ugly hump concealed angel's wings. Can it be that all the ugly things in our lives have in them angel's wings? Can it be that even our sin, our ugly sin, can be turned to good; could it conceal angels' wings?

This is the glorious promise of conversion: God is able to make all things work together for good. Even

the sinful years, the ugly years, need not be wasted but can result in good. Is this not a most comforting assurance? For many of us our ugly years were numerous, and they cause deep remorse. They may have struck at the prime of our lives and ministries. For so long we have grieved them, feeling that many years of ministry were wasted. But the love of God dawns upon us, and with it comes a most amazing promise and a new hope: What we cannot redeem, God can; and what we cannot erase, God will.
—Norman Shawchuck

  In 1966 a retrospective of Picasso's paintings was exhibited in Cannes, France. Hundreds of his works, from the first he did as an adolescent beginner to the latest of the master, who was then eighty-five years old, graced the walls of the gallery. The old man himself roamed about, enjoying the show more than anyone. One report told of a woman who stopped him and said, "I don't understand. Over there, the beginning pictures—so mature, serious and solemn—then the later ones, so different, so irrepressible. It almost seems as though the dates should be reversed. How do you explain it?"

"Easily," replied Picasso, eyes sparkling. "It takes a long time to become young."
—From *Alive in Christ* by Maxie Dunnam

  One of the great lies of our day is that conversion is instant, like fast food. God can zap us and we're saved. It is all free. It costs nothing. Take it and run. This is what Bonhoeffer calls "cheap grace." Punch in at church. Grab a sacrament and run. Season your conversation with "praise the Lord" and you're among the saved.

One of the great truths of our day is that conversion is ongoing. Conversion is the process in which we are given opportunity upon opportunity to accept the free gift of salvation. Salvation is a free gift, yes, but it's costly. It's "costly grace." It costs us our lives lived passionately. The road to conversion is not a fast food line. When Saul was knocked down by that flash of lightning, that was not conversion. That was just God getting his attention. The conversion came as he groped his way in blindness to Ananias, able to see with interior eyes because he had no external eyes to depend on. His conversion continued day after day as he began to give meaning to his new name, Paul. He was still in the process of conversion when he was on his way to Rome in chains.

—From *A Tree Full of Angels* by Macrina Wiederkehr

❧ We shouldn't put down people who show great euphoria and excitement after a born again or religious experience. They're right. Suddenly the world makes sense for them. Suddenly it's okay, despite the absurdity, the injustice, the pain. Life is now so spacious that we can even absorb the contradictions. God is so great, so bottomless, so empty, that God can absorb even the contraries, even the collision of opposites. Thus salvation often feels like a kind of universal amnesty, a total forgiveness of ourselves and all other things.

—From *Everything Belongs* by Richard Rohr

❧ Many assert that John Wesley was the world's most influential social reformer of his day. While some will question the depth of his influence, none question his remarkable ability to link piety with justice and to translate doctrine into daily living. From the early days at Oxford until a few days before his death, Wesley was about the ministry of caring for the poor, the oppressed, and the imprisoned. And all of this while living a rigorous life of prayer, study, and reflection.

This commitment to neighbor and passion to proclaim the gospel story was so great that John and Charles rode in a cart with a condemned prisoner so that they could sing and pray on the way to the hangman's scaffold. . . .

Holy living is a direct result of and inseparable from a holy heart. To experience Christian perfection is to live as Jesus lived. It is to be obedient to the One proclaimed as Savior and Lord. Matthew 25 is a text to be taken seriously. To know Christ and to be known by Christ means to walk with Christ in the everyday business of life.

—From *A Wesleyan Spiritual Reader* by Rueben P. Job

᪣ We are rich and strong, good and holy, beneficent and benignant, by answered prayer. It is not the mere performance, the attitude, nor the words of prayer, which bring benefit to us, but it is the answer sent direct from heaven. Conscious, real answers to prayer bring real good to us. This is not praying merely for self, or simply for selfish ends. The selfish character cannot exist when the prayer conditions are fulfilled.

It is by these answered prayers that human nature is enriched. The answered prayer brings us into constant and conscious communion with God, awakens and enlarges gratitude, and excites the melody and lofty inspiration of praise. Answered prayer is the mark of God in our praying. It is the exchange with heaven, and it establishes and realizes a relationship with the unseen.

—From *The Possibilities of Prayer* by Edward M. Bounds

Fifth Sunday after Pentecost (Ordinary Time)
Sunday between June 19 and 25
(If after Trinity Sunday; otherwise turn to next Sunday.)

34: Signs and Wonders

Affirmation
God delivers and rescues,
> he works signs and wonders in heaven and on
> earth (Dan. 6:27).

Petition
Teach me your way, O LORD,
> that I may walk in your truth;
> give me an undivided heart to revere your name.
I give thanks to you, O Lord my God, with my whole
> heart,
> and I will glorify your name forever.
For great is your steadfast love toward me;
> you have delivered my soul from the depths of
> Sheol (Ps. 86:11-13).

Sacred Reading: anthology or other selected reading

Daily Scripture Readings

Sunday	A.	Genesis 21:8-21; Psalm 86:1-10, 16-17; Romans 6:1-11; Matthew 10:24-39
	B.	1 Samuel 17:1, 4-11; Psalm 9:9-20; 2 Corinthians 6:1-13; Mark 4:35-41
	C.	1 Kings 19:1-4, 8-15; Psalm 42; Galatians 3:23-29; Luke 8:26-39
Monday		Acts 3:1-10
Tuesday		John 9:1-12
Wednesday		Isaiah 35:1-4
Thursday		Isaiah 35:5-10
Friday		Acts 19:11-20
Saturday		Acts 12:6-11

Prayer: thanksgiving, petition, intercession, praise, and offering

Reflection: silent (listening to God), written (journaling)

God's Promise
For you shall go out in joy,
      and be led back in peace;
the mountains and the hills before you
      shall burst into song,
      and all the trees of the field shall clap their hands
      (Isa. 55:12).

My Response
O LORD, you are my God;
      I will exalt you, I will praise your name;
for you have done wonderful things,
      plans formed of old, faithful and sure (Isa. 25:1).

Readings for Reflection

❧ The dramatic change in the lives of people touched by the power and presence of God through the early church proved to be a nearly irresistible magnet, drawing many to believe in and follow Jesus Christ. Besides the miraculous healing of a blind beggar (Acts 3), many signs and wonders done among the people (Acts 5:12 ff.) caught the attention of those outside and those inside this young church. It was clear to observers and participants: God was at work transforming individuals and communities through this new movement. It was also clear that many not only wanted to see what was going on but longed for such salvation, healing, and wholeness in their own lives.

Today people still look for evidence of God's transforming presence in the church and in the world. When they find that evidence, they often turn toward it, seeking to be close to the God who is obviously at work changing lives in such dramatic ways. They are drawn because they want to be close to God, and often they seek their own transformation and salvation. The congregation where signs and wonders are evident is the congregation that finds new people coming to be touched by that transforming presence of God.

In Acts we read of transformation that leads from sinfulness to holiness of life. The kind of transformation that leads from selfishness to sharing, from uselessness to usefulness, from sickness to health, and from death to life is the transformation many seek. This transformation is promised in the Gospels by the One who came that all might have life and have it abundantly.

Where are the signs and wonders of God's active and transforming presence most visible today? How can you and I make ourselves and the entire church more available, thus permitting those signs and wonders to occur within and through our lives? One way the early church made itself available was by always giving an unqualified yes when God invited obedience, witness, and service. Can we do as much?
—Rueben P. Job

❧ Money, I never think of it. It always comes. The Lord sends it.

We do his work. He provides the means.

If he does not give us the means, that shows that he does not want the work. So why worry?
—From *My Life for the Poor* by Mother Teresa

❧ *To think that God could put an idea into someone's mind and that person could comprehend that idea and immediately act upon it with unquestioning determination is the most remarkable wonder of all!*

A second wonder is that God has given all of us this capacity. God communicates with all of us! We get little nudges—feelings that this or that should be done or not done; we get hunches and leadings, signs and signals, and sometimes direct messages.
—From *Yearning to Know God's Will* by Danny E. Morris

❧ St. Francis was a radical in his day—was even per-
ceived as a heretic—because he offered a fresh view of
the Christian life by living as a beggar, believing in
providence, and closely following the teaching of the
Gospel. But what was also unusual about him was that
he reformed his own religion from within the institu-
tional Church rather than by breaking away from it.
Mother Teresa's life has many similarities to that of
Francis. Her path is also through poverty, simplicity
and adherence to the teachings of Christ, and because
of this she has been viewed as a progressive in the present fundamentalist framework of the patriarchal
Church. Yet she preaches her love and peace in action
in a world still lacking in strong female leaders and
from one of the largest and poorest and most polluted
cities in Asia.
—Lucinda Vardey in *Mother Teresa: A Simple Path*
comp. by Lucinda Vardey

❧ Our work is constant, our homes are full. The problems of the poor continue, so our work continues. Yet
everyone, not just the Missionaries of Charity, can do
something beautiful for God by reaching out to the
poor people in their own countries. I see no lack of hesi-
tation in helping others. I see only people filled with
God's love, wanting to do works of love. This is the
future—this is God's wish for us—to serve through
love in action, and to be inspired by the Holy Spirit to
act when called.
—Mother Teresa in *Mother Teresa: A Simple Path* comp.
by Lucinda Vardey

❧ Prayer is not an indifferent or a small thing. It is not
a sweet little privilege. It is a great prerogative, far-
reaching in its effects. Failure to pray entails losses far
beyond the person who neglects it. Prayer is not a mere
episode of the Christian life. Rather the whole life is a
preparation for and the result of prayer. In its condition,
prayer is the sum of religion. Faith is but a channel of

prayer. Faith gives it wings and swiftness. Prayer is the lungs through which holiness breathes. Prayer is not only the language of spiritual life, but makes its very essence and forms its real character.

—From *The Possibilities of Prayer* by Edward M. Bounds

ᴥ Now, Jesus himself was and is a joyous, creative person. He does not allow us to continue thinking of our Father who fills and overflows space as a morose and miserable monarch, a frustrated and petty parent, or a policeman on the prowl.

One cannot think of God in such ways while confronting Jesus' declaration, "He that has seen me has seen the Father." One of the most outstanding features of Jesus' personality was precisely an abundance of joy. This he left as an inheritance to his students, "that their joy might be full" (John 15:11). And they did not say, "Pass the aspirin," for he was well known to those around him as a happy man. It is deeply illuminating of kingdom living to understand that his steady happiness was not ruled out by his experience of sorrow and even grief.

So we must understand that God does not "love" us without liking us—through gritted teeth—as "Christian" love is sometimes thought to do. Rather, out of the eternal freshness of his perpetually self-renewed being, the heavenly Father cherishes the earth and each human being upon it. The fondness, the endearment, the unstintingly affectionate regard of God toward all his creatures is the natural outflow of what he is to the core—which we vainly try to capture with our tired but indispensable old word *love*.

—From *The Divine Conspiracy* by Dallas Willard

ᴥ Salute Paula and Eustochium, who, whatever the world may think, are always mine in Christ. Salute Albina, your mother, and Marcella, your sister; Marcellina also, and the holy Felicitas; and say to them all: "We must all stand before the judgment seat of Christ, and there shall be revealed the principle by which each has lived."

And now, illustrious model of chastity and virginity, remember me, I beseech you, in your prayers, and by your intercessions calm the waves of the sea.
—From "Letter 45—to Asella" by Jerome

Sixth Sunday after Pentecost (Ordinary Time)
Sunday between June 26 and July 2

35: Encountering Opposition

Affirmation
When they heard these things, they became enraged and ground their teeth at Stephen. But filled with the Holy Spirit, he gazed into heaven and saw the glory of God and Jesus standing at the right hand of God. "Look," he said, "I see the heavens opened and the Son of Man standing at the right hand of God!" (Acts 7:54-56).

Petition
Then they dragged him out of the city and began to stone him; and the witnesses laid their coats at the feet of a young man named Saul. While they were stoning Stephen, he prayed, "Lord Jesus, receive my spirit." Then he knelt down and cried out in a loud voice, "Lord, do not hold this sin against them." When he had said this, he died (Acts 7:58-60).

Sacred Reading: anthology or other selected reading

Daily Scripture Readings

Sunday	A.	Genesis 22:1-14; Psalm 13; Romans 6:12-23; Matthew 10:40-42
	B.	2 Samuel 1:1, 17-27; Psalm 130; 2 Corinthians 8:7-15; Mark 5:21-43
	C.	2 Kings 2:1-2, 6-14; Psalm 77:1-2, 11-20; Galatians 5:1, 13-25; Luke 9:51-62
Monday		Acts 4:1-12
Tuesday		Acts 5:17-21
Wednesday		Acts 8:1-3
Thursday		Acts 11:19-26

| Friday | Luke 11:14-23 |
| Saturday | 1 Peter 4:12-19 |

Prayer: thanksgiving, petition, intercession, praise, and offering

Reflection: silent (listening to God), written (journaling)

God's Promise
The Lord said to him, "Go, for he is an instrument whom I have chosen to bring my name before Gentiles and kings and before the people of Israel; I myself will show him how much he must suffer for the sake of my name" (Acts 9:15-16).

My Response
For we do not have a high priest who is unable to sympathize with our weaknesses, but we have one who in every respect has been tested as we are, yet without sin. Let us therefore approach the throne of grace with boldness, so that we may receive mercy and find grace to help in time of need (Heb. 4:15-16).

Readings for Reflection

❧ Those who seek to follow Jesus will encounter opposition. It follows as surely as night follows day. The opposition may arise within ourselves; it may arise among the followers of Jesus; or it may arise in the world. It may be subtle, blatant, mild, or severe. But opposition is sure to come, so the issue is not whether it will appear but how we respond to opposition.

Following Jesus was not easy in the first century, and it is not easy in the twenty-first century. The level of opposition to Jesus from within his own family and his own religious group surprised his early followers. Two thousand years later we understand a little more about human personality, but the level of opposition to Jesus and his followers still surprises us.

We may be able to understand the opposition of the Roman government, but it is hard to understand the opposition of a religious community that claimed to be seeking God and faithfulness to God just as Jesus was. And yet, opposition still comes today from within the church *as well as* from without. How are we to face opposition when it comes? Squarely, humbly, openly, and with all the faith we can muster.

To commit to following Jesus is to commit myself to a lifelong journey of being led where Jesus wants me to go and not necessarily where I want to go. This situation often causes opposition within myself. Jesus may call me to do what I do not normally and easily do. Jesus may ask me to wait or remain silent when I wish to speak or move on. In each of these cases I experience opposition within to what Jesus calls me to do and to be.

External opposition can arise when God calls for an action that is not what the church wants or what the world wants. Am I to follow Jesus? If so, I will face and feel opposition. And yet, the only course for faithfulness is to follow where Jesus leads. May God always guide us, and may we have the grace to follow Jesus as faithfully when we face opposition as when we face affirmation, affection, and acclaim.

—Rueben P. Job

ᴥ About the same time, in the reign of Commodus, our condition became more favorable, and through the grace of God the churches throughout the entire world enjoyed peace, and the word of salvation was leading every soul from every race of [humanity] to the devout worship of the God of the universe. So that now at Rome many who were highly distinguished for wealth and family turned with all their household and relatives unto their salvation.

But the demon who hates what is good, being malignant in his nature, could not endure this, but prepared himself again for conflict, contriving many devices against us. And he brought to the judgment seat Apollonius, of the city of Rome, a man renowned among the faithful for learning and philosophy, having stirred up one of his servants, who was well fitted for such a purpose, to accuse him.

But this wretched man made the charge unseasonably, because by a royal decree it was unlawful that informers of such things should live. And his legs were broken immediately, Perennius the judge having pronounced this sentence upon him.

But the martyr, highly beloved of God, being earnestly entreated and requested by the judge to give an account of himself before the Senate, made in the presence of all an eloquent defense of the faith for which he was witnessing. And as if by decree of the Senate he was put to death by decapitation; an ancient law requiring that those who were brought to the judgment seat and refused to recant should not be liberated.

—From "How Apollonius Suffered Martyrdom at Rome" by Eusebius

❧ One of the early Christian writers describes the first stage of solitary prayer as the experience of a man who, after years of living with open doors, suddenly decides to shut them. The visitors who used to come and enter his home start pounding on his doors, wondering why they are not allowed to enter. Only when they realize that they are not welcome do they gradually stop coming. This is the experience of anyone who decides to enter into solitude after a life without much spiritual discipline. At first, the many distractions keep presenting themselves. Later, as they receive less and less attention, they slowly withdraw.

—From *Making All Things New* by Henri J. M. Nouwen

❧ During one of the unfortunate wars between India and Pakistan, an Indian army officer was captured and kept incommunicado in Karachi till the end of the war, when he was set free, came back to India and told his

experience. During his captivity, he said, he was allowed to read newspapers and listen to the radio, but, of course, only Pakistani newspapers and radio stations. Accordingly he heard and read day by day news of the war which said repeatedly that India was losing on all fronts, and was about to be defeated. That was all the information he had. And yet, as he himself told when he was free in India recollecting his past captivity, he refused to believe even then that his country was losing, and was sure in his heart, in spite of all the constant propaganda to the contrary, that India was winning the war all along. And that was the fact. India was winning, and in a few days obtained the final victory that forced the peace. The experience of that gallant officer, when I read it in the press, gave me an example of how faith works in us . . . if only we too are proud of our heavenly citizenship, and gallant patriots of the Kingdom. All the information we receive is adverse and contrary to our beliefs. The Enemy is winning. Honesty does not pay, to tell the truth only creates problems, violence always gets the upper hand, and goodness has no place left in this troubled world. Those are the news we read and hear day by day and hour by hour. The Kingdom is being defeated, and there is no hope of victory. And yet, in our heart of hearts, we know that that is not true. In spite of all the enemy propaganda we know deep down in our conscience that the Kingdom is winning, that truth prevails, that honesty pays, and Jesus is King. This is heavenly patriotism, which is divine faith. Let us wait in joyful patience for the final news, and when victory comes we will tell our experience.
—From *Faith for Justice* by Carlos G. Valles

❧ A casual glimpse at the life of John Wesley may lead us to believe that life for him was without opposition. He knew where God was calling him to go, who God was calling him to be, and the rest was simple. In retrospect, we may think that he chose a difficult way of discipleship, but that once the decision was made, and in spite of personal hardship, there was little internal or external opposition.

A deeper gaze at his life and ministry as revealed through his writing and the testimony of those who wrote about him suggests that he faced real opposition from the beginning until the end. Life was not simple or easy. The struggle for faithful discipleship resulted in opposition within his own life and opposition from those who could not agree with the way he had chosen. The search for authentic discipleship led him to go far beyond the common understanding or practice of the Christian faith, and this going beyond the commonly accepted way often led to opposition.

—From *A Wesleyan Spiritual Reader* by Rueben P. Job

❧ The powers of this world do not want to see their authority and control usurped by another, even if that other is God. To preach a message and practice a life of authentic discipleship will make us uncomfortable and make others anxious and sometimes hostile. We are not above the struggle of what it means to follow Jesus. The complex issues of life do not lend themselves to easy answers. It is not easy to know with certainty the path we are to follow. And often, after careful discernment, the direction we hear is not the way we would have chosen. There is often resistance within us to the way we are convinced God is calling us to travel. It is a strenuous journey of faith that permits us to say with Mary, "Here am I, the servant of the Lord; let it be with me according to your word" (Luke 1:38).

We should not expect instantly to be where Mary was in her witness. Neither should we think that there is something wrong with us because we struggle with internal or external opposition. Self examination and the help of a faithful spiritual guide are ways to test our perceptions with reality.

—From *A Wesleyan Spiritual Reader* by Rueben P. Job

❧ The good news is that the scriptures, tradition, the experience of the saints, and our own experience tell us that it is possible to face the unknown and even to face opposition without fear and without defeat. To expect a life without struggle is unrealistic. But it is realistic to expect God's help in living an authentic and joyful life as a Christian. To daily declare our love for God and neighbor, to give ourselves as fully as we can to God, and to ask for God's help in living an authentic life of faith is to be prepared to meet any and all opposition. Once we have given all of life to God, we have nothing to lose. We have everything because God has us.

—From *A Wesleyan Spiritual Reader* by Rueben P. Job

❧ The cup of suffering has many shapes and a variety of contents. In our tradition, the cup has special significance. It is a communal cup, meant for sharing. Abandonment at a time of suffering is the deepest of tragedies. Each time we pass the wine of the Eucharist, we are reminded of our communal relationships and our responsibility to the whole body. We are reminded that our sharing is to continue in our picking up the burdens of the larger community.

Draining the cup of suffering is the final test of our sincerity in claiming discipleship. We can expect no right or left hand seats of honor, no prerogatives of power or monopoly on truth, no thrones, no outsiders. But we can have the privilege of holding one another, broken and bruised, in the embrace of our circle, of keeping watch with the dying or keeping vigil with the condemned, of walking alongside the exiled and the weary, of standing at the foot of the cross, not in despair or in bitterness, but open to the miracle of pending resurrection. And, finally, of waiting hopefully for our own welcome into life. Wholeness at last!

—From *Seek Treasures in Small Fields* by Joan Puls

❧ The more I see of conflict in the church, the more I am moved by persons who allow conflict to become the occasion of their growth. And wherever several persons allow personal growth to happen, their collective growth may begin to reshape the community of which they are a part. To say this is in no way to make light of the number of church and denominational conflicts that swirl about us. It is to say, though, that Jesus seeks to form us even in the places of greatest friction. In the midst of division and hurt, he can draw us toward maturity in fresh and formative ways. This formation can take place whether we happen to be the focal point of a conflict; its anguished observer; or, in some formally defined role, are present to the situation as "conflict manager."

In matters of conflict, Jesus shapes his community fundamentally by pointing it toward a healing intent. Nowhere in the Gospels does Jesus deny conflict. At no time, in his own actions or in his counsel to others, does he ignore its presence or imply that conflict itself is evil. However, Jesus unceasingly encourages his followers to reach after wholeness.

—From *Discovering Community* by Stephen V. Doughty

❧ "You are Peter, and on this rock I will build my church," said Jesus to Simon Peter (Matt. 16:18). I had always envisioned this as the rock-strengthened church standing firm against all the onslaughts and batterings of hell's forces. "Not so," a scientist who was also a lay minister once told me, "I see that rock of the church not standing still, waiting to be attacked, but thrown by God, flying through the air, crashing into the gates of evil to release those trapped there." What an insight!

—From *Forgiveness, the Passionate Journey* by Flora Slosson Wuellner

Seventh Sunday after Pentecost (Ordinary Time)
Sunday between July 3 and July 9

36: Praying for Boldness

Affirmation
When they had prayed, the place in which they were
gathered together was shaken; and they were all filled
with the Holy Spirit and spoke the word of God with
boldness (Acts 4:31).

Petition
Now, Lord, look at their threats, and grant to your servants to speak your word with all boldness, while you
stretch out your hand to heal, and signs and wonders
are performed through the name of your holy servant
Jesus (Acts 4:29-30).

Sacred Reading: anthology or other selected reading

Daily Scripture Readings

Sunday	A.	Genesis 24:34-38, 42-49, 58-67; Psalm 45:10-17; Romans 7:15-25; Matthew 11:16-19, 25-30
	B.	2 Samuel 5:1-5, 9-10; Psalm 48; 2 Corinthians 12:2-10; Mark 6:1-13
	C.	2 Kings 5:1-14; Psalm 30; Galatians 6:1-16; Luke 10:1-11, 16-20
Monday		Acts 4:23-31
Tuesday		Romans 15:1-6
Wednesday		Acts 15:14-21
Thursday		Philippians 1:1-11
Friday		Acts 5:12-16
Saturday		Ephesians 6:18-20

Prayer: thanksgiving, petition, intercession, praise,
and offering

Reflection: silent (listening to God), written (journaling)

God's Promise
And this is the boldness we have in him, that if we ask anything according to his will, he hears us. And if we know that he hears us in whatever we ask, we know that we have obtained the requests made of him (1 John 5:14-15).

My Response
It is my eager expectation and hope that I will not be put to shame in any way, but that by my speaking with all boldness, Christ will be exalted now as always in my body, whether by life or by death. For to me, living is Christ and dying is gain. If I am to live in the flesh, that means fruitful labor for me; and I do not know which I prefer. I am hard pressed between the two: my desire is to depart and be with Christ, for that is far better; but to remain in the flesh is more necessary for you. Since I am convinced of this, I know that I will remain and continue with all of you for your progress and joy in faith (Phil. 1:20-25).

Readings for Reflection

⁊ Living in a multicultural world, the disciples easily could have remained silent about their dramatic encounter with God in Jesus Christ. In a world of many religions, they might understandably have been timid about even mentioning their faith in Jesus Christ. In a time when allegiance to the official religion often was demanded, they would have found it so much simpler to go along with the crowd. In a time when advocacy of any new religion was dangerous, they would have been so much safer to hide any evidence of faith in Jesus Christ.

However, these very risks and dangers that could have sent the disciples running in fact prompted them to pray for boldness to declare the gospel. They did not ask for security, relief from persecution, or the demise of the opposition. They asked for boldness to declare the gospel. They were not longing for their own safety; they were longing for faithfulness. And as soon as their prayers subsided, the place where they were gathered was shaken and they were all filled with the Holy Spirit and spoke the word of God with boldness (Acts 4:31). Their prayers were instantly answered.

How often has the Christian community of which you are a member prayed for boldness to declare the gospel? Probably not very often since we don't place great value on boldness to declare the gospel. But what if we did? What difference would it make in our lives, our congregations, and the communities in which we live? The early disciples found that praying for boldness gave them the wisdom, the faith, and the power to live faithful and effective lives. What are we praying for today?

—Rueben P. Job

❧ Any difficulty, any dilemma, can be surmounted by whole-hearted prayer. A given difficulty can only confront you on its own level. Rise above that level through prayer and meditation and the difficulty will melt away.

—From *Power Through Constructive Thinking* by Emmet Fox

❧ The church and the world need saints. They need saints more than they need more canny politicians, more brilliant scientists, more grossly overpaid executives and entrepreneurs, more clever entertainers and talk-show hosts. Are there any on the horizon now that Mother Teresa is no longer with us, either of the extraordinary or of the ordinary kind? I think there are. Maybe I should say that there are saints "aborning" by God's grace. There are those whose lives have been irradiated by God's grace, who seek not to be safe but to be faithful, who have learned how to get along in adversity, who are joyful, who are dream filled, and above all, who are prayerful. That is what the church and the world need most. It begins with you.

—From *Spiritual Preparation for Christian Leadership* by E. Glenn Hinson

❧ True prayer begins with God who moves our spirit, as the Gospel song tells us, to seek Him seeking us. To believe that we who pray take the initiative is a conceit born of pride! The impulse to pray always begins with God. We may either choose to obey or ignore that impulse, but the impulse itself always begins with God. Through our prayers He reveals that His will is wholly Love, and that our response to that will must be love as well. Even our love for God draws its energy from the source of Love itself, which is God.

This Love cannot be mediated through knowledge, but must be revealed to love. It is not reasonable to forgive infinitely, as our Savior demands. Knowledge can never produce the will to forgive but Love working within us can and does. Our life, unless it be transformed by this Love, will never produce the fruits of Love. The person who continually prays finds his or her life transformed from one of "knowing" to one of believing, and from one ruled by the many selves to one lived according to God's will, which is Love.

Yet the self—the deepest self—is the clay from which God may fashion a vessel for His love. The person who prays discovers that the deepest self is the clay which must be shaped, molded and fired by Love. This God-created entity is what Christian tradition calls the soul.

The starting point for prayer is to place the self in the hands of God. This process, whether long or short, is an arduous one, which the mystics call purgation. This is the clay's surrender to the potter, the surrender of the vanquished to the conqueror as yet unseen, and the lover's surrender to the beloved hidden behind the veil.

This yielding may begin hesitatingly, reluctantly, and with apprehension, but over time these misgivings must give way to the joy of that new awareness that comes of spiritual rebirth.

—From *Crossing the Border* by Russell M. Hart

❧ Since I first entered on the religious life, I have looked on God as the *Goal* and *End* of all the thoughts and affections of the soul. As a novice, during the hours appointed for prayer I labored to arrive at a conviction of the truth of the Divine Being, rather by the light of faith than by the deductions of the intellect, and by this short and certain method I grew in the knowledge of this *Object* of Love, in Whose Presence I resolved evermore to abide. Possessed thus entirely with the greatness and the majesty of this INFINITE BEING, I went straightway to the place which duty had marked out for me—the kitchen. There, when I had carried out all that called for me, I gave to prayer whatever time remained, as well before my work as after. Before beginning any task I would say to GOD, with child-like trust: "O GOD, since Thou art with me, and it is Thy will that I must now apply myself to these outward duties, I beseech Thee, assist me with Thy grace that I may continue in Thy Presence; and to this end, O LORD, be with me in this my work, accept the labor of my hands, and dwell within my heart with all Thy Fullness." Moreover, as I wrought, I would continue to hold familiar converse, offering to [GOD] my little acts of service, entreating the unfailing succour of [GOD's] grace. When I had finished, I would examine how I had performed my duty: if I found well, I gave [GOD] thanks; if ill, I besought [GOD's] pardon, and without losing heart I set my spirit right, and returned anew unto [GOD's] Presence, as though I had never wandered from [GOD]. Thus, by rising after every fall, and by doing all in faith and love, without wearying, I have come to a state in which it would be as little possible for me not to think of GOD, as it was

hard to discipline myself thereto at the beginning.
—From *The Spiritual Maxims of Brother Lawrence*

❧ Life is full of perils and of hidden reefs, on which we shall make shipwreck without the continual succour of the grace of God. Yet how can we ask for it, unless we are with [God]? How can we be with [God], unless our thoughts are ever of [God]? How can [God] be in our thoughts, unless we form a holy habit of abiding in [God's] Presence, there asking for the grace we need each moment of our life?

If you would go forward in the spiritual life, you must avoid relying on the subtle conclusions and fine reasonings of the unaided intellect. Unhappy they who seek to satisfy their desire therein! The Creator is the great teacher of Truth. We can reason laboriously for many years, but fuller far and deeper is the knowledge of the hidden things of Faith and of [God], which [God] flashes as light into the *heart* of the humble.

Nothing can give us so great relief in the trials and sorrows of life, as a loving intercourse with God; when such is faithfully practiced, the evils that assail the body will prove light to us. God often ordains that we should suffer in the body to purify the soul, and to constrain us to abide with [God]. How can anyone whose life is hid with God, and whose only desire is God, be capable of feeling pain?
—From *The Spiritual Maxims of Brother Lawrence*

❧ There can be no substitute, no rival for prayer; it stands alone as the great spiritual force, and this force must be imminent and acting. It cannot be dispensed with during one generation, nor held in abeyance for the advance of any great movement—it must be continuous and particular, always, everywhere, and in everything. We cannot run our spiritual operations on the prayers of the past generation. *Many persons believe in the efficacy of prayer, but not many pray.* Prayer is the easiest and hardest of all things; the simplest and the sublimest; the weakest and the most powerful; its results lie outside the range of human possibilities—they are limited only by the omnipotence of God.

Few Christians have anything but a vague idea of the power of prayer; fewer still have any experience of that power. The Church seems almost wholly unaware of the power God puts into her hand; this spiritual *carte blanche* on the infinite resources of God's wisdom and power is rarely, if ever, used—never used to the full measure of honoring God. It is astounding how poor the use, how little the benefits. Prayer is our most formidable weapon, but the one in which we are the least skilled, the most averse to its use. We do everything else for the heathen save the thing God wants us to do; the only thing which does any good—makes all else we do efficient.

—From *Purpose in Prayer* by Edward M. Bounds

ᶬ In Authoritative Prayer we are calling forth the will of the Father upon the earth. Here we are not so much speaking *to* God as speaking *for* God. We are not asking God to do something; rather, we are using the authority of God to command something done.

—From *Prayer: Finding the Heart's True Home* by Richard J. Foster

ᶬ How beautiful it is to see relationships in which asking and receiving are a joyful and loving way of life. Often we see those who cherish one another each seriously or playfully trying to outgive the other. That is how relationships should be. Of course we must never eliminate the asking side of the relationship. A balance must be kept, for giving is not the same as imposition. That is why God does not just give us what we need without being asked. Prayer is nothing but a proper way for persons to interact. Thus Jesus very naturally moves in Matt. 7:7-11 from asking for what you want of others to asking for what you want from your Father, the one in the heavens.

These two relationships, he clearly taught, are on a continuous line.
—From *The Divine Conspiracy* by Dallas Willard

❧ Biblical spirituality inspires acts of courage born of commitment to God. Such courage does not call persons to do the impossible but faithfully and selflessly to do what they can when they could have chosen otherwise. Lent recalls the courage of Jesus who "set his face to go to Jerusalem" (Luke 9:51), in spite of understanding what awaited him there. Jesus' example invokes courage today as you and I translate words of commitment to God into freely chosen actions that place others above self—and God above all, for trust of God opens the door to courage.
—From *Neglected Voices* by John Indermark

❧ God is active in the world and in our lives in many ways. We may feel the mystery of God as we view storm clouds brewing over a blue ocean. We may experience the love of God when we are comforted by a friend. We may be filled with the compassion of God as we attend a conference on the plight of the homeless. We may be blessed by the peace of God during prayer or troubled by the challenges of God as we study the Bible. God comes to us in both our conscious and our unconscious experiences, for God is in all of life.
—From *Journaling* by Anne Broyles

37: *Audacious Prayers/Perfect Response*

Affirmation

There he found a man named Aeneas, who had been bedridden for eight years, for he was paralyzed. Peter said to him, "Aeneas, Jesus Christ heals you; get up and make your bed!" And immediately he got up. And all the residents of Lydda and Sharon saw him and turned to the Lord (Acts 9:33-35).

Petition

While Peter was kept in prison, the church prayed fervently to God for him. . . . Peter, bound with two chains, was sleeping between two soldiers, while guards in front of the door were keeping watch over the prison. Suddenly an angel of the Lord appeared and a light shone in the cell. He tapped Peter on the side and woke him, saying, "Get up quickly." And the chains fell off his wrists (Acts 12:5-7).

Sacred Reading: anthology or other selected reading

Daily Scripture Readings

Sunday	A.	Genesis 25:19-34; Psalm 119:105-112; Romans 8:1-11; Matthew 13:1-9, 18-23
	B.	2 Samuel 6:1-5, 12-19; Psalm 24; Ephesians 1:3-14; Mark 6:14-29
	C.	Amos 7:7-17; Psalm 82; Colossians 1:1-14; Luke 10:25-37
Monday		Acts 4:32-37
Tuesday		Acts 9:32-35
Wednesday		Acts 13:48-52
Thursday		2 Corinthians 1:3-11
Friday		2 Corinthians 8:1-15
Saturday		2 Thessalonians 3:1-5

Prayer: thanksgiving, petition, intercession, praise, and offering

Reflection: silent (listening to God), written (journaling)

God's Promise

Be strong and bold; have no fear or dread of them, because it is the LORD your God who goes with you; he will not fail you or forsake you. . . . It is the LORD who goes before you. He will be with you; he will not fail you or forsake you. Do not fear or be dismayed (Deut. 31:6, 8).

My Response

Peter came to himself and said, "Now I am sure that the Lord has sent his angel and rescued me from the hands of Herod and from all that the Jewish people were expecting" (Acts 12:11).

Readings for Reflection

❧ Remarkable things happened when the early church prayed. The fourth chapter of the book of Acts records just one of those audacious prayers and the nearly unbelievable events that followed a time of very bold prayer. The threat of opposition was real; the disciples knew they faced the same dangers that had taken the life of Jesus. So they prayed for boldness to speak the gospel truth and for the active healing presence of God to be evident in their midst and in their ministry.

The scripture says that signs and wonders gave evidence of God's activity in the midst of this new community of followers of Jesus Christ. One of those dramatic signs was the incredible community that formed around Jesus Christ. "Not a needy person among them" (Acts 4:34) is a sign and wonder that we long for in every community. Many sold land and goods, then brought the proceeds and laid it at the disciples' feet. The disciples "distributed to each as any had need" (Acts 4:35). Such love and generosity were certainly additional remarkable signs of God's activity in the midst of the early church.

The miraculous healings brought about as the apostles declared the gospel also revealed God's presence and action in the church community. The willingness to relinquish property and wealth for the good of all was even more compelling than the healing received by the sick who were brought to the apostles. The results of the apostles' prayer was evident to those within the church and astounded observers from afar, who were then drawn to this contagious and joyful community. May our prayers be as audacious and God's response in our midst as dramatic and transforming.
—Rueben P. Job

☙ It is answered prayer which brings praying out of the realm of dry, dead things, and makes praying a thing of life and power. It is the answer to prayer which brings things to pass, changes the natural trend of things, and orders all things according to the will of God. It is the answer to prayer which takes praying out of the regions of fanaticism, and saves it from being Eutopian, or from being merely fanciful. It is the answer to prayer which makes praying a power for God and for [us], and makes praying real and divine.
—From *The Possibilities of Prayer* by Edward M. Bounds

☙ What the world longs for from the Christian religion is the witness of men and women daring enough to be different, humble enough to make mistakes, wild enough to be burned in the fire of love, real enough to make others see how unreal they are. Jesus, son of the living God, anoint us with fire this day. Let your Word not shine in our hearts, but let it burn. Let there be no division, compromise, or holding back. Separate the

mystics from the romantics, and goad us to that daredevil leap into the abyss of your love.
—From *Reflections for Ragamuffins* by Brennan Manning

❧ Prayer is not controlled. We are the ones controlled, called upon to submit to a mysterious inward process, to be carried beyond ourselves without ever knowing clearly what carries us or where we are going.
—From *Toward God* by Michael Casey

❧ Prayer is larger than any of us. It is less a question of bringing prayer into our hearts than of bringing our hearts into prayer; not drawing water from the sea to fill a bath, but being immersed in an immense ocean and becoming one with it.
—From *Toward God* by Michael Casey

❧ If prayer is a force at all, it cannot be possible to pray without something happening.
—From *Power Through Constructive Thinking* by Emmet Fox

❧ There is no end to a prayer. It echoes on forever in your soul. Long after the visible demonstration has been made and forgotten, the prayer that produced it continues to work for your spiritual advancement, for the creative power of a God thought is unlimited and eternal.
—From *Power Through Constructive Thinking* by Emmet Fox

❧ Many of us have absorbed tacit or explicit taboos about what we are permitted to bring into prayer. We may have learned, for instance, that doubt, anger, hatred, or despair were inappropriate to express to God. Yet we know what happens to human relationships when negative feelings are suppressed. Communication becomes artificial or breaks down; the two parties become emotionally estranged; intimacy becomes impossible. Why should we imagine it is different with God? In prayer, we need to speak whatever truth is in us: pain and grief, fear and disappointment, yearning and desire, questions and doubt, hope and faith, failure and weakness, praise and thanks, despair and sorrow, anger and, yes, even hatred.

—From *Soul Feast* by Marjorie J. Thompson

❧ It takes practice to learn not to censor our prayer. But trying to keep secrets from God is like the three-year-old who covers her eyes and declares, "You can't see me." God sees into our hearts more clearly than we do. Indeed, God is the one who prompts us to look at what we have swept under the rug of our repressions and rationalizations. The Spirit awakens us to what lies hidden within—sometimes gently, sometimes with a jolt, but always so God can work with our conscious consent to free us for growth.

—From *Soul Feast* by Marjorie J. Thompson

❧ Most of us pray that God will do something *to* us
    or *for* us,
    But God wants to do something *in* us and
        through us.
    That can be done only through our cooperation,
    Through our yielding to [God] in Receptive Prayer,
    First in quietness; then in action.
    God can give [God's self] to us for [God's] purpose
only as we give ourselves to [God]. [God] does not ask
for a death of self but for the death of self-centeredness.
[God] asks for the self's surrender and its offering to
be used in [God's] service.

—From *Receptive Prayer* by Grace Adolphsen Brame

❧ We weep
    that we may have the strength to live.
    We wail
    that we may have the power to speak

of these things
in the times to be.

Let not the days come
when we will mourn
for having given life
for having birthed
for having hoped.

Let not the days come
when we bid
the mountains fall
or the hills
to cover us.

Bid them, rather, to dance
For having loved so well.
Bid them, rather, to fly
for having dreamed so long.
—From *Sacred Journeys* by Jan L. Richardson

38: Principles and Practices of Disciples

Affirmation

A disciple is not above the teacher, nor a slave above the master; it is enough for the disciple to be like the teacher, and the slave like the master. . . . So have no fear of [persecutors]; for nothing is covered up that will not be uncovered, and nothing secret that will not become known. What I say to you in the dark, tell in the light; and what you hear whispered, proclaim from the housetops. Do not fear those who kill the body but cannot kill the soul; rather fear him who can destroy both soul and body in hell. Are not two sparrows sold for a penny? Yet not one of them will fall to the ground apart from your Father. And even the hairs of your head are all counted. So do not be afraid; you are of more value than many sparrows (Matt. 10:24-31).

Petition

I appeal to you therefore, brothers and sisters, by the mercies of God, to present your bodies as a living sacrifice, holy and acceptable to God, which is your spiritual worship. Do not be conformed to this world but be transformed by the renewing of your minds, so that you may discern what is the will of God—what is good and acceptable and perfect (Rom. 12:1-2).

Sacred Reading: anthology or other selected reading

Daily Scripture Readings

Sunday	A.	Genesis 28:10-19; Psalm 139:1-12, 23-24; Romans 8:12-25; Matthew 13:24-30, 36-43
	B.	2 Samuel 7:1-14; Psalm 89:20-37; Ephesians 2:11-22; Mark 6:30-34, 53-56

	C.	Amos 8:1-12; Psalm 52; Colossians 1:15-28; Luke 10:38-42
Monday		Acts 4:32-37
Tuesday		Romans 15:1-5
Wednesday		Philippians 1:27-30
Thursday		Mark 16:19-20
Friday		1 Peter 3:8-12
Saturday		1 Peter 3:13-22

Prayer: thanksgiving, petition, intercession, praise, and offering

Reflection: silent (listening to God), written (journaling)

God's Promise
The LORD will command the blessing upon you in your barns, and in all that you undertake; he will bless you in the land that the LORD your God is giving you. The LORD will establish you as his holy people, as he has sworn to you, if you keep the commandments of the LORD your God and walk in his ways (Deut. 28:8-9).

My Response
In Caesarea there was a man named Cornelius, a centurion of the Italian Cohort, as it was called. He was a devout man who feared God with all his household; he gave alms generously to the people and prayed constantly to God (Acts 10:1-2).

Readings for Reflection
ﺨ The way early disciples lived mystified people around them because the disciples seemed to live in another world. The principles that guided them clearly differed from those that guided others. They practiced a way of life both beautiful and mysterious. Their lives made sense only if one knew that they were living by the power and guidance of God. Their lives were

governed by the reign of God and not by the press of politics or the call of culture. They were different because they chose to live their lives in obedience to and in the presence of God. Their radical love for God and neighbor resulted in dramatic actions that perplexed all who observed them.

When we move securely into the reign and presence of God, our lives also take on a beautiful and mysterious quality because God's presence and principles are being expressed in all that we are and in all that we do. Our actions prompt sometimes gratitude and sometimes perplexity in others. They prompt sometimes joy and gratitude within our lives and sometimes weariness when our radical actions are misunderstood.

But we are not alone. The first-generation Christians lived this radical faith every day. Their actions caught the world's attention both positively and negatively, but their actions—like ours—were not calculated to bring a response; rather, their actions and ours are a *response*. A response to God's amazing grace that has apprehended us in Jesus Christ. An amazing grace that accepts us, assures us, sustains us, and always holds us close in the embrace of divine love. Such radical grace prompts a radical response.
—Rueben P. Job

✴ Remember for whom you work: Whether you work for a private company, the government, a large corporation, or yourself, the true disciple understands that he or she ultimately is working for God in that place. "Whatever your task, put yourselves into it, as done for the Lord and not for your masters, since you know that from the Lord you will receive the inheritance as your reward; you serve the Lord Christ" (Col. 3:23-24).
—Norman Shawchuck

✴ The persons and ministries of John the Baptist and of Jesus himself, both rich in the practice of activities designed to strengthen the spirit, were held constantly before [early Christians]. So, wherever early Christians looked they saw examples of the practice of solitude, fasting, prayer, private study, communal study, worship, and sacrificial service and giving—to mention only some of the more obvious disciplines for spiritual life.

These early Christians really did arrange their lives very differently from their non-Christian neighbors, as well as from the vast majority of those of us called Christians today. We are speaking of their overall style of life, not just what they did under pressure, which frequently was also astonishingly different.

—From *The Spirit of the Disciplines* by Dallas Willard

❧ Discipline in the Christian life is not a luxury. Without it we become confused, lose our way, compromise our principles, and discover that we are not the people we had intended to be. No one is so sturdy in the faith that the temptation to surrender bit by bit does not erode conviction. Days go by and we discover that, instead of growing in grace in these days, we have wasted them.

These "means" to whose use we are tied . . . are a positive set of directions for the Christian life, often called the "means of grace.". . . These means of grace are not a method of deserving God's grace, but a pattern by which we enable ourselves to be receptive to grace and remove the barriers that God permits us to erect as the price of our freedom. These tools, or aids, are ways by which we open ourselves to God's free grace. In using them, we shape our lives in order to become open to God's presence. They give our Christian pilgrimage a definite shape, in an age in which there is a general sense of loss of direction and confusion about right and wrong, along with an accompanying sense of God's absence.

—From *Reformed Spirituality* by Howard L. Rice

❧ The Church is in the world to save the world. It is a tool of God for that purpose; not a comfortable religious club established in fine historical premises. Every one of its members is required, in one way or another, to co-operate with the Spirit in working for that great end: and much of this work will be done in secret and invisible ways. We are transmitters as well as receivers. Our contemplation and our action, our humble self-opening to God, keeping ourselves sensitive to His music and light, and our generous self-opening to our fellow creatures, keeping ourselves sensitive to their needs, ought to form one life: mediating between God and His world, and bringing the saving power of the Eternal into time. We are far from realizing all that human spirits can do for one another on spiritual levels if they will pay the price; how truly and really our souls interpenetrate, and how impossible and un-Christian it is to "keep ourselves to ourselves."
—From *The Spiritual Life* by Evelyn Underhill

❧ Where I live my little segment of time, I must live it in the light of the fact that all of the vast complex of which my little segment is a part, gives to my little segment its meaning. Therefore, I cannot say about my life that it is of no account, I cannot say of the time that I am living that nothing seems to be happening, because this is not one of the great and tempestuous or creative moments in human history or in the history of worlds. My time is my time, and I must live my time with as much fullness and significance as I am capable of, because my little segment of time is all the time that I have. I cannot wait to begin living meaningfully when I will have more time, because all the time that I can ever experience is the time interval of my moment, so that my minutes, my hours, my days, my months, must be full of my flavor and my meaning.

Therefore, I will bring to my day, as commonplace and insignificant as it may seem, the fullest mind, the greatest purpose, and the most significant intent of

which I am capable, because my time is not merely mine, but because my time is in [God's] hands as well.
—From *The Mood of Christmas* by Howard Thurman

❧ Jesus was broken on the cross. He lived his suffering and death not as an evil to avoid at all costs but as a mission to embrace. We too are broken. We live with broken bodies, broken hearts, broken minds, or broken spirits. We suffer from broken relationships.

How can we live our brokenness? Jesus invites us to embrace our brokenness as he embraced the cross and live it as part of our mission. He asks us not to reject our brokenness as a curse from God that reminds us of our sinfulness but to accept it and put it under God's blessing for our purification and sanctification. Thus, our brokenness can become a gateway to new life.
—From *Bread for the Journey* by Henri J. M. Nouwen

❧ Jesus remains Lord by being a servant.

The beloved disciple presents a mind-bending image of God, blowing away all previous conceptions of who the Messiah is and what discipleship is all about. What a scandalous reversal of the world's values! To prefer to be the servant rather than the lord of the household is the path of downward mobility in an upwardly mobile culture. To taunt the idols of prestige, honor, and recognition, to refuse to take oneself seriously or to take seriously others who take themselves seriously, and to freely embrace the servant lifestyle—these are the attitudes that bear the stamp of authentic discipleship.

The stark realism of John's portrait of Christ leaves no room for romanticized idealism or sloppy sentimentality. Servanthood is not an emotion or mood or feeling; it is a decision to live like Jesus. It has nothing to do with what we feel; it has everything to do with what we *do*—humble service. To listen obediently to Jesus— "If I, then, the Lord and Master, have washed your feet, you should wash each other's feet"—is to hear the heartbeat of the Rabbi John knew and loved.

When being is divorced from doing, pious thoughts become an adequate substitute for washing dirty feet.
—From *Reflections for Ragamuffins* by Brennan Manning

❧ The Christian Gospels do not encourage anyone to believe that he or she can choose both the palace and the lotus: both mammon and God (Matt. 6:24). The Gospels are for men and women of free hearts and free wills who must decide for themselves as to where they will bestow their love and allegiance. The Gospels give few particulars as to conduct and choices; they give, rather, the basic principles that each person must apply for him or herself. They only lay the pruning saw at the foot of the tree. The Gospels confront us with One who pierces us by his bottomless love and caring. One who compels us to decide for ourselves what in our lives is incongruous with his love.
—From *Dimensions of Prayer* by Douglas V. Steere

❧ A couple of years ago I read a story that has taken on great metaphorical significance for me. The setting is Christmas Eve in Chicago in the 1920s, before the stock market crash. Two businessmen are rushing to catch the 6:00 P.M. commuter train for home. On the train platform a young handicapped boy is selling papers and other goods he can pick up and resell for a bargain at a small stand. The first man emerges on the platform. He runs into the boy, knocking him and his stand over. Hurling a few choice curse words at the boy, the man continues on to catch his train. A few seconds later the second man emerges on the platform. He sees the boy and his stand knocked down. He immediately helps the boy up and tries to gather up some of his goods. The man reaches in his billfold and pulls out a five-dollar bill. He gives it to the boy, saying he hopes it will help cover part of the boy's losses. Wishing the boy a "Merry Christmas," he turns to catch his train. The boy yells after him, "Say, Mister, are you

Jesus Christ?" Red-faced and embarrassed, the man answers, "No, but I try to be like him."

Both men are made in the image of God, but only one man is living in the likeness of Jesus Christ. It is not enough as a Christian to claim being made in our Creator's image; we are called to be conformed to the likeness of Christ.

—From *Climbing the Sycamore Tree* by Ann Hagmann

&❧ Let us, then, not only call Him Lord, for that will not save us. For He saith, "Not everyone that saith to Me, Lord, Lord, shall be saved, but he that worketh righteousness." Wherefore, brethren, let us confess Him by our works, by loving one another, by not committing adultery, or speaking evil of one another, or cherishing envy; but by being continent, compassionate, and good. We ought also to sympathize with one another, and not be avaricious. By such works let us confess Him, and not by those that are of an opposite kind. And it is not fitting that we should fear [others], but rather God.

—From "The Second Epistle of Clement"

Tenth Sunday after Pentecost (Ordinary Time)
Sunday between July 24 and July 30

39: At the Table with Jesus

Affirmation
You are those who have stood by me in my trials; and
I confer on you, just as my Father has conferred on me,
a kingdom, so that you may eat and drink at my table
in my kingdom, and you will sit on thrones judging
the twelve tribes of Israel (Luke 22:28-30).

Petition
Holy Father, protect them in your name that you have
given me, so that they may be one, as we are one. . . . I
am not asking you to take them out of the world, but
I ask you to protect them from the evil one. They do
not belong to the world, just as I do not belong to the
world. Sanctify them in the truth; your word is truth
(John 17:11, 15-17).

Sacred Reading: anthology or other selected reading

Daily Scripture Readings

Sunday	A.	Genesis 29:15-28; Psalm 128; Romans 8:26-39; Matthew 13:31-33, 44-52
	B.	2 Samuel 11:1-15; Psalm 14; Ephesians 3:14-21; John 6:1-21
	C.	Hosea 1:2-10; Psalm 85; Colossians 2:6-15; Luke 11:1-13
Monday		Luke 22:14-23
Tuesday		John 21:9-14
Wednesday		Luke 15:15-24
Thursday		Luke 24:36-43
Friday		1 Corinthians 11:23-26
Saturday		Revelation 19:6-10

Prayer: thanksgiving, petition, intercession, praise, and offering

Reflection: silent (listening to God), written (journaling)

God's Promise
Simon, Simon, listen! Satan has demanded to sift all of you like wheat, but I have prayed for you that your own faith may not fail; and you, when once you have turned back, strengthen your brothers" (Luke 22:31-32).

My Response
And [Peter] said to him, "Lord, I am ready to go with you to prison and to death!" (Luke 22:33).

Readings for Reflection

❧ I have always been intrigued with Luke's choice of words as he describes the Passover meal Jesus shared with his disciples on the eve before his suffering and death (Luke 22:14-23). According to Luke, Jesus said that he "eagerly desired" to share the meal with the disciples before his suffering. Jesus was confronting the greatest challenge of his life and ministry, and yet he longed for a holy time of sharing and breaking bread. I have wondered why Jesus was so eager for this time at table with the disciples. Could it be that he needed to be with those closest to him as they affirmed God's presence and plan for him and the disciples? To spend quality time with those we love is a wonderful gift of healing and strength to all of us, and Jesus deserved this holy fellowship for comfort and strength.

Or did Jesus want to say something more to the disciples? He did declare again that it was his last meal until the kingdom of God would fully arrive. He did tell them that he was providing a new covenant for them and for the world. And perhaps most significantly, he told them by words and acts that his life and theirs were cradled and safely sheltered in God's care.

Today Jesus invites you and me to come to the table. We are now invited to sit with Jesus, to listen to him speak to us, teach us, and bless us. In holy time and holy place he reminds us once again that his body is given for us and that his blood is poured out for us. What good news it is that the sacrifice of his life replaces the darkness of my life with the purity and light of his own.

Perhaps you are not able literally to be at the table with Jesus every day. But in your time of prayer as in your time of work and leisure you can remember that Jesus eagerly desires to be with you. And wherever you are, you may hear his words, "I have eagerly desired this time with you," and then accept his invitation to holy fellowship.

—Rueben P. Job

❧ To identify the movements of the Spirit in our lives, I have found it helpful to use four words: taken, blessed, broken and given. These words summarize my life as a priest because each day, when I come together around the table with members of my community, I take bread, bless it, break it, and give it. These words also summarize my life as a Christian because, as a Christian, I am called to become bread for the world: bread that is taken, blessed, broken and given. Most importantly, however, they summarize my life as a human being because in every moment of my life somewhere, somehow the taking, the blessing, the breaking and the giving are happening.

I must tell you at this point that these four words have become the most important words of my life. Only gradually has their meaning become known to me, and I feel that I won't ever know their full profundity. They are the most personal as well as the most universal words. They express the most spiritual as well as the most secular truth. They speak about the most divine as well as the most human behavior. They reach high as well as low, embrace God as well as all people. They succinctly express the complexity of life and embrace its ever-unfolding mystery. They are the keys to understanding not only the lives of the great prophets of Israel and the life of Jesus of Nazareth, but also our own lives. I have chosen them not only because they are so deeply engraved in my being, but also because, through them, I have come into touch with the ways of becoming the Beloved of God.

—From *Life of the Beloved* by Henri J. M. Nouwen

❧ Maybe we are not used to thinking about the Eucharist as an invitation to Jesus to stay with us. We are more inclined to think about Jesus inviting us to his house, his table, his meal. But Jesus wants to be invited. Without an invitation he will go on to other places. It is very important to realize that Jesus never forces himself on us. Unless we invite him, he will always remain a stranger, possibly a very attractive, intelligent stranger with whom we had an interesting conversation, but a stranger nevertheless.

—From *With Burning Hearts* by Henri J. M. Nouwen

❧ The Christian life flourishes in community. Corporate worship, study, fellowship, and action are the soil in which authentic faith takes root and grows toward maturity. . . .

Worship is one of the most profound experiences of life for humankind. For Christians, gathering around the Lord's Table, the baptismal font, and the scriptures are essential elements of an authentic life of worship. The congregation where scripture, liturgy, music, persons in quest of communion with God, and spirit-filled leadership come together will provide nurture and sustenance to all who experience its life.

—From *Spiritual Life in the Congregation* by Rueben P. Job

❧ Let me share an example of ministering to the Lord in the moment of *his* adversity. This happened in Chicago's South Side on Holy Thursday night. I wrote in my journal: "The adoration of the Lord Jesus in the Eucharist began with a heaviness within me. It's freezing outside; the chapel is cold; my mind is opaque; but foremost is the nagging doubt about my own sincerity." Earlier in the day I sensed a tug in the direction of nonacceptance, when I read, "Where the Spirit of the Lord is, there is freedom." Do I really want to be free? Do I honestly desire a Kingdom lifestyle? What are the real tendencies and desires of my heart? Do I long more than anything else to be God's man? To serve rather than be served? To pray when I could play? Be slow to speak, Brennan, be cautious to answer. . . . I felt confusion and discouragement tiding within me.

Then a beautiful thing happened. I realized that the only reason I was at prayer was because I wanted to be with my friend. The doubt and uncertainty vanished. I knew I wanted to comfort Jesus in his loneliness and fear in the Garden. I wanted to watch not an hour but the whole night with him. The only words that formed on my lips were those of the little boy Willie-Juan in the fairy tale I had written the year past. Over and over I whispered, "I love you, my friend."

—From *Reflections for Ragamuffins* by Brennan Manning

❧ When Jesus took the bread, blessed it, broke it and gave it to his disciples, he summarized in these gestures his own life. Jesus is chosen from all eternity, blessed at his baptism in the Jordan River, broken on the cross, and given as bread to the world. Being chosen, blessed, broken, and given is the sacred journey of the Son of God, Jesus the Christ.

When we take bread, bless it, break it, and give it with the words, "This is the Body of Christ," we express our commitment to make our lives conform to the life of Christ. We too want to live as people chosen, blessed, and broken and thus become food for the world.

—From *Bread for the Journey* by Henri J. M. Nouwen

❧ What can we say about God's love? We can say that God's love is unconditional. God does not say, "I love you, if. . ." There are no *ifs* in God's heart. God's love for us does not depend on what we do or say, on our looks or intelligence, on our success or popularity. God's love for us existed before we were born and will exist after we have died. God's love is from eternity to eternity and is not bound to any time-related events or circumstances. Does that mean that God does not care what we do or say? No, because God's love wouldn't be real if God didn't care. To love without condition does not mean to love without concern. God desires to enter into relationship with us and wants us to love God in return.

Let's dare to enter into an intimate relationship with God without fear, trusting that we will receive love, and always more love.

—From *Bread for the Journey* by Henri J. M. Nouwen

❧ When Jesus begins his public ministry, one of the first things he does is to find companions, those individuals who will share his life and ministry in a special way. Whenever Jesus faces a difficult situation, he gathers these companions around himself—sometimes all twelve, sometimes only a few. Jesus Christ, the Son of God, the Savior of the world, needed the companionship of others. Even he, as strong and powerful and good as he was, couldn't go it alone.

We can't go it alone either. We cannot face the challenges of life without the support of others. This need for companionship is one we must never be ashamed of. We must never think, "If I were more mature, I could stand on my own two feet." Or, "If my faith were stronger, I wouldn't have to rely so much on others." No, our need for companionship, fellowship, friendship, is in the very fabric of our human psyche. It is yet one more way that we are made in the image and likeness of God.

—From *Abundant Treasures* by Melannie Svoboda

To live in Christ is to give all that we are, have, and hope to become to God's gracious direction. This is to enter into "fellowship" with God in a new and nurturing way—a way that leads to assurance of salvation and life abundant and eternal. It is a way that leads to the confidence and comfort that only companionship with Jesus Christ can bring. And it is a way that leads to definite and decisive response on the part of the believer.

—From *A Wesleyan Spiritual Reader* by Rueben P. Job

It is time for the Lord's Supper. We look toward the altar with the Lord's table beautifully prepared with the best that we have. The table is covered with a white damask cloth, a memorial gift used only for Holy Communion. Beside the gold-plated cross, the symbolic light of the world flickers in two false candles, constant in size with no messy drips. Our eyes shift to the silk flowers whose blooms, scentless and seedless, won't wilt or die. The pastor breaks the bread and blesses it, saying the words of old. Then as the pastor reaches across the chalice to set down the bread, the long full sleeves of the robe drag, and one sleeve catches on the chalice and tips it. There is just an instant before the chalice is uprighted.

But it in that instant, the red wine spills. It runs across the beautiful cloth and seeps under the candlesticks and reaches the cross. It begins to bleed down the front overhang of the white cloth. Everyone in the congregation can see the spilled blood of Christ dripping, staining, trickling where it will. In the midst of the high holy feast is a lowly holy error. The blood of Christ is *poured* out. And perhaps there is a smile as the Holy One welcomes us to the table, for the tipped chalice co-incidentally reminds us that the blood of Christ—that amazing love of the new covenant—cannot be controlled, restrained, confined, contained.

—From *Wilderness Wanderings* by Marilyn Brown Oden

❧ Most of us do not remember the Lord's Supper after Sunday any more than we remember Sunday's shaving or applying make-up or feeding the dog. It affects weekdays, nevertheless, the way any note inserted into a song affects the entire melody. From the perspective of the one God who listens to the whole melody of our lives, it adds unmistakable beauty to each day.
—From *A Wakeful Faith* by J. Marshall Jenkins

❧ The symbolism and power of the Eucharist change how we think about food, the breaking of bread, and who is welcome at the table. Once we have broken bread at the Lord's table, we cannot help but take bread out to those who have no bread at all. At the Lord's table, there is plenty of elbow room. We find ourselves sitting next to those who would normally be strangers. The hungry find themselves filled. The family of Christ shares fully in their father's board.
—From *Yours Are the Hands of Christ* by James C. Howell

Eleventh Sunday after Pentecost (Ordinary Time)
Sunday between July 31 and August 6

40: *Teach Us to Pray*

Affirmation
Ask, and it will be given you; search, and you will find; knock, and the door will be opened for you. For everyone who asks receives, and everyone who searches finds, and for everyone who knocks, the door will be opened (Matt. 7:7-8).

Petition
Answer me when I call, O God of my right!
>You gave me room when I was in distress.
>Be gracious to me, and hear my prayer (Ps. 4:1).

Sacred Reading: anthology or other selected reading

Daily Scripture Readings

Sunday	A.	Genesis 32:22-31; Psalm 17:1-7, 15; Romans 9:1-5; Matthew 14:13-21
	B.	2 Samuel 11:26–12:13; Psalm 51:1-12; Ephesians 4:1-16; John 6:24-35
	C.	Hosea 11:1-11; Psalm 107:1-9, 43; Colossians 3:1-11; Luke 12:13-21
Monday		Luke 11:1-13
Tuesday		Jeremiah 33:1-9
Wednesday		John 17:1-11
Thursday		Matthew 6:1-15
Friday		Psalm 118:1-9
Saturday		Matthew 7:7-11

Prayer: thanksgiving, petition, intercession, praise, and offering

Reflection: silent (listening to God), written (journaling)

God's Promise
Call to me and I will answer you, and will tell you great and hidden things that you have not known (Jer. 33:3).

My Response
Teach me, O LORD, the way of your statutes,
    and I will observe it to the end.
Give me understanding, that I may keep your law
    and observe it with my whole heart (Ps. 119:33-34).

Readings for Reflection

❧ As far as we know, the disciples never asked Jesus to teach them how to fish, preach, teach, communicate, or multiply loaves. They did ask him to teach them how to pray. Was it because they didn't need to make a living, teach, catch fish, or communicate? Probably not! Perhaps the disciples saw the remarkable relationship that Jesus enjoyed with his Abba and wanted something like it in their own lives. They too wanted to know the confidence, peace, security, and love that Jesus found in this relationship with God.

Perhaps the disciples also noted that prayer was a priority for Jesus; in fact, his whole life seemed to be built around this priority. In crisis, in need, and when perplexed and weary, Jesus could be found praying. Prayer was not an additive to life; it was a way of life for Jesus.

Perhaps too the disciples saw dramatic results as the consequence of the life of prayer that Jesus lived. They did see loaves multiplied, individuals healed, storms stilled, and peace descending on many. Whatever the reason, the disciples apparently believed that praying was one of their most important lessons to be learned.

The benefit of that teaching is available to us today as we reflect on the words and life of Jesus. And the relationship with God that enriched and sustained the life of Jesus is available to us as well. I desire the trust,

serenity, confidence, and deep peace that seemed to flow from the life of Jesus at every moment. Teach me to pray.
—Rueben P. Job

❧ To pray well I must first find out where I am. Self-knowledge is never procured cheaply. To pray well I need to face up to realities about myself, that I would prefer to ignore: my anxieties, fears, private griefs, failures, lovelessness, my utter lack of resources. To accept the truth about what I am, as also the truth about other human beings, demands courage. If I do not pray well, it is usually because I lack that kind of courage.
—From *Toward God* by Michael Casey

❧ Prayer is not primarily saying words or thinking thoughts. It is, rather, a stance. It's a way of living in the Presence. It is, further, a way of living in awareness of the Presence, even enjoying the Presence. The full contemplative is not just aware of the Presence, but trusts, allows, and delights in it.
—From *Everything Belongs* by Richard Rohr

❧ You see, I've done a lot of work for the Church— I'm aware of it. It has been my only thought, my only care. I have raced hard and covered as many miles as the most committed missionary. At a certain point it occurred to me that what the Church lacked was not work, activity, the building of projects or a commitment to bring in souls. What was missing, *or at least was scarce, was the element of prayer, meditation, self-giving, intimacy with God, fidelity to the Holy Spirit and the conviction that [Christ] was the real builder of the Church:* in a word, the supernatural element. Let me make myself clear: people of action are needed in the Church but we have to be very careful that their action *does not smother the more delicate but much more important element of prayer.*

If action is missing and there is prayer, the Church lives on, it keeps on breathing, but if prayer is missing and there is only action, the Church withers and dies.
—From *Letters to Dolcidia: 1954–1983* by Carlo Carretto

☙ If this idea that prayer consists of attention to God seems strange to us, perhaps it is because we have given up the discipline and no longer really know how to pray. In most of our praying, our attention is neither focused nor on God. What we attend to is largely our own selves, and this in a rather generalized and ambiguous way. Prayer, both public and private, and particularly among Protestants, tends to be almost totally prayer of petition. We have some need, and we pray that it will be met. We are in some trouble, and we pray that God will take it away. Even when we do pray prayers of praise, thanksgiving, and confession, we do so with our attention turned to what we are pleased with, thankful for, and guilty of. We find it extremely difficult to allow our praise, thanks, confession, petition, and intercession to be formed by attention to God, and awfully easy to allow the God to whom we pray to become a mere reflection of our own concerns. At least this is what I experience myself as a prayer and what I perceive in most public worship. "Simple attentiveness" is most difficult. It is also very important.
—From *Vision and Character* by Craig R. Dykstra

☙ Those who receive the Lord's blessing are those who, in the course of their lives, are able to pay attention to the hungry, the thirsty, the stranger, the ill, and the imprisoned. It turns out that, unwittingly, they had all along been attending to God in Christ. Prayer, in its implicit form, is the act of attention to realities that are before us. By such acts, we attend, indirectly, to God. Through such acts, God's very self is made known to us, and we are thus more able to pray explicitly.
—From *Vision and Character* by Craig R. Dykstra

❧ The one condition that precedes *every* kind of prayer is being present to God with conscious awareness. God is always present with us, whether or not we can feel this reality. In a very real sense, then, the foundation of all prayer is being present to the presence of God. Quaker writer and teacher Douglas Steere speaks of "being present where we are" and "not too elsewhere."
—From *Soul Feast* by Marjorie J. Thompson

❧ We can also no longer escape the realization that the ministry of intercession requires time of every Christian, but most of all of the pastor who has the responsibility of a whole congregation. Intercession alone, if it is thoroughly done, would consume the entire time of daily meditation. So pursued, it will become evident that intercession is a gift of God's grace for every Christian community and for every Christian. Because intercession is such an incalculably great gift of God, we should accept it joyfully. The very time we give to intercession will turn out to be a daily source of new joy in God and in the Christian community.
—From *Life Together* by Dietrich Bonhoeffer

❧ Pray for us: we value your prayers as worthy to be heard, since you go to God with so great an offering of unfeigned love, and of praise brought to [God] by your works. Pray that in us also these works may shine, for [God] to whom you pray knows with what fullness of joy we behold them shining in you. Such are our desires.
—From "Letter 41" by Saint Augustine

❧ There are two movements which must be plainly present in every complete spiritual life. The energy of its prayer must be directed on the one hand towards God; and on the other towards men. The first movement embraces the whole range of spiritual communion between the soul and God: in it we turn towards

Divine Reality in adoration, bathing, so to speak, our souls in the Eternal Light. In the second we return, with the added peace and energy thus gained, to the natural world; there to do spiritual work for and with God for other men.

Thus prayer, like the whole of man's inner life, "swings between the unseen and the seen." Now both these movements are of course necessary in all Christians; but the point is that the second will only be well done where the first has the central place. The deepening of the soul's unseen attachments must precede, in order that it may safeguard, the outward swing towards the world.

—From *Concerning the Inner Life* by Evelyn Underhill

❧ Shared prayer adds power to the work of intercession. Christians dare to believe that God needs and wants our prayers, our compassionate intercession for one another and for the world. Through our prayers for one another, circumstances are changed and the work of the kingdom is done. An individual may feel overwhelmed by the needs of the world, or even the needs of a single congregation, but there is strength in numbers. Individuals gain courage for the task of intercession when the community prays together, aware of Christ's presence among those gathered in his name. And the person for whom prayers are offered feels the added force of multiple prayers.

—From *Praying Together* by Martha Graybeal Rowlett

41: Who Is This Who Forgives Sinners?

Affirmation
"I have come to call not the righteous but sinners to repentance" (Luke 5:32).

Petition
In my distress I cry to the LORD,
    that he may answer me:
"Deliver me, O LORD,
    from lying lips,
    from a deceitful tongue" (Ps. 120:1-2).

Sacred Reading: anthology or other selected reading

Daily Scripture Readings

Sunday	A.	Genesis 37:1-4, 12-28; Psalm 105:1-6, 16-22, 45; Romans 10:5-15; Matthew 14:22-33
	B.	2 Samuel 18:5-9, 15, 31-33; Psalm 130; Ephesians 4:25–5:2; John 6:35, 41-51
	C.	Isaiah 1:1, 10-20; Psalm 50:1-8, 22-23; Hebrews 11:1-3, 8-16; Luke 12:32-40
Monday		Luke 7:36-50
Tuesday		Matthew 9:2-8
Wednesday		Psalm 103:1-14
Thursday		Acts 10:34-43
Friday		Isaiah 1:18-20
Saturday		Colossians 1:9-14

Prayer: thanksgiving, petition, intercession, praise, and offering

Reflection: silent (listening to God), written (journaling)

God's Promise
The LORD is merciful and gracious,
     slow to anger and abounding in steadfast love.
He will not always accuse,
     nor will he keep his anger forever.
He does not deal with us according to our sins,
     nor repay us according to our iniquities.
For as the heavens are high above the earth,
     so great is his steadfast love toward those who fear
          him;
as far as the east is from the west,
     so far he removes our transgressions from us.
As a father has compassion for his children,
     so the LORD has compassion for those who fear
          him (Ps. 103:8-13).

My Response
I long for your salvation, O LORD,
     and your law is my delight.
Let me live that I may praise you,
     and let your ordinances help me.
I have gone astray like a lost sheep; seek out your
          servant,
     for I do not forget your commandments
          (Ps. 119:174-176).

Readings for Reflection

❧ There are some things that only God can do. We
look at the rise of violence around the globe or the rising tide of population and hunger and know that some
of these problems are so deep-seated that without
God's help they will not be resolved. Then we look into
our own hearts and know that sin—our failure to do
what we want to do and our doing what we know we
do not want to do—can only be remedied with God's
help. We are not the first to discover these truths.

     When Jesus had dinner at Simon's house (Luke
7:36-50), a woman identified as a known sinner came

and washed the feet of Jesus with her tears, drying his feet with her hair. The rest of the dinner crowd was astonished and outraged. Why did this righteous man not recognize who this woman was? And if he did recognize who she was, why did he not rebuke her? Jesus then pointed out that her love was greater and demonstrated love more beautifully than that of the host. Jesus then declared in the hearing of all that the woman was forgiven. She was cleansed and sent on her way with Jesus' blessing.

The dinner guests were still astounded. They knew that only God could forgive sins, and they were not yet able to believe that this carpenter's son was also son of God. Jesus said that the woman was saved by her faith, but the rest of the guests missed out on the divine gift of forgiveness and the blessing of peace Jesus was offering.

The good news Christians tell one another and the world is that only God can wipe away the failures, errors, and missed opportunities that sometimes plague us. We cannot wipe away or forgive our sins or those of another. But God can, and therein lies our hope, joy, and peace—a message we proclaim to all.
—Rueben P. Job

  Our experience of grace represents a certain natural progression in the Christian life. Initially divine grace surrounds us without our conscious knowledge. We are simply immersed in God's unconditional, ever-present love. God works to protect us from spiritual danger and "woos" us in the unconscious infancy of our faith, calling us to be aware of grace. Once we have become fully conscious of a faith decision and choose to receive God's forgiving love in Jesus Christ, we experience the grace of justification. At this point the experience of grace helps us know that we belong not to ourselves but to our faithful Savior, Jesus Christ. We understand that righteousness before God is not something we earn; it can be received only as a gift. As the Spirit builds on the foundation of justification, we gradually grow in holiness of life, or sanctification. This experience of grace leads us to bear the fruits of the Spirit and to exercise the gifts of the Spirit.

—From *Companions in Christ: Participant's Book,* Part 1 by Rueben P. Job and Marjorie J. Thompson

❧ This is hard. It is perhaps not so hard to forgive a single great injury. But to forgive the incessant provocations of daily life—to keep on forgiving the bossy mother-in-law, the bullying husband, the nagging wife, the selfish daughter, the deceitful son—how can we do it? Only, I think, by remembering where we stand, by meaning our words when we say in our prayers each night "Forgive us our trespasses as we forgive those that trespass against us!" We are offered forgiveness on no other terms. To refuse it is to refuse God's mercy for ourselves. There is no hint of exceptions.

—From *Fern-Seed and Elephants* by C. S. Lewis

❧ I believe with all my heart that the mystery of forgiveness is the entire Gospel. When you "get" forgiveness, you get it. We use the phrase "falling in love." I think forgiveness is almost the same thing. It's a mystery we fall into: the mystery is God. God forgives all things for being imperfect, broken, and poor. Not only Jesus but all the great people who pray that I have met in my life say the same thing. That's the conclusion they come to. The people who know God well, the mystics, the hermits, those who risk everything to find God, always meet a lover, not a dictator. God is never found to be an abusive father or a tyrannical mother, but always a lover who is more than we dared hope for. How different than the "account manager" that most people seem to worship.

—From *Everything Belongs* by Richard Rohr

❧ It is hard to speak of beauty without speaking of Saint Francis. In his personality was mirrored a generous measure of the transcendent beauty of God. If God is an illimitable ocean of beauty, Francis was a small spring shooting up, such as the world had never seen before. His gestures are the revelation of his soul. One day he arrives in the village square. A large crowd follows him. As everyone knows, the village priest has not been living a life of rectitude. As Francis reaches the square, the priest by chance happens out of the church. The crowd watches and waits. What will Francis do? Denounce the priest for the scandal he has created, sermonize the villagers on human frailty and the need for compassion, simply pretend he doesn't see the priest and continue on his way? No. He steps forward, kneels in the mud, takes the priest's hand, and kisses it. That's all. And that is magnificent. Toward the end of his life, Francis gathers two branches -- one represents a violin, the other a bow. And what a marvelous melody he plays. Interiorly, of course. But what is the music of Mozart and Bach beside this? The words and gestures of Francis are manifestations of a soul completely surrendered to God. As we see the beauty streaming from his soul, one realizes anew the truth of the words of Leon Bloy, "The only real sadness in life is not to be a saint."

—From *Reflections for Ragamuffins* by Brennan Manning

   ❦ Community is not possible without the willingness to forgive one another "seventy-seven times" (see Matt. 18:22). Forgiveness is the cement of community life. Forgiveness holds us together through good times and bad times, and it allows us to grow in mutual love. . . .

To forgive another person from the heart is an act of liberation. We set that person free from the negative bonds that exist between us. We say, "I no longer hold your offense against you." But there is more. We also free ourselves from the burden of being the "offended one." As long as we do not forgive those who have wounded us, we carry them with us or, worse, pull them as a heavy load. The great temptation is to cling in anger to our enemies and then define ourselves as being offended and wounded by them. Forgiveness, therefore, liberates not only the other but also ourselves. It is the way to the freedom of the children of God.

—From *Bread for the Journey* by Henri J. M. Nouwen

❧ A discussion of Christian prayer that leaves out the final movement of forgiveness would be a travesty. There is nothing that God cannot heal, and God's forgiveness is given before we even approach God. Nowhere is this more tellingly described than in the Old Testament story of the father King David weeping over his son Absalom who has perhaps come to his death because he did not believe his father could ever forgive his treason: "O my son Absalom, my son, my son Absalom!" (2 Sam. 18:33).

Forgiveness is a condition in which the sin of the past is not altered, nor its inevitable consequences changed. Rather in forgiveness a fresh act is added to those of the past, which restores the broken relationship and opens the way for the one who forgives and the one who is forgiven to meet and communicate deeply with each other in the present and future. Thus, forgiveness heals the past, though the scars remain and the consequences go on. . . . It is taken into the fresh act of outgoing renewal and there it is healed.

The whole witness of Jesus' life and death is to the unfathomable depths of God's forgiveness. English poet and artist William Blake cites the capacity of Jesus to forgive another, and to reenter vulnerably into the deepest relation with another, as the strongest evidence of his being God in the flesh. For only so could someone be truly able to forgive others.

—From *Dimensions of Prayer* by Douglas V. Steere

42: Do You Want to Get Well?

Affirmation
Very truly, I tell you, anyone who hears my word and
believes him who sent me has eternal life, and does not
come under judgment, but has passed from death to
life (John 5:24).

Petition
Have mercy on me, O God,
      according to your steadfast love;
according to your abundant mercy
      blot out my transgressions.
Wash me thoroughly from my iniquity,
      and cleanse me from my sin.

For I know my transgressions,
      and my sin is ever before me (Ps. 51:1-3).

Sacred Reading: anthology or other selected reading

Daily Scripture Readings

Sunday	A.	Genesis 45:1-15; Psalm 133; Romans 11:1-2, 29-32; Matthew 15:21-28
	B.	1 Kings 2:10-12; 3:3-14; Psalm 111; Ephesians 5:15-20; John 6:51-58
	C.	Isaiah 5:1-7; Psalm 80:1-2, 8-19; Hebrews 11:29–12:2; Luke 12:49-56
Monday		John 5:1-18
Tuesday		Matthew 9:2-8
Wednesday		Matthew 9:18-26
Thursday		Matthew 9:27-31
Friday		Luke 17:11-19
Saturday		Psalm 32

Prayer: thanksgiving, petition, intercession, praise, and offering

Reflection: silent (listening to God), written (journaling)

God's Promise
Very truly, I tell you, the hour is coming, and is now here, when the dead will hear the voice of the Son of God, and those who hear will live. For just as the Father has life in himself, so he has granted the Son also to have life in himself; and he has given him authority to execute judgment, because he is the Son of Man. Do not be astonished at this; for the hour is coming when all who are in their graves will hear his voice and will come out—those who have done good, to the resurrection of life, and those who have done evil, to the resurrection of condemnation (John 5:25-29).

My Response
One man was there who had been ill for thirty-eight years. When Jesus saw him lying there and knew that he had been there a long time, he said to him, "Do you want to be made well?" The sick man answered him, "Sir, I have no one to put me into the pool when the water is stirred up; and while I am making my way, someone else steps down ahead of me." Jesus said to him, "Stand up, take your mat and walk." At once the man was made well, and he took up his mat and began to walk (John 5:5-9).

Readings for Reflection

❧ *Do you want to get well?* is a shocking question. Of course I want to be well! But then on closer reflection I am forced to ask, *Do I really want to get well?* At times I am so attached to my illness (today we could also say addiction) that I prefer illness to health. Possibly my illness (addiction) keeps me from facing the real problem or my real self. My illness could be the crutch I have used to hide or circumvent deeper spiritual problems.

The question also shocks because it reminds me that I am a participant in my road to health. God may indeed bring miraculous, sudden, or slow healing with or without the benefit of modern medicine. But it appears that God does not bring healing unless I desire to be whole. So once again I am reminded that I am partner with God. I am asked to participate in the healing process. Even in the miraculous healing I am asked to be a full participant.

In the passage where this question is posed (John 5:1-18) Jesus gives instructions to "take up your bed and walk." The mental desire to be well now shifts to a physical act. I am asked to take some specific actions to open the doors to healing. Do I want to be well? Yes, yes, even if it means taking up my bed and carrying what has been carrying me. I am indeed helpless on my own, and I am indeed invincible with God. God does have the ability to make me whole once again. In obedience I will take up my bed and walk on the pathway to wholeness.

—Rueben P. Job

❧ Thirty-eight years is a long time to be unwell. After so long, you might get used to being sick, and develop some strong habits to keep yourself infirm. After all, when you are stuck in a closet of ill health—and everyone around you is also used to being unwell—then being sick seems like the thing to do. If you decide to get well, all the other infirm people will complain about it.

This is the way it was for the man described in John 5:1-16. He felt at home in his infirmity, as did all the others who occupied the surrounding porticos. They were all unwell, and they spent all their time waiting but not seeing that their most serious illness was that they were "at home" in their ill health. They would have felt quite naked had they suddenly found themselves exposed to wellness. And so Jesus had to remind this man that there was another alternative: "Do you really want to get well?"

The man's response tells it all, as he reels off a long list of excuses:

I don't have anyone to put me into the water.

When the angel comes to stir the water, someone gets there ahead of me.

So you see, all I can do is remain unwell for another year.

But I am faithful. I have been waiting for thirty-eight years.

Go ahead! Blame circumstances, blame the angel, blame the other sick people around you for not letting you in first. . . . Do you realize the waters that need to be stirred are inside you? Just once why don't you get up and get there first? If you listen carefully at this moment, you may just hear Jesus saying to you in the portico of your heart, "Get up! . . . Pick up your mat and walk!"

—Norman Shawchuck

⊃ Show, then, your wound to the Physician that [God] may heal it. Though you show it not, [God] knows it, but waits to hear your voice. Do away your scars by tears. Thus did that woman in the Gospel, and wiped out the stench of her sin; thus did she wash away her fault, when washing the feet of Jesus with her tears.

Would that Thou, Lord Jesus, mightest reserve for me the washing off from Thy feet of the stains contracted since Thou walkest in me! O that Thou mightest offer to me to cleanse the pollution which I by my deeds have caused on Thy steps! But whence can I obtain living water, wherewith I may wash Thy feet? If I have no water I have tears, and whilst with them I wash Thy feet I trust to cleanse myself. Whence is it that Thou shouldst say to me: "His sins which are many are forgiven, because he loved much"? I confess that I owe more, and that more has been forgiven me who have been called to the priesthood from the tumult and strife of the law courts and the dread of public administration; and therefore I fear that I may be found ungrateful, if I, to whom more has been forgiven, love less.

—From "On Repentance" by Saint Ambrose

☙ You have been wounded in many ways. The more you open yourself to being healed, the more you will discover how deep your wounds are. You will be tempted to become discouraged, because under every wound you uncover you will find others. Your search for true healing will be a suffering search. Many tears still need to be shed.

But do not be afraid. The simple fact that you are more aware of your wounds shows that you have sufficient strength to face them.

The great challenge is *living* your wounds through instead of *thinking* them through. It is better to cry than to worry, better to feel your wounds deeply than to understand them, better to let them enter into your silence than to talk about them.

—From *The Inner Voice of Love* by Henri J. M. Nouwen

☙ The choice you face constantly is whether you are taking your hurts to your head or to your heart. In your head you can analyze them, find their causes and consequences, and coin words to speak and write about them. But no final healing is likely to come from that source. You need to let your wounds go down into your heart. Then you can live them through and discover that they will not destroy you. Your heart is greater than your wounds. . . .

Think of each wound as you would of a child who has been hurt by a friend. As long as that child is ranting and raving, trying to get back at the friend, one wound leads to another. But when the child can experience the consoling embrace of a parent, she or he can live through the pain, return to the friend, forgive, and

build up a new relationship. Be gentle with yourself, and let your heart be your loving parent as you live your wounds through.
—From *The Inner Voice of Love* by Henri J. M. Nouwen

≈ We have to train ourselves to recognize how we're giving an "affective charge" to an offense, how we are *getting energy* from mulling over someone else's mistakes. We can build a case with no effort at all. We wrap and embellish and by the time our twenty minutes of "prayer" are over, we have a complete case. The verdict is in: the other person is guilty. And wrong besides. And because the other is wrong, we are right. "Scapegoating" is when we displace the issue and project it over *there* instead of owning it *here*, too. Only the contemplative mind can recognize its own complicity and participation in this great mystery of evil. The contemplative mind holds the tension and refuses to ease itself by projecting evil elsewhere.
—From *Everything Belongs* by Richard Rohr

≈   Faith to be healed I surely have
          (And faith can all things do);
     Thou art Omnipotent to save,
          And Thou art willing too;
     The God who in thy feeble days
          Of flesh didst show thy power,
     The sick to cure, the dying raise,
          And bid the grave restore.
     —From *The Unpublished Poetry of Charles Wesley*, Vol. 3

Fourteenth Sunday after Pentecost (Ordinary Time)
Sunday between August 21 and August 27

43: Repentance

Affirmation
The people who sat in darkness
  have seen a great light,
and for those who sat in the region and
      shadow of death
  light has dawned."
From that time Jesus began to proclaim, "Repent, for the kingdom of heaven has come near" (Matt. 4:16-17).

Petition
Help me, Lord God, to fulfill my good intention and your holy service. Starting today, let me begin perfectly, for what I have done so far is nothing.
—From *The Imitation of Christ* by Thomas à Kempis

Sacred Reading: anthology or other selected reading

Daily Scripture Readings

Sunday	A.	Exodus 1:8–2:10; Psalm 124; Romans 12:1-8; Matthew 16:13-20
	B.	1 Kings 8:1, 6, 10-11, 22-30, 41-43; Psalm 84; Ephesians 6:10-20; John 6:56-69
	C.	Jeremiah 1:4-10; Psalm 71:1-6; Hebrews 12:18-29; Luke 13:10-17
Monday		Mark 1:14-15
Tuesday		Luke 5:27-32
Wednesday		Luke 24:44-49
Thursday		Acts 2:37-42
Friday		Romans 2:1-11
Saturday		2 Peter 3:8-13

Prayer: thanksgiving, petition, intercession, praise, and offering

Reflection: silent (listening to God), written (journaling)

God's Promise
I baptize you with water for repentance, but one who is more powerful than I is coming after me; I am not worthy to carry his sandals. He will baptize you with the Holy Spirit and fire. His winnowing fork is in his hand, and he will clear his threshing floor and will gather his wheat into the granary; but the chaff he will burn with unquenchable fire (Matt. 3:11-12).

My Response
Now when they heard this, they were cut to the heart and said to Peter and to the other apostles, "Brothers, what should we do?" Peter said to them, "Repent, and be baptized every one of you in the name of Jesus Christ so that your sins may be forgiven; and you will receive the gift of the Holy Spirit. For the promise is for you, for your children, and for all who are far away, everyone whom the Lord our God calls to him.". . . So those who welcomed his message were baptized, and that day about three thousand persons were added. They devoted themselves to the apostles' teaching and fellowship, to the breaking of bread and the prayers (Acts 2:37-39, 41-42).

Readings for Reflection

᪾ Whenever we see a person whose life is exemplary in every way, we are drawn to live like that. When we see clarity and purity of motive, generous attitude, unobtrusive service, righteous acts, and righteous motives, we want to turn our lives in that direction. It is easy to understand the obedient response of those who heard Jesus call the disciples, crowds, and sinners in general to repent and believe. Here was purity and righteousness beyond compare calling all to repent, or turn their lives in the direction that his life modeled so well.

The good news is that we can live those exemplary lives. We can repent—turn our lives toward God. We can turn away from everything that keeps us from God and from living within God's reign. You and I can repent and believe. But it is not always easy. To repent, or turn our lives in another direction, requires our will, our effort, and our faith as we call on God to supply the strength to turn toward God in all aspects of our living. And to believe in the unseen Companion who calls us to goodness and fills us with goodness is difficult when all those visible companions tend to discount the divine companionship promised to all who believe.

What will it mean for you to repent and believe? Only you can fill in the details. But Jesus promises the power and presence to enable you to live the good life, a life in harmony with God.

—Rueben P. Job

❧ O God, I surrender to you the habits and sins that, like frost, chill my soul and cause your life-giving energy to cease its flow in me. Uproot me from the weed patches of evil wherein I have chosen to sink my roots. Plant me instead in your field of righteousness.

Direct the searchlight of your love into every crevice of my life that I may see to journey from this long winter of sin, to once again flourish in the summer of your goodness and love.

Send the gracious showers of your forgiveness to break the long drought of spiritual aridity that has shriveled my soul, and grant, my Lord, that I may become more like you and less like my shadowy self.

This day I pledge to you and to myself that I will begin even now to pursue right thinking and right living, but my God, I need your help. Amen.

—Norman Shawchuck

❧ But as that grace operates, it cannot (save through a miracle of the same grace) be other than painful, and God does not perform continual miracles in the order of grace any more than in the order of nature. It would be as great a miracle to see one full of self die suddenly to self-consciousness and self-interest as it would be to see a child go to bed a mere child and rise up the next morning [an adult] of thirty! God hides [God's] work beneath a series of imperceptible events, both in grace and nature, and thus [God] subjects us to the mysteries of faith. Not only does [God] accomplish [this] work gradually, but [God] does it by—the most simple and likely means, so that its success appears natural to [us]. Otherwise all that God does would be as a perpetual miracle, which would overthrow the life of faith by which [God] would have us exist.

—From *The Royal Way of the Cross: Letters and Spiritual Counsels of Francois de Salignac de la Mothe-Fénelon*

❧ So it is to insure that the operation of grace may remain a mystery of faith that God permits it to be slow and painful. [God] makes use of the inconstancy, the ingratitude of men [and women], the disappointments, the failures which attend human prosperity, to detach us from the creature and its good things. [God] opens our eyes by letting us realize our own weakness and evil in countless falls. It all seems to go on in the natural course of events, and this series of apparently natural causes consumes us like a slow fire. We would much rather be consumed at once by the flames of pure love, but so speedy a process would cost us nothing. It is utter selfishness that we desire to attain perfection so cheaply and so fast.

—From *The Royal Way of the Cross: Letters and Spiritual Counsels of Francois de Salignac de la Mothe-Fénelon*

❧ My beginning advice to you is this: Always read the Scriptures with a heart ready to repent. Receive the storm that repentance brings. Let the holy winds toss you to and fro. You will be awakened to new depths as you wrestle with the life forces within. What seems like violence at first will lead you gently into the eye of God where all is calm and quiet, like the eye of a hurricane. When you finally surrender and stop fighting the winds, you will be carried by angels into the eye of God. There, you will rest in peace and learn to see like God. It will be the great harvest of contemplation—through the storm into the quiet.

—From *A Tree Full of Angels* by Macrina Wiederkehr

❧ If our problem is really sin—a fundamental breach in human existence—then repentance, not self-improvement, is the first requirement. This is the biblical view of the foundations of morality. The prophets, John the Baptist, Jesus, and Paul all beckoned their hearers to a new life by calling them first to give up the old in repentance (Mark 1:15; Luke 13:3, 5; Acts 26:20; Rom. 2:4; 2 Cor. 7:9-10). Repentance is the absolutely inescapable first step of the Christian moral life. Without repentance, the Christian moral life is impossible.

—From *Vision and Character* by Craig R. Dykstra

❧ Repentance . . . requires two things: humility and trust. Repentance requires the humility involved in the confession that I am a sinner, one whose life is not whole and who lacks the power both to find either the direction to wholeness or the resources for wholeness on my own. Repentance requires trust in a power that can and will ultimately sustain and establish me if I let go of myself into that power's hands. Without both trust and humility, repentance is impossible.

—From *Vision and Character* by Craig R. Dykstra

❧ Watchfulness is a spiritual method which, if sedulously practiced over a long period, completely frees us with God's help from impassioned thoughts, impassioned words and evil actions. It leads, in so far as this

is possible, to a sure knowledge of the inapprehensible God, and helps us to penetrate the divine and hidden mysteries. It enables us to fulfil every divine commandment in the Old and New Testaments and bestows upon us every blessing of the age to come. It is, in the true sense, purity of heart, a state blessed by Christ when He says: "Blessed are the pure in heart, for they shall see God" (Matt. 5: 8); and one which, because of its spiritual nobility and beauty -- or, rather, because of our negligence -- is now extremely rare among monks. Because this is its nature, watchfulness is to be bought only at a great price. But once established in us, it guides us to a true and holy way of life.
—From *The Philokalia*

❧ Wherefore [Jesus Christ] who inspired you with this thought is assuredly doing what he promised to his disciples when they were grieved, not for themselves, but for the whole human family, and were despairing of the salvation of any one, after they heard from him that it was easier for a camel to go through the eye of a needle than for [someone who is] rich to enter into the kingdom of heaven. [Jesus] gave them this marvellous and merciful reply: "The things which are impossible with [mortals] are possible with God." [Jesus Christ], therefore, with whom it is possible to make even the rich enter into the kingdom of heaven, inspired you with that devout anxiety which makes you think it necessary to ask my counsel on the question how you ought to pray. For while [Jesus] was yet on earth, he brought Zaccheus, though rich, into the kingdom of heaven, and, after being glorified in his resurrection and ascension, he made many who were rich to despise this present world, and made them more truly rich by extinguishing their desire for riches through his imparting to them his Holy Spirit. For how could you desire so much to pray to God if you did not trust in [God]? And how could you trust in [Christ] if you were fixing your trust in uncertain riches, and neglecting the wholesome exhortation of the apostle: "Charge them that are rich in this world that they be not high-minded, nor trust in uncertain riches, but in the living God, who giveth us richly all things to enjoy; that they do good, that they be rich in good works, ready to distribute, willing to communicate, laying up in store for themselves a good foundation, that they may lay hold on eternal life"?

—From "Letter 130—to Proba" by Saint Augustine

  ❧ Patient and Forgiving God, I need to ask your forgiveness for much, although I know I am your child. You have forgiven me for everything in Christ, but I continue to stumble and fall like a little child. Christ reigns in my heart, but pride emerges in the shadow of my spiritual progress; self-will, idolatry, and love of the world assault my soul; desire and love of praise, jealousy, and envy crowd my thoughts. I feel terrible about the darkness remaining in my heart. While my words and actions seem to be good and pure, my intentions and motives are sometimes self-serving and anything but godly. Sometimes I feel utterly helpless, and I know it is a grand illusion to think I can expel pride, selfishness, and inbred sin on my own.

I trust you to deliver me from this sin that remains, just as you have freed me from the power of evil in my life. Not only are you willing, you are able to liberate me fully. You want me to grow from faith to faith and to feel the power of Christ every moment.

In repentance I feel remaining sin; by faith I receive your power to purify my heart and cleanse my hands.

In repentance I realize the consequences of my brokenness; by faith I am conscious of Christ's pleading for me and your liberating pardon.

In repentance I recognize my helplessness; by faith I accept your mercy and experience your grace. By your grace you free me from bondage to outward sin, and the power of inward sin is broken while not entirely destroyed.

When you accepted me as a part of your family through Christ, I felt as though I was born again. The change in my life was amazing. But I need to experience your life-changing love over and over again in order to grow into the fullness of your love. Amen.

—From *Praying in the Wesleyan Spirit* by Paul W. Chilcote

44: *Living Water*

Affirmation

Then he said to me, "It is done! I am the Alpha and the Omega, the beginning and the end. To the thirsty I will give water as a gift from the spring of the water of life. Those who conquer will inherit these things, and I will be their God and they will be my children" (Rev. 21:6-7).

Petition

Then Jesus said to them, "Very truly, I tell you, it was not Moses who gave you the bread from heaven, but it is my Father who gives you the true bread from heaven. For the bread of God is that which comes down from heaven and gives life to the world." They said to him, "Sir, give us this bread always." Jesus said to them, "I am the bread of life. Whoever comes to me will never be hungry, and whoever believes in me will never be thirsty" (John 6:32-35).

Sacred Reading: anthology or other selected reading

Daily Scripture Readings

Sunday	A.	Exodus 3:1-15; Psalm 105:1-6, 23-26, 45; Romans 12:9-21; Matthew 16:21-28
	B.	Song of Solomon 2:8-13; Psalm 45:1-2, 6-9; James 1:17-27; Mark 7:1-8, 14-15, 21-23
	C.	Jeremiah 2:4-13; Psalm 81:1, 10-16; Hebrews 13:1-8, 15-16; Luke 14:1, 7-14
Monday		John 4:7-15
Tuesday		Exodus 17:1-7
Wednesday		Isaiah 12:1-6
Thursday		John 7:37-39

| Friday | Revelation 7:13-17 |
| Saturday | Isaiah 42:1-9 |

Prayer: thanksgiving, petition, intercession, praise, and offering

Reflection: silent (listening to God), written (journaling)

God's Promise

On the last day of the festival, the great day, while Jesus was standing there, he cried out, "Let anyone who is thirsty come to me, and let the one who believes in me drink. As the scripture has said, 'Out of the believer's heart shall flow rivers of living water'" (John 7:37-38).

My Response

And all ate the same spiritual food, and all drank the same spiritual drink. For they drank from the spiritual rock that followed them, and the rock was Christ (1 Cor. 10:3-4).

Readings for Reflection

❧ Have you ever been extremely thirsty? If you have experienced deep thirst, you know how wonderful and refreshing cool water can be. We can live for many days without food but only a short time without water. When the Samaritan woman encountered Jesus at Jacob's well, she was searching for that which would quench her body's thirst for life-giving and life-sustaining water. In the presence of Jesus she recognized a deeper thirst, the thirst for God. And it was to this thirst that Jesus offered living water and the promise that her thirst for God could be satisfied.

The thirst for God is universal because we have been created with a longing for the Creator. This desire to know and be known by the One who made us and loves us is often ignored, denied, and finally buried under a multitude of pursuits and interests. But then some event in life invites or forces us to pause, and the desire for God comes rushing back to our awareness. And once again we know that real life is impossible without the companionship of the One who first gave us the gift of life and who sustains us even now. We know for certain that we need living water; we need what only God can give if we are to really live.

Today Jesus continues to offer living water, a way, and a companionship that can quench our thirst for God. Our part is to recognize the deep need for God within us and to offer hospitality to the One who seeks to fill and satisfy that need. Like the psalmist, our souls thirst for God. The good news we share is that through Jesus Christ our thirst can be satisfied.

—Rueben P. Job

❧ I think of prayer in essence as having two motions. *The first motion is one of response.* It is opening like a flower opening to the morning sunshine to allow God's love energies to flow into your inner chamber. You may know that many flowers close up at night, folding their petals in. When it begins to become daylight, they open just a little. Then as the sun's rays strike them, they open a little more and a little more until they are wide open.

"God is love," an apostle writes (1 John 4:8). Theologically, you must say, God's love energies brought the world into being. God's love energies sustain the world. God's love energies are directing the world toward some meaningful end. And the same love energies are constantly pouring on you. That is true even though you cannot see God in the same way that the sun's energy is bathing the earth even when you cannot see it, when it is on the other side of the earth. Were that not true, you would be a block of ice.

God, you see, is the initiator of this communion. If you will think about it a moment, you will quickly realize why that is true. Physicists today are pointing out that our sun is one of millions of suns in our galaxy and our galaxy is one of more than 150 billion galaxies. Our God is a God of 150 billion-plus galaxies! And when I think about that, my mouth gapes open in awe.

Yet God's greatness is not the most awesome discovery. The most awesome is what we learn from revelation—that the God of 150 billion-plus galaxies cares about me, about you, grains of sand on an endless seashore. That, you see, is what the whole of revelation tells us, that God, the God of this vast universe, loves us with an infinite love. "While we were still sinners, Christ died for us. That proves God's love," the Apostle Paul put it (Rom. 5:8, author's translation).

—From *Spiritual Preparation for Christian Leadership* by E. Glenn Hinson

᭟ We can be energized and motivated by our personal experience of God, so that we have both the vision and the strength to go out and engage in acts of risk-taking on behalf of others. Our own experience becomes the source for our motivation for involvement with others. Our freedom from self-centeredness is freedom to care more fully for them. As we are met by God's love, we are compelled to share that love by our actions. Thus our prayer becomes the force that empowers us to engage the world. We move back and forth between being renewed in silence and quiet by ourselves, reading the Bible and praying, and then carrying that new energy out into the world with vigor. This back-and-forth pattern is a central way in which the spiritual experience of the individual is related to the activity of the disciple. The movement back and forth may be daily or weekly, or it may follow some other pattern. Some people are so heavily involved with the world that they find it necessary to take a day a month for personal retreat.

—From *Reformed Spirituality* by Howard L. Rice

᭟ In other words, the resurrection needs to be experienced as present risenness. If we take seriously the

word of the risen Christ, "Know that I am with you always; yes, to the end of time" (Matt. 28:20), we should expect that [Christ] will be actively present in our lives. If our faith is alive and luminous, we will be alert to moments, events and occasions when the power of resurrection is brought to bear on our lives. Self-absorbed and inattentive, we fail to notice the subtle ways in which Jesus is snagging our attention.
—From *Abba's Child* by Brennan Manning

❧ Thomas Merton insists that there is no union with God without transformation. Paradoxically, the person who has struggled with personal transformation and become psychologically stronger is the person who can be empty and receptive before God. It is the prepared personality that is less resistant to God's love. This vulnerability is an act of strength, since we no longer need to hold tightly to a false self that protects us from our inner pain and fears. We are free at last. We can surrender to God, who is everywhere and always present, and can actively respond as the occasion requires. We have the ease to rest in God in whom we have been found.
—From "Participating in the New Creation" by Mary Conrow Coelho in *The Weavings Reader*

❧ The future is in God's hands, not yours. God will rule it accordingly to your need. But if you seek to forecast it in your own wisdom, you will gain nothing but anxiety and anticipation of inevitable trouble. Try only to make use of each day; each day brings its own good and evil, and sometimes what seems evil becomes good if we leave it to God, and do not forestall [God] with our impatience.
—From *The Royal Way of the Cross: Letters and Spiritual Counsels of Francois de Salignac de la Mothe-Fénelon*

❧ Be sure that God will grant you whatever time you need to attain to Him. Perhaps [God] may not give you as much as you would like for your own plans, or to please yourself under the pretext of seeking spiritual perfection, but you will find that neither time nor opportunity for renunciation of self and self-pleasing will be lacking. All other time is lost, however well spent it may seem.

—From *The Royal Way of the Cross: Letters and Spiritual Counsels of Francois de Salignac de la Mothe-Fénelon*

❧ The biblical promise that if we truly seek, we shall find God is the basis for the journey of the spiritual life. In spite of the difficulties along the way, the times of dryness when nothing seems to be happening, the discouragement and distraction that come to us all, and the times of falling back and wondering if we have made any progress at all, the journey is one from which we cannot turn back. The testimony of the saints of all the ages is that the journey is worth it; that God really is love; and that the love God offers is the most important reality that can be known by any of us. Such knowledge enables a person to have tremendous power to take what happens, to surmount great difficulties, and to grow in the face of tragedy and deep disappointment.

The fruit of the spiritual life is not easily attained. The process of growing in grace is sometimes difficult. It requires persistence which never comes easily for any of us. The old part of us, the part that wants to go it alone and maintain control, keeps asserting itself. There are times when we want to go back to being unaware and half dead. God requires honesty from us, and such honesty can be painful. Because God knows us better than we know ourselves, pretending will not work. God's knowledge of us demands that we come to terms with who we really are.

—From *Reformed Spirituality* by Howard L. Rice

❧ The goal of the Christian life is union with Christ, but such union is only dimly and occasionally realized

in this life by most of us. Nevertheless, the pilgrimage toward the goal is one of joyful discovery that Christ is with us whether or not we realize that presence. We are given new opportunities for relationship with others along the way. We find new possibilities within us that we had not thought possible. The adventure of the Christian life is one that demands all we can give it. But the testimony of the ages is that the goal of the adventure is well worth the struggle. The hungry heart of the pilgrim is fed along the way.
—From *Reformed Spirituality* by Howard L. Rice

❧ Each of us is born into inextricably interwoven kinships, community systems, and global infrastructures that connect us with all humankind—past, present, and future. Each of us inherits a complex private, social, and cultural collective consciousness from external sources and from authorities with which we can identify. Yet beyond this conscious knowledge may reside a reservoir of inherited collective unconsciousness that remains largely unknown but awaits discovery.

Because our individual stories are deeply embedded in history and traditions that extend across many centuries, generations, and cultures, all of us unconsciously know more than we think we know. Because we have acquired and received knowledge and accumulated wisdom from ancient and modern sources, all of us can do and be more than we consciously think. Inherited memories from sources beyond our knowing link us to all generations of humankind. And because we are surrounded by so great a cloud of witnesses, all of us have received an inherited faith that first lived in our ancestors and now lives in us. Through them more of God's spiritual nature has been passed on to us than we can ever imagine or intuit. We cannot fully grasp this kind of collective knowing by rational means only. It comes to us through faith. Perhaps Jesus had this same experience. Luke's Gospel tells us that Jesus increased in wisdom, in years, and in favor with God and people (2:52).

—From *Mother Roots* by Helen Bruch Pearson

45: No Condemnation

Affirmation

For I am convinced that neither death, nor life, nor angels, nor rulers, nor things present, nor things to come, nor powers, nor height, nor depth, nor anything else in all creation, will be able to separate us from the love of God in Christ Jesus our Lord (Rom. 8:38-39).

Petition

Therefore, do not let sin exercise dominion in your mortal bodies, to make you obey their passions. No longer present your members to sin as instruments of wickedness, but present yourselves to God as those who have been brought from death to life, and present your members to God as instruments of righteousness. For sin will have no dominion over you, since you are not under law but under grace (Rom. 6:12-14).

Daily Scripture Readings

Sunday	A.	Exodus 12:1-14; Psalm 149; Romans 13:8-14; Matthew 18:15-20
	B.	Proverbs 22:1-2, 8-9, 22-23; Psalm 125; James 2:1-10, 14-17; Mark 7:24-37
	C.	Jeremiah 18:1-11; Psalm 139:1-6, 13-18; Philemon 1-21; Luke 14:25-33
Monday		Romans 8:1-11
Tuesday		John 8:1-11
Wednesday		1 John 3:18-24
Thursday		Psalm 34:11-22
Friday		Romans 8:31-39
Saturday		James 2:8-13

Prayer: thanksgiving, petition, intercession, praise, and offering

Reflection: silent (listening to God), written (journaling)

God's Promise
There is therefore now no condemnation for those who are in Christ Jesus . . . for if you live according to the flesh, you will die; but if by the Spirit you put to death the deeds of the body, you will live. For all who are led by the Spirit of God are children of God (Rom. 8:1, 13-14).

My Response
What then are we to say about these things? If God is for us, who is against us?. . .Who will separate us from the love of Christ? Will hardship, or distress, or persecution, or famine, or nakedness, or peril, or sword? As it is written,

> "For your sake we are being
>   killed all day long;
> we are accounted as sheep to
>   be slaughtered."

No, in all these things we are more than conquerors through him who loved us (Rom. 8:31, 35-37).

Readings for Reflection

❧ Condemnation is a heavy burden to bear. No matter the source of the condemnation and no matter the reason, condemnation crushes the life out of us all when given the opportunity. Many of us live our lives condemned because we have been unable or unwilling to permit that burden to be removed. Sometimes the condemnation is self-imposed, and we just cannot forgive ourselves for what seems to be, in our own estimation, some great failure. Sometimes the condemnation comes from outside ourselves for failures in the eyes of others. Whether these failures are relatively insignificant or enormous, the burden of condemnation is hard to bear. Therefore the words of Jesus—"Neither do I condemn you. Go your way, and from now on do not sin again" (John 8:11)—are music to our ears. To know that we do not need to carry the failures of the past into the future is good news indeed. Jesus came not to condemn the world but to save the world (John 3:17). The good news for all of us declares that the chains binding us to past failures can be broken; we can be set free to live all our tomorrows without condemnation.

Stop and think for a moment about all those memories that keep invading your consciousness to convince you that you are condemned. And then remember these words of the New Testament: "Who is to condemn? It is Christ Jesus, who died, yes, who was raised, who is at the right hand of God, who indeed intercedes for us" (Rom. 8:34). There is no condemnation for those who walk with Christ.

Today offer all the condemnations of the past and present—silly and substantial—to God in Christ Jesus and hear the words of Jesus addressed to you: "Neither do I condemn you. Go your way, and from now on do not sin again." And now give thanks to God that you are free of the burden of condemnation.
—Rueben P. Job

& It may sound paradoxical, but no man is condemned for anything he has done; he is condemned for continuing to do wrong. He is condemned for not coming out of the darkness, for not coming to the light, the living God, who sent the light, His Son, into the world to guide him home.
—From *Creation in Christ* by George Macdonald

& I was terrified of God as a child; and though it took me a long time to admit it to myself, when I came to pray, I was still terrified of God as an adult. "Only trust God," I would hear people say. Trust God! I could hardly imagine sitting in God's presence as the person I actually was without feeling crushed with shame. Whatever I told myself I believed about God's loving me, what I really thought was that what God really liked doing was weighing up and judging every one of my faults, sins, flaws, and errors.

Only as an adult was I able at last to believe that God really isn't very interested in judging everything I do, and that God truly does love the very person I am, as God loves all people. How that happened I've told elsewhere. What I need to say here, however, is this: I believe we do awful damage to ourselves when we tell ourselves and others that God loves us in spite of who we are, and then on top of everything else, exhort ourselves to love God in return. As a child, I used to feel such fear and despair that I couldn't "have faith" and love God no matter how hard I tried. Now, I often think, gratefully, that the very fact that I couldn't was a gift of God's grace. What would it have done to me if I had managed to love the very God I believed found everything about me contemptible? What does it do to any of us? If nothing else, the use of such "in spite of" language of judgment keeps us from being able to be truthful with ourselves in God's presence. Certainly, it prevents us thriving and enjoying the presence of God as God meant us to do.

The first assumption that I make, therefore, is that God loves me as God loves all people, without qualification. The second is related to it, and it was also a long time coming to me. According to such great early Christian teachers of the first five centuries whom I teach, such as Irenaeus, Athanasius, Anthony, and Gregory of Nyssa, all human beings are created in the image of God. To them, to be in the image of God means that all of us are made for the purpose of knowing and loving God and one another and of being loved in turn, not literally in the same way God knows and loves, but in a way appropriate to human beings.
—From *In Ordinary Time* by Roberta C. Bondi

❧ That which is unforgiven holds us captive. We are imprisoned by the hatred and malice we clutch in our hearts. I do not mean to suggest that forgiveness is easy or even that it is a swift process. No. When wrongs have been committed the last thing one wants, or even should do is claim that the transgression should be overlooked. The aftermath of betrayal or injury is unavoidably rage, hate, self-blame, flight, and fight. It is a long and painful process to move through the stages of healing that must occur for forgiveness to begin. The injury must be named and claimed as part of you, the pain allowed to work for you, the injurer must rightly be blamed, and power and strength returned to the injured. Then, knowing you have experienced pain and overcome it, forgiveness can come as a free act.

—From *The Time Between* by Wendy M. Wright

❧ Forgiveness can be the great cleansing action that allows one to begin again. Retribution or restitution is not enough. They serve as payback but they do not allow for the deep scouring that is necessary to truly start anew. The ancient Israelites knew the principle well for they instituted the practice of the Sabbath year. Each seventh year was set aside so that all could begin over again: fields lay follow and all debts were forgiven. This crucial period of rest was seen as necessary for the harmonious functioning of society and the fertility of the land. The earth can be depleted, our societies become imbalanced and unjust. Similarly, as individuals and as families we require a time of absolution so that we might truly begin again and become fertile fields that yield a rich harvest.

The prayer most identified with Christianity, the one taught to us by Jesus himself, incorporates the crucial insight that forgiveness is a key ingredient as we live into the promised kingdom.

—From *The Time Between* by Wendy M. Wright

ɚ Recently I was in a doctor's office ... when a young mother with long brown hair and a gentle face entered, pushing in a wheelchair a child three or four years old. The child obviously was disabled: her hands unable to grasp anything, her arms and legs flailing helplessly, her eyes unable to hold focus. Her voice could not make syllables but only squeals or little wails. The mother positioned the child's chair so that they were face-to-face. She began softly singing and doing the hand motions to "The Itsy Bitsy Spider" directly in front of the child's face, to attract her attention. She repeated it over and over, sometimes catching the child's hand and kissing it, stroking her hair; she looked into the child's eyes and whispered, with enormous tenderness, "I love you." For a moment, I felt like an unwitting intruder into a sacred space.

Is this how we are, I wondered, before our God who wants to love us just this tenderly? Our limbs flailing aimlessly, unable to unify our energies to respond to the gift of life we have been given; our eyes unable to focus on the love God tries over and over in so many ways to reveal to us; our voices unable to respond coherently to this God whom our minds cannot comprehend? And is that why we so often turn to the word *mercy* when we want to speak of our God?

When God's love touches us in our neediness, the sorrow and suffering inherent in the human condition, we name it mercy. Mercy is perhaps the loveliest of all God's qualities. This is the love that reaches into the dark space of our flailing and our failing, our losing and our dying. Mercy enters that space, picks us up and holds us tenderly until we are healed. Little by little, this love draws our groping hands and wasted energies to purposeful service; it looks directly into our uncomprehending eyes, hears our futile wail, and says, *"No matter, I love you anyway. Come on. . . ."* And so mercy brings us to ever-new life.

—From "Living in the Mercy" by Elaine M. Prevallet in *Weavings* September/October 2000

ᏋᏃ Those to whom spiritual guidance is entrusted should only lay bare [a person's] faults as God prepares the heart to see them. One must learn to watch a fault patiently, and take no external measure until God begins to make it felt by the inward conscience. Nay, more: one must imitate God's own way of dealing with the soul, softening [God's] rebuke, so that the person rebuffed feels as if it was rather self-reproach, and a sense of wounded love, than God rebuking. All other methods of guidance, reproving impatiently, or because one is vexed at infirmities, smack of earthly judgments, not the correction of grace. It is imperfection rebuking the imperfect: it is a subtle, clinging self-love, which cannot see anything to forgive in the self-love of others. The greater our own self-love, the more severe critics we shall be. Nothing is so offensive to a haughty, sensitive, self-conceit as the self-conceit of others. But, on the contrary, the love of God is full of consideration, forbearance, condescension, and tenderness. It adapts itself, waits, and never moves more than one step at a time. The less self-love we have, the more we know how to adapt ourselves to curing our neighbor's failings of that kind; we learn better never to lance without putting plenty of healing ointment to the wound, never to purge the patient without feeding [the patient], never to risk an operation save when nature indicates its safety. One learns to wait years before giving a salutary warning; to wait till Providence prepares suitable external circumstances, and grace opens the heart. If you persist in gathering fruit before it is ripe, you simply waste your labor.

—From *The Royal Way of the Cross: Letters and Spiritual Counsels of Francois de Salignac de la Mothe-Fénelon*

ᏋᏃ In the strange and challenging world of the Bible, where very little is only what it appears to be, the real explanation for the force shaping the course of things is gathered up in one radiant word: *mercy*. Creation in its entirety is a work of God's love and though it is fractured by every sort of strife, it cannot escape the gravity of mercy. God's mercy fills the earth (Ps. 33:5), an outpouring of costly care that is not merely one among several of God's possible dispositions toward misery and need. Mercy is the deepest quality of God's love, the most encompassing movement of God's heart, the most stunningly unexpected evidence of God's generosity, the most enduring commitment of God's sovereignty. . . . Flexible and strong, mercy is capable of bearing sorrow's weight and of supporting every honest effort to build new life.

"Be merciful, just as your Father is merciful" (Luke 6:36). The one who speaks these words became like us so that experiencing in him the full embodiment of God's mercy, we might desire to become like God. With Jesus, mercy would be the touchstone of our judgments and the measure of our conduct (Ps. 36:5-7). Yet surely God continues to regret the mystifying stubborn-heartedness that imprisons us in the small circle of our own counsel: "O that my people would listen to me, that Israel would walk in my ways!" (Ps. 81:13).

"Blessed are the merciful, for they will receive mercy" (Matt. 5:7). In the paradoxical economy of God's realm, what is freely given away often returns greatly multiplied (Mark 6:30-44). The real explanation for such abundance where we would expect depletion is mercy.

—From "Editor's Introduction" by John S. Mogabgab
  in *Weavings* September/October 2000

46: Making Room for God

Affirmation

If you offer your food to the hungry
    and satisfy the needs of the afflicted,
then your light shall rise in the darkness
    and your gloom be like the noonday.
The LORD will guide you continually,
    and satisfy your needs in parched places,
    and make your bones strong;
and you shall be like a watered garden,
    like a spring of water,
    whose waters never fail (Isa. 58:10-11).

Petition

He said to them, "When you pray, say:
Father, hallowed be your name.
    Your kingdom come.
    Give us each day our daily bread.
    And forgive us our sins,
        for we ourselves forgive everyone
            indebted to us.
    And do not bring us to the time of trial"
    (Luke 11:2-4).

Sacred Reading: anthology or other selected reading

Daily Scripture Readings

Sunday	A.	Exodus 14:19-31; Psalm 114; Romans 14:1-12; Matthew 18:21-35
	B.	Proverbs 1:20-33; Psalm 19; James 3:1-12; Mark 8:27-38
	C.	Jeremiah 4:11-12, 22-28; Psalm 14; 1 Timothy 1:12-17; Luke 15:1-10
Monday		Matthew 6:16-18

Tuesday	Ezra 8:21-23
Wednesday	Luke 2:36-38
Thursday	Acts 13:1-3
Friday	Acts 14:21-23
Saturday	Isaiah 58:6-9

Prayer: thanksgiving, petition, intercession, praise, and offering

Reflection: silent (listening to God), written (journaling)

God's Promise
Is not this the fast that I choose:
   to loose the bonds of injustice,
   to undo the thongs of the yoke,
to let the oppressed go free,
   and to break every yoke? . . .
Then you shall call, and the LORD will answer;
   you shall cry for help, and he will say, Here I am
      (Isa. 58:6, 9).

My Response
Then Jesus was led up by the Spirit into the wilderness to be tempted by the devil. He fasted forty days and forty nights, and afterwards he was famished. The tempter came and said to him, "If you are the Son of God, command these stones to become loaves of bread." But he answered, "It is written,
 'One does not live by bread alone,
      but by every word that comes
         from the mouth of God'" (Matt. 4:1-4).

Readings for Reflection

❧ How can I make room in my life for the things that really matter? This question plagues most adults in the developed world. We have so many things, so many activities, so many opportunities, and so many responsibilities. Is it possible to find a place for God in our busy lives? Many have answered the question with a resounding no. Others have answered by filling every moment of every day with activity until there is no time even to think about God. Others yearn to find that sacred space and time but just don't know how or where to look.

The saints who have gone before us left a legacy of experience in living with God. One learning they pass on to us is the value of fasting as a spiritual discipline. Fasting makes room for God in our lives. The discipline required to relinquish food or entertainment or anything else can often be the opening that admits God more fully into our lives.

Is there a way for you to find regular time and place for God in your life without fasting or giving up some things? Probably not. Therefore the real question becomes, What do you feel called to give up in order to find room for God in your life? Fasting for a season may give you the space, time, and energy to make room for God in your busy life.

—Rueben P. Job

  ❧ My God, I lift my face toward you now like a hungry child asking to be fed. My soul is starved; my flesh yearns for the touch that only you can give. Come to me, O God, and stay with me; I abandon myself into your hands. Do with me as you will, and whatever you do with me, I thank you. I am prepared for anything; I will accept everything so long as your will is accomplished in the totality of my living.

My God, I give myself to you, placing myself in your hands as a gift of love. It is necessary for me to give myself to you in confidence and without reserve because I love you, and I know you love me also.

Reach down inside me now, O God, and change the gears that race and roar. In place of turmoil give me peace; in place of frenzy give me patience. Then shall I be more like Jesus, who taught us to make room for you in our hectic days.

Teach me, God, to make room for you in all the events and affairs of my days. Then I shall find rest. Then I will be at peace with my self and with you.
—Norman Shawchuck

❧ The house of my soul is too small for you to enter: make it more spacious by your coming. It lies in ruins: rebuild it. Some things are to be found there which will offend your gaze; I confess this to be so and know it well. But who will clean my house? To whom but yourself can I cry, *Cleanse me of my hidden sins, O Lord, and for those incurred through others pardon your servant?* I believe, and so I will speak. You know everything, Lord. Have I not laid my own transgressions bare before you to my own condemnation, my God, and have you not forgiven the wickedness of my heart? I do not argue my case against you, for you are truth itself; nor do I wish to deceive myself, lest my iniquity be caught in its own lies. No, I do not argue the case with you, because *if you, Lord, keep the score of our iniquities, then who, Lord, can bear it?*
—From *The Confessions* by Saint Augustine

❧ Solitude is obviously intended to be far more than just being physically alone. It is the way we form a habit of retreat, creating a space and a time when God can speak to us. Perhaps you are fortunate enough to have some place in your house that could become a place of retreat. Some people have a favorite walk that becomes a "prayer walk." Every large city, despite the noise and crowds, has places of great solitude and peace. Often city center churches are examples of this. What is certain is that if we create a place where we can regularly turn to God, [God] will meet us there. There, as Amma Syncletica said, "it is possible to be a solitary in one's mind while living in a crowd." Time spent with God in solitude will always bring a harvest. The problems we have outside the solitude will seem different when we return to them refreshed and strengthened. The surer sense of our relationship with Christ that solitude brings spills over into everything else we do. When Moses came down from his solitude on Mount Sinai, his face shone (Exod. 34:29-35). For you, too, solitude can be a place of transfiguration, a meeting place with the living God.

—From *The Interior Mountain* by Simon Peter Iredale

❧ In fasting, we abstain in some significant way from food and possibly from drink as well. This discipline teaches us a lot about ourselves very quickly. It will certainly prove humiliating to us, as it reveals to us how much our peace depends upon the pleasures of eating. It may also bring to mind how we are using food pleasure to assuage the discomforts caused in our bodies by faithless and unwise living and attitudes— lack of self-worth, meaningless work, purposeless existence, or lack of rest or exercise. If nothing else, though, it will certainly demonstrate how powerful and clever our body is in getting its own way against our strongest resolves. . . .

Persons well used to fasting as a systematic practice will have a clear and constant sense of their resources in God. And that will help them endure deprivations of *all* kinds, even to the point of coping with them easily and cheerfully.

—From *The Spirit of the Disciplines* by Dallas Willard

❧ By participating in Christian disciplines, we live out our desire and intention to cooperate with the Holy Spirit. As we do so, we are encouraged, instructed, healed, challenged, loved, renewed, and beckoned to God and godly living.

While it is true that God is in every when and where and that many other things besides disciplines contribute to our deepening relationship with God, we discover that it makes a meaningful difference in everyday life when we set aside time, space, and ourselves to be more fully present with and attentive and responsive to God. Disciplines are like faithful companions on the way. The benefit we seek and desire most is deepening companionship with God. We come away from other pursuits to listen for the still, small voice that is our best friend, our beloved Savior, the Holy One, our Creator, God.

—From *Holy Invitations* by Jeannette A. Bakke

❧ "Asceticism" refers to practices or disciplines that require considerable effort on our part to learn and continue to perform. One who is ascetical is well schooled in the disciplines of the spiritual life. The principal form of Christian asceticism is fasting, which means to refrain from food and drink for a specific period of time for a spiritual motive. The fathers [and mothers] of the Church express two reasons for fasting: as preparation for prayer (since Jesus fasted and prayed in the New Testament) and as a way to identify with the poor. The primitive form of fasting is to omit all eating of solid foods for a specific period of time, usually a day or two.

The decision to give up a meal is a choice to step back from a routine dependence upon food and drink in order to gain perspective on the relationship between material food and spiritual nourishment. The pangs of physical hunger lead us to a new hunger for God, and our own tendency to use creation in selfish and pragmatic ways is uncovered. Thus an increase of time spent in prayer goes hand in hand with fasting, which emphasizes the experience of emptiness and dependence upon God. Many serious Christians fast from solid foods one day a week. . . .

Abstaining from a particular food for a spiritual motive is another common form of asceticism, for example, from meat on certain days of the week or in the season of Lent or Advent. Again, this discipline gives us some freedom from our likes and dislikes and helps us to see the patterns of gratification that may be dominating us, cluttering our lives with imaginary need. The presumption of both fasting and abstaining is that all of creation is good and is intended for our enjoyment. We let go of one good thing to experience another good; in this case, our intention is to look more intensely at God and to state, in this ritual way of fasting and abstaining, our highest priorities. Fasting and abstention are spiritual disciplines that quickly and effectively clarify those priorities for us. In the first place, we are mortified to discover how thoroughly captured we are by our physical needs, but the empty "space" left by fasting and abstaining is graciously filled with God and a new sensitivity to the needs of [God's] people.

—From "Getting Ready to Pray: The Practice of Spiritual Disciplines" by Gabriel O'Donnell in *Spiritual Traditions for the Contemporary Church*

꙰ What I most desire for you is a certain calmness which recollection, detachment, and love of God alone can give. St. Augustine says that whatever we love outside God, so much the less do we love [God]. It is as a brook whence part of the waters is turned aside. Such a diversion takes away from that which is God's and thence arise harassment and trouble. God would have all, and [God's] jealousy cannot endure a divided heart. The slightest affection apart from [God] becomes a hindrance, and causes estrangement. The soul can only look to find peace in love without reserve.

—From *The Royal Way of the Cross: Letters and Spiritual Counsels of Francois de Salignac de la Mothe-Fénelon*

꙰ Dear Jesus, during this day help me quiet all the thoughts that fill my head—where I must go, whom I must see, and what I must do. In their place, give me a sense of your order, your peace, and your time.

Help me to understand that you are in control, and I can trust you with my day. Help me to realize that nothing on my to-do list is important if it is not what you want me to do.

I give all my tasks to you and trust you to bring

order to them. In these moments, dear Jesus, come to me, be with me, and free me from the tyranny of "to do."
—From *Quiet Spaces* by Patricia F. Wilson

❧ When Jesus encountered the hemorrhaging woman, he set aside the levitical cleanliness laws that had kept this suffering woman separated from the larger community for twelve long years (Matt. 9:20-22; Mark 5:25-34; Luke 8:43-48). Her touch did not offend him nor was he concerned it had made him unclean. Instead he called attention to the fact that she had touched him and that her faith—not his—had made her well. Choosing love and healing to meet human need, Jesus restored the woman's rightful place into the fellowship of the Israelites by calling her "Daughter," perhaps recalling the honored memory of another "daughter" of Israel, Bathsheba.
—From *Mother Roots* by Helen Bruch Pearson

47: Compassion for the World

Affirmation

I will ransom them from the power of the grave;
I will redeem them from death.
O Death, I will be your plagues!
O Grave, I will be your destruction!
Pity is hidden from My eyes (Hos. 13:14, NKJV).

Petition

Take words with you
    and return to the LORD;
say to him,
    "Take away all guilt;
accept that which is good,
    and we will offer
    the fruit of our lips (Hos. 14:2).

Sacred Reading: anthology or other selected reading

Daily Scripture Readings

Sunday	A.	Exodus 16:2-15; Psalm 105:1-6, 37-45; Philippians 1:21-30; Matthew 20:1-16
	B.	Proverbs 31:10-31; Psalm 1; James 3:13–4:3, 7-8; Mark 9:30-37
	C.	Jeremiah 8:18–9:1; Psalm 79:1-9; 1 Timothy 2:1-7; Luke 16:1-13
Monday		Mark 6:30-44
Tuesday		Matthew 9:35-38
Wednesday		Isaiah 61:1-7
Thursday		Isaiah 61:8-11
Friday		Luke 7:11-17
Saturday		Matthew 14:13-21

Prayer: thanksgiving, petition, intercession, praise, and offering

Reflection: silent (listening to God), written (journaling)

God's Promise

I will heal their disloyalty;
    I will love them freely,
    for my anger has turned from them.
I will be like the dew to Israel;
    he shall blossom like the lily,
    he shall strike root like the forests of Lebanon.
His shoots shall spread out;
    his beauty shall be like the olive tree,
    and his fragrance like that of Lebanon.
They shall again live beneath my shadow,
    they shall flourish as a garden;
they shall blossom like the vine,
        their fragrance shall be like the wine of Lebanon
            (Hos. 14:4-7).

My Response

Come, let us return to the LORD; for it is he who has torn, and he will heal us; he has struck down, and he will bind us up. . . . Let us know, let us press on to know the LORD; his appearing is as sure as the dawn; he will come to us like the showers, like the spring rains that water the earth (Hos. 6:1, 3).

Readings for Reflection

❧ Jesus was often prompted by compassion to act on behalf of those who were suffering loss, disease, and hunger. It seems inevitable that those who follow Jesus must also show compassion in all of their decisions and actions. This is especially true of those who relate to people suffering hunger, disease, and death. The followers of Jesus cannot ignore the needy of the world, and neither can we look away from the needs of the world. If our lives are modeled after the one we claim to follow, we will, as Jesus did, look with compassion upon all who cross our paths. Looking with compassion requires the further step of seeking to alleviate the pain that prompted our compassion.

Colossians 3:12 has provided a source of guidance and strength for my life for many years. "As God's chosen ones, holy and beloved, clothe yourselves with compassion, kindness, humility, meekness, and patience." The author of Colossians calls the followers of Jesus to clothe themselves with these five incredible qualities, and the first of them is compassion. As chosen ones, it is the only option. To be chosen as God's beloved can only evoke gratitude and goodness. Therefore our response of compassion for the world is really a response to God's unqualified love for us. How could we respond in any other way?

Jesus saw a need, had compassion, then sought to remedy the need. As Christians we seek to model our lives after Jesus. The pain of the world draws forth our compassion and our effort to remedy the need.

As God's beloved, pray this week for eyes to see the needs around you and for compassion that will prompt actions to meet those needs with loving remedy.
—Rueben P. Job

❧ I always explain to the sisters, "It is Christ you tend in the poor. It is his wounds you bathe, his sores you clean, his limbs you bandage. See beyond appearances, hear the words Jesus pronounced long ago. They are still operative today: *What you do to the least of mine, you do it to me.* When you serve the poor, you serve our Lord Jesus Christ."
—From *My Life for the Poor* by Mother Teresa

❧ I was at a meeting of the Superiors General in Europe.
They talked only of changing the structures of society, organizing things in a different way.
It all came to nothing. It did not do something for

the poor, or preach Christ to those without religion, to those totally ignorant of God.

I was happy when it was all over.

—From *My Life for the Poor* by Mother Teresa

❧ To go where healing love is needed, and give it in a way in which it can be received, often means acting in the teeth of our own interests and preferences, even religious interests and preferences. Christ risked his reputation for holiness by healing on the Sabbath; he touched the unclean and dined with the wrong people; he accepted the love and companionship of a sinner (that most wonderful of all remedies for the wounds of sin). He loved with God's love and so went straight to the point: What can I do to restore my fellow creature and how?

—From *The Light of Christ* by Evelyn Underhill

❧ Following the way of forgiveness prepares us to go one step further. Something more is asked of us by Jesus: "Go and learn the meaning of the words, 'I desire mercy, not sacrifice.' I did not come to call the righteous, but sinners" (Mt 9:13 [NAB]).

This "something more" is compassion. Once we grasp the depth of God's merciful love for us, he wants us to express that same compassion for others. This is the balm that softens the scars of sinfulness and suffering. As we show mercy to others, so they will extend the blessing to us in turn.

Ask yourself some revealing questions: *Do I sense the presence of the suffering Christ in others? Do I share their pain? Am I aware of their vulnerability? Do I know that the need for mercy is often hidden under a mask of self-sufficiency, coldness, and indifference?*

—From *Divine Guidance* by Susan Muto and Adrian Van Kaam

❧ Compassionate people often inspire others to be compassionate. I feel this way whenever I meditate on the life of Jesus. I marvel at how Jesus was so consistently compassionate when he met the ill, the grieving, the hungry, the oppressed. He is often described as being "deeply moved in spirit" or feeling compassion for the people. Jesus touched torn and tattered people with an amazing awareness of their woundedness. The vastness of his ability to love and be loved is phenomenal.

I've also been inspired by compassionate people in history such as Dorothy Day, Mahatma Ghandi, Etty Hillesum, Tom Dooley, Mother Teresa, and Albert Schweitzer. I was in awe as I read about the English spiritual writer, Caryll Houselander. Psychologists would bring their mentally and emotionally ill patients whom they could not cure to live with Caryll because they were astounded at the affect her compassionate presence had on them. Caryll accepted and loved the patients and this made a dramatic healing impact on their health.

When I look at the lives of compassionate people I see some common characteristics. They often have significant suffering or painful life events of their own, a generous heart, a non-blaming and non-judging mind, a passionate spirit, a willingness to sacrifice their life, a keen empathy, and a love that embraces the oneness of all creation.

I invite you to think about your teachers of compassion today. Who has taught you how to offer the cup of compassion to others?

—From *The Cup of Our Life* by Joyce Rupp

꙯ If there is one notion that is central to all great religions it is that of "compassion." The sacred scriptures of the Hindus, Buddhists, Moslems, Jews, and Christians all speak about God as the God of compassion. In a world in which competition continues to be the dominant mode of relating among people, be it in politics, sports, or economics, all true believers proclaim compassion, not competition, as God's way. . . .

Compassion, to be with others when and where they suffer and to willingly enter into a fellowship of the weak, is God's way to justice and peace among people. Is this possible? Yes, it is, but only when we dare to live with the radical faith that we do not have to compete for love, but that love is freely given to us by the One who calls us to compassion.

—From *Here and Now* by Henri J. M. Nouwen

   ❧ One of the few things John Wesley feared was the accumulation of wealth. As a biblical scholar and a practical theologian he was convinced that to follow Jesus Christ meant involvement with, and ministry among and to, the poor. This conviction led him to live on a modest income even when his writing was producing significant return. His solution was to give away all but the money he needed to buy the essentials.

This understanding of the relationship between following Christ and involvement with the poor led him to some unusual practices. It was not uncommon for him to beg in order to raise money for the poor. . . .

Not only did Wesley beg on behalf of the poor, he preached to them and found ways to be with them. His journal is filled with entries that describe his experiences of visiting the poor, the prisoner, the sorrowing and the suffering. The false stereotypes of the day were shattered as he came to work with and to know the poor and the needy of the world. Had he ignored God's urging to ministry with the poor he would have missed a large segment of the population that turned toward Christ through the Methodist movement. He would also have missed living and witnessing to a balanced faith that emphasized love for God and love for neighbor in very simple and practical ways.

—From *A Wesleyan Spiritual Reader* by Rueben P. Job

Nineteenth Sunday after Pentecost (Ordinary Time)
Sunday between September 25 and October 1

48: When Nothing Goes Our Way

Affirmation
For I, the LORD your God,
    hold your right hand;
it is I who say to you, "Do not fear,
    I will help you."

Do not fear, you worm Jacob,
    you insect Israel!
I will help you, says the LORD;
    your Redeemer is the Holy One
        of Israel (Isa. 41:13-14).

Petition
When nothing goes our way
Look at me, O God!
Do not remove your gaze from me,
Hold me near to you,
Lest I pass away and am no more.

Sacred Reading: anthology or other selected reading

Daily Scripture Readings

Sunday	A.	Exodus 17:1-7; Psalm 78:1-4, 12-16; Philippians 2:1-13; Matthew 21:23-32
	B.	Esther 7:1-6, 9-10; 9:20-22; Psalm 124; James 5:13-20; Mark 9:38-50
	C.	Jeremiah 32:1-3, 6-15; Psalm 91:1-6, 14-16; 1 Timothy 6:6-19; Luke 16:19-31
Monday		Mark 6:45-52
Tuesday		Acts 8:2-8
Wednesday		Acts 9:1-9
Thursday		Acts 27:13-26

| Friday | Philippians 1:12-14, 27-30 |
| Saturday | Matthew 14:22-33 |

Prayer: thanksgiving, petition, intercession, praise, and offering

Reflection: silent (listening to God), written (journaling)

God's Promise
But now thus says the LORD,
he who created you, O Jacob,
    he who formed you, O Israel:
Do not fear, for I have redeemed you;
    I have called you by name,
        you are mine.
When you pass through the waters, I will be with you;
    and through the rivers, they shall not
        overwhelm you;
when you walk through fire you shall not be burned,
    and the flame shall not consume you.
For I am the LORD your God,
    the Holy One of Israel, your Savior.
I give Egypt as your ransom,
    Ethiopia and Seba in exchange for you
        (Isa. 43:1-3).

My Response
Answer me quickly, O Lord; my spirit fails. Do not hide your face from me, or I shall be like those who go down to the pit. Let me hear of your steadfast love in the morning, for in you I put my trust. Teach me the way I should go, for to you I lift up my soul.

Readings for Reflection

❦ There are those times in our lives when nothing seems to go as we planned. Times when day after day we are faced with difficulties and darkness no matter how much we long for lighter loads and light for our pathway. There are other times when we come from a spectacular high moment and suddenly find ourselves hanging on to hope by our fingernails. While such a situation can be distressing, it is good to remember that we are not the first to experience darkness, difficulty, or disappointing surprises in the midst of faithful and sunny days.

Chapter 6 in Mark's Gospel reports the rejection Jesus encountered in his hometown, the first missionary venture of the twelve, the death of John the Baptist, feeding the five thousand, Jesus' walking on the water, and the healing in Gennesaret. In this one chapter we are confronted with the widest range of human emotion and experience, great miracles as well as great disappointment.

Our lives may be a bit steadier and the peaks and valleys a little more subdued than what Jesus and the twelve experienced. However, we do live through those periods when nothing seems to go our way, when the winds of life seem to be against us, when we are working hard but getting nowhere. So it was with the disciples as they strained at the oars against an adverse wind. Then Jesus appeared to them and uttered the words we all want to hear in the terror of our personal storm: "Take heart, it is I; do not be afraid" (Mark 6:50). The storm was over the moment Jesus was recognized by the disciples, and soon the men found themselves at their destination.

One of the best times for us to cultivate the nearness of God emerges when nothing is going our way. Such an experience may sharpen our ability to see God at work in our midst and in our lives. Remember that we are not alone when things are not going our way, as we are not alone when things are going our way. Each situation gives us opportunity to pay attention to God's presence and call for God's help.

—Rueben P. Job

❧ My first monastic Triduum [three days of prayer] occurred well over a decade ago. This Easter, it was I who preached the homily at the Resurrection Eucharist. What can one add to a liturgy that celebrates the resurrection promise into fact? I tried. The scripture for the day was simple enough: the story of two disciples running to a vacant tomb, then returning to their homes (John 20:1-10). For them, I suggested, the resurrection had not yet occurred—for when it does, one can never go home again. Even Judas could not escape the Easter event. He hanged himself. But tradition tells us that on Holy Saturday Jesus "descended into hell." This time it must have been Jesus who kissed Judas, repeating the same words as in the garden: "Friend, why are you here?" But this time they became a resurrection invitation to Judas: "Follow me." Jesus knows the way out, even out of hell. Together they walked, and all of creation walked with them—through the Red Sea to death's other side. If at Easter the slaughtered lamb becomes the Good Shepherd, then God's final word to everything must be "Yes!" (2 Cor. 1:19).
—From *A Season in the Desert* by W. Paul Jones

❧ Adam is one of the men who introduced me into the community of L'Arche Daybreak and led me into a whole spirituality of weakness which has transformed my life. Living together with Adam at L'Arche Daybreak has profoundly influenced my prayer, my sense of myself, my spirituality, and my ministry. Adam, the man who suffers from severe epilepsy, and whose life has seemingly been limited because of his many disabilities, has touched the lives of hundreds of L'Arche assistants, visitors, and friends. As my friend and housemate he has reached into the depths of my heart and has touched my life beyond words.
—From *Sabbatical Journey* by Henri J. M. Nouwen

❧ Just after I had fallen asleep at the Dayspring, Ann called and said, "Henri, Adam has died." Adam's life—

and mission—had come to its end. I thought of Jesus' words "It is fulfilled." Fifteen minutes later I was back at the hospital. Adam lay there, completely still, at peace. Rex and Jeanne and Ann were sitting beside the bed touching Adam's body. There were tears, tears of grief but also of gratitude. We held hands, and, while touching Adam's body, we prayed in thanksgiving for the thirty-four years of his life and for all that he had brought to us in his great physical weakness and incredible spiritual strength.

—From *Sabbatical Journey* by Henri J. M. Nouwen

☙ Joy does not come from positive predictions about the state of the world. It does not depend on the ups and downs of the circumstances of our lives. Joy is based on the spiritual knowledge that, while the world in which we live is shrouded in darkness, God has overcome the world. Jesus says it loudly and clearly: "In the world you will have troubles, but rejoice, I have overcome the world."

The surprise is not that, unexpectedly, things turn out better than expected. No, the real surprise is that God's light is more real than all the darkness, that God's truth is more powerful than all human lies, that God's love is stronger than death.

—From *Here and Now* by Henri J. M. Nouwen

☙ Our desire for equilibrium can become an idolatrous attempt to deny a large part of what life is about. The advertising industry achieves a good deal of its success through the message that if only we opt for this or that product, our needs and longings will be satisfied. We learn that life is not yet perfect, but we can fix it by obtaining the right house, floor polish, insurance policy, or therapy. In other words, we are encouraged to believe that there is something wrong with us if things are out of kilter and that life is meant to be lived on a plateau of happiness. The psalms give the lie to this kind of thinking by encouraging us to robustly deal with life as it really is and to find God in disorientation as well as harmony.

It is both a relief and a challenge to comprehend that there is no place where God is not. Psalm 139 speaks of the attempt to escape the Creator by soaring into the heavens, going into the depths, or sinking into the horizon where sea and sky meet. The sense that God is behind, in front, and above, laying a hand upon the one who feels searched out and known, makes the omnipresence of the Creator into a felt reality. I pray this psalm and I have to ask "Who am I? How can I respond to this all-encompassing presence of God?" In my time and place I am on holy ground, and as I allow myself to be held in that moment of awareness, I must respond with what is truly in my heart. I tell God that I am afraid, relieved, filled with gratitude, or over-whelmed by a sense of being invaded.

—From "Sing a New Song" by Elizabeth J. Canham in
Communion, Community, Commonweal

❧ The seasons of our life will condition our response to the God who encounters us in the psalms. Again, Psalm 139 is a good example. When I feel that I am in a precarious place, I will be relieved to know that God surrounds me, but when I am caught up in prideful ambition, I may wish that a distance could be placed between us. The psalm raises my awareness of what is going on for me at that moment and, in the process, puts me in touch with the Source of my life. It offers no magic "fix" but sets me to the task of figuring out the most appropriate response to the One who loved me into being. Often that response will be an invitation to change.

—From "Sing a New Song" by Elizabeth J. Canham in
Communion, Community, Commonweal

❧ In learning to accept the consequences of living as a Christian, most of us trip on the cracks and "fall flat on our face" once in a while. Fortunately we do not all have to experience that literally! We eventually learn that "for those who love God all things work together unto good," and we relax a bit. Until we repeatedly experience the truth of that statement, the words are only words we have heard, but as we struggle to ascend the "upgrades" in our lives and find that the view from the top of the mountain was well worth the effort, the words become conviction.

—From *Symbols of Inner Truth* by Carole Marie Kelly

❧ Any serious attempt to practice a simple but radical discipleship is certain to bring opposition today. We, as Wesley before us and as the saints before him, also know the struggle of internal and external opposition. In a time when division, violence, lust, and greed are the acclaimed way of life, the proclamation of the gospel of Jesus Christ and the attempt to live out that gospel will stir up opposition within and without.

—From *A Wesleyan Spiritual Reader* by Rueben P. Job

❧ God desires that we be abundantly fruitful and acts to help this happen. With enduring faithfulness and intimate knowledge of our capacities, the heavenly Vinedresser provides opportunities for us to shed the excess burdens that inhibit our full maturation in God's service. "Every branch that bears fruit he prunes to make it bear more fruit" (John 15:2). The Bible sometimes describes this process of intensive nurture using the image of a parent exercising constructive discipline with a child. The purpose is not to erase our uniqueness or subdue our vitality, but rather to give us a share in God's own holiness (Heb. 12:10) and thereby to become "fully-developed, complete, with nothing missing" (James 1:3, JB).

Pruning can certainly be uncomfortable. It strips us of what is non-essential to the power of God's life rising within us. But it also gathers and focuses energies previously dispersed in draining distractions or even apparently worthy commitments. Pruning concentrates the savor of the fruit we bear, for it proceeds from inward peace and promotes outward goodness. Therefore the effect of the Vinedresser's skilled hands is always a power of life greater than that which we would or could choose on our own.

—From "Editor's Introduction" by John S. Mogabgab in *Weavings* September/October 2001

Twentieth Sunday after Pentecost (Ordinary Time)
Sunday between October 2 and October 8

49: *When Jesus Slips Away*

Affirmation

Do not let your hearts be troubled. Believe in God, believe also in me. In my Father's house there are many dwelling places. If it were not so, would I have told you that I go to prepare a place for you? And if I go and prepare a place for you, I will come again and will take you to myself, so that where I am, there you may be also (John 14:1-3).

Petition

Make us worthy, Lord, to serve you and all the world's people who live and die in loneliness, hunger, poverty, and sickness. Give them through our hands this day their daily bread, and by our understanding love, give them peace and joy. Amen.

Sacred Reading: anthology or other selected reading

Daily Scripture Readings

Sunday	A.	Exodus 20:1-4, 7-9, 12-20; Psalm 19; Philippians 3:4-14; Matthew 21:33-46
	B.	Job 1:1; 2:1-10; Psalm 26; Hebrews 1:1-4; 2:5-12; Mark 10:2-16
	C.	Lamentations 1:1-6; Psalm 137; 2 Timothy 1:1-14; Luke 17:5-10
Monday		Luke 24:28-35
Tuesday		1 Thessalonians 1:2-10
Wednesday		Acts 1:6-11
Thursday		Mark 16:1-8
Friday		Psalm 105:1-6
Saturday		Psalm 90

Prayer: thanksgiving, petition, intercession, praise, and offering

Reflection: silent (listening to God), written (journaling)

God's Promise
Peace I leave with you; my peace I give to you. I do not give to you as the world gives. Do not let your hearts be troubled, and do not let them be afraid. You heard me say to you, "I am going away, and I am coming to you." If you loved me, you would rejoice that I am going to the Father, because the Father is greater than I (John 14:27-28).

My Response
His disciples said, "Yes, now you are speaking plainly, not in any figure of speech! Now we know that you know all things, and do not need to have anyone question you; by this we believe that you came from God" (John 16:29-30).

Readings for Reflection

✦ Many theologians declare that God cannot be absent from creation or creature without both ceasing to exist. Trying to convince the broken and empty-hearted of this truth is not an easy task. Why did the author of Psalms and Jesus feel forsaken and alone? The answer is not easy to find, especially for those who experience the absence of God more readily than they experience the presence of God. Jesus was able to move from that forsaken feeling to the confidence and trust of a child as he placed his life and his death fully in the care of God. And the resurrection becomes the final proof that God can be trusted.

Jesus' journey from that forsaken feeling to confident trust gives hope to us in our times of loneliness and fear of being forsaken. If the theologians are right and God never does forsake us, we can remind ourselves frequently of God's presence. Establishing a way of life that intentionally makes us present to God is one way of removing the feeling of God's absence. Regular times of daily prayer and regular times of corporate worship offer opportunities to establish a relationship of companionship with the One who made us and loves us.

If the theologians are wrong and God does indeed become distant and absent, our response will be the same as we call upon God to rescue us from our aloneness, confident that the One who always responds in love and wisdom will restore our sense of companionship. The biblical witness and the witness of the saints who have gone before us testify that God does not leave us alone. Even the apparent final absence of death is not a plunge into darkness but a movement into the light of ultimate companionship with God. So the words of Jesus become our own, "Father, into your hands I commend my spirit" (Luke 23:46).
—Rueben P. Job

❧ I am beginning now to see how radically the character of my spiritual journey will change when I no longer think of God as hiding out and making it as difficult as possible for me to find [God], but, instead, as the one who is looking for me while I am doing the hiding.
—From *The Return of the Prodigal Son* by Henri J. M. Nouwen

❧ We may say that there are three reasons for which this journey made by the soul to union with God is called night. The first has to do with the point from which the soul goes forth, for it has gradually to deprive itself of desire for all the worldly things which it possessed by denying them to itself; the which denial and deprivation are, as it were, night to all the senses of man. The second reason has to do with the mean, or the road along which the soul must travel to this union—that is, faith, which is likewise as dark as night to the understanding. The third has to do with the point to which it travels—namely, God, Who, equally, is dark night to the soul in this life. These three nights must pass through the soul—or, rather, the soul must pass through them—in order that it may come to Divine union with God.

—From *Ascent of Mount Carmel* by Saint John of the Cross

❧ These three parts of the night are all one night; but, after the manner of night, it has three parts. For the first part, which is that of sense, is comparable to the beginning of night, the point at which things begin to fade from sight. And the second part, which is faith, is comparable to midnight, which is total darkness. And the third part is like the close of night, which is God, the which part is now near to the light of day.

—From *Ascent of Mount Carmel* by Saint John of the Cross

❧ There is always a night shift and sooner or later we are put on it. The praise does not cease with the fading of the light, but goes on through the spiritual night as well as the spiritual day. And if you are picked for the night shift—well, praise the Lord. Lift up your hands in the dark sanctuary of your soul when you are tempted to wonder what is the good of it all, and praise the Lord! And *the Lord, maker of heaven and earth, will bless you from Zion.*

—From *The Fruits of the Spirit* by Evelyn Underhill

❧ We took him too much for granted. Perhaps we all take each other too much for granted. The routines of life distract us; our own pursuits make us oblivious; our anxieties and sorrows, unmindful. The beauties of the familiar go unremarked. We do not treasure each other enough.

[Eric] was a gift to us for twenty-five years. When the gift was finally snatched away, I realized how great it was. Then I could not tell him. An outpouring of letters arrived, many expressing appreciation for Eric. They all made me weep again: each word of praise a stab of loss.

How can I be thankful, in his gone-ness for what he was? I find I am. But the pain of the *no more* outweighs the gratitude of the *once was*. Will it always be so?

I didn't know how much I loved him until he was gone.

Is love like that?

—From *Lament for a Son* by Nicholas Wolterstorff

   ❧ How shall I call upon my God, my God and my Lord, when by the very act of calling upon him I would be calling him into myself? Is there any place within me into which my God might come? How should the God who made heaven and earth come into me? Is there any room in me for you, Lord, my God? Even heaven and earth, which you have made and in which you have made me -- can even they contain you? Since nothing that exists would exist without you, does it follow that whatever exists does in some way contain you? But if this is so, how can I, who am one of these existing things, ask you to come into me, when I would not exist at all unless you were already in me? Not yet am I in hell, after all, but even if I were, you would be there too; for if I descend to the underworld, you are there. No, my God, I would not exist, I would not be at all, were you not in me. Or should I say, rather, that I should not exist if I were not in you, from whom are all things, through whom are all things, in whom are all things? Yes, Lord, that is the truth, that is indeed the truth. To what place can I invite you, then, since I am in you? Or where could you come from, in order to come into me? To what place outside heaven and earth could I travel, so that my God could come to me there, the God who said, *I fill heaven and earth?*

—From *The Confessions* by Saint Augustine

๛ For many of us . . . the great and poignant challenge is precisely to see God on earth. . . . We labor to discern meaning in the mess of hectic days, to find God in the torque of stressful work, demanding family life, and complicated friendships. And when the days of travail are upon us, when suffering consumes our energy and despair spreads its unwelcome scent around us, how can we live faithfully before God in the chaos of God's apparent absence? Paul's image is apt: We see God on earth as if through a glass or mirror, but darkly (1 Cor. 13:12). It is not simply that what we are able to see is a mere reflection of the real thing. This reflection is also distorted, obscure, maddeningly enigmatic.

Jesus lived to its fullest our pained bewilderment. A terrible longing to see God surges through those shattering words the crucified Messiah recalled from the Psalter: "My God, my God, why have your forsaken me?" (Matt. 27:46; Ps. 22:1). This cry of desolation, unthinkable from him who so intimately knew God as "Abba," reveals how completely Jesus is one with us in our need to see God nearby when the mists of the incomprehensible or intolerable overtake us. But more is revealed in Jesus' anguish than his solidarity with suffering humanity. His darkening passage into death illumines with the intensity of a lightening bolt God's pledge to be unconditionally present for us. In that molten moment, the cross of God's most unbearable absence is also the cradle of God's most intense presence, the birthplace of a new creation. In this new creation, the One who chose to become one with us establishes the astonishing possibility of our becoming one with the risen Christ. By grace through faith, we may even share the mind of Christ (1 Cor. 2:16; Phil. 2:5) and therefore also begin to see life with the vision of Christ. As we experience a deepening participation in the mind of Christ, our capacity to see God on earth is expanded, although not without continued struggle.
—From "Editor's Introduction" by John S. Mogabgab in *Weavings* March/April 1998

Twenty-first Sunday after Pentecost (Ordinary Time)
Sunday between October 9 and October 15

50: Eating the Bread of Anxious Toil

Affirmation
Happy is everyone who fears the LORD,
  who walks in his ways.
You shall eat the fruit of the labor of your hands;
  you shall be happy, and it shall go well with you
    (Ps. 128:1-2).

Petition
Pray then in this way:
Our Father in heaven,
  hallowed be your name.
  Your kingdom come.
  Your will be done,
    on earth as it is in heaven.
  Give us this day our daily bread.
  And forgive us our debts,
    as we also have forgiven our debtors.
  And do not bring us to the time of trial,
    but rescue us from the evil one (Matt. 6:9-13).

Sacred Reading: anthology or other selected reading

Daily Scripture Readings

Sunday	A.	Exodus 32:1-14; Psalm 106:1-6, 19-23; Philippians 4:1-9; Matthew 22:1-14
	B.	Job 23:1-9, 16-17; Psalm 22:1-15; Hebrews 4:12-16; Mark 10:17-31
	C.	Jeremiah 29:1, 4-7; Psalm 66:1-12; 2 Timothy 2:8-15; Luke 17:11-19
Monday		Mark 8:14-21
Tuesday		Psalm 127:1-2
Wednesday		2 Corinthians 11:16-33

Thursday	John 6:25-34
Friday	Philippians 4:15-20
Saturday	Matthew 6:25-34

Prayer: thanksgiving, petition, intercession, praise, and offering

Reflection: silent (listening to God), written (journaling)

God's Promise
Do not worry about anything, but in everything by prayer and supplication with thanksgiving let your requests be made known to God. And the peace of God, which surpasses all understanding, will guard your hearts and your minds in Christ Jesus (Phil. 4:6-7).

My Response
The LORD is my shepherd, I shall not want.
  He makes me lie down in green pastures;
he leads me beside still waters. . . .

You prepare a table before me
  in the presence of my enemies;
you anoint my head with oil;
  my cup overflows.
Surely goodness and mercy shall follow me
  all the days of my life,
and I shall dwell in the house of the LORD
  my whole life long (Ps. 23:1-2, 5-6).

Readings for Reflection

ॐ I didn't want it to happen but it did. Before I knew it, anxiety found its way into my restless heart and robbed me of the peace promised to all who place their trust in God. Ah, so that is the reason for my anxious heart: I forgot to trust in God!

Many demands upon our time and many opportunities waiting to be explored often fill our lives too full

with activities and distractions. When this happens it is not surprising that we grow anxious and lose our sense of peace and tranquility. Today remember that God and God alone is able to care for all that exists; we can trust our smallest and largest concern to the wisdom and love of God. Peace, hope, calm, and joy are the fruits of placing our confidence in God. May these gifts be yours in abundance.
—Rueben P. Job

❧ As we grow older, we tend to become control freaks. We need to control everybody and everything, moment by moment, to be happy. If the now has never been full or sufficient, we will always be grasping, even addictive or obsessive. If you're pushing yourself and others around, you have not yet found the secret of happiness. It's okay as it is. This moment is as perfect as it can be. The saints called it the "sacrament of the present moment."
—From *Everything Belongs* by Richard Rohr

❧ When the Master invited the Governor to practice meditation and the Governor said he was too busy, this is the reply he got: "You put me in mind of a man walking blindfolded into the jungle—and being too busy to take the blindfold off."
   When the Governor pleaded lack of time, the Master said, "It is a mistake to think that meditation cannot be practiced for lack of time. The real reason is agitation of the mind."
—From *Taking Flight* by Anthony de Mello

❧ How often people today cry out in exasperation or despair, "I just don't have enough time!" There is so much to do: earn a living, fulfill a vocation, nurture relationships, care for dependents, exercise, clean the house. Moreover, we hope to maintain sanity while doing all this, and to keep growing as faithful and loving people at the same time. We are finite, and the demands seem too great, the time too short. . . .

Puritan Sabbath keepers agreed that "good Sabbaths make good Christians." They meant that regular, disciplined attention to the spiritual life was the foundation of faithfulness. Another dimension of the saying opens up if we imagine a worshiping community helping one another step off the treadmill of work-and-spend and into the circle of glad gratitude for the gifts of God. Taken this way, good Sabbaths make good Christians by regularly reminding us of God's creative, liberating, and redeeming presence, not only in words but also through a practice we do together in response to that presence.

—From "Keeping Sabbath" by Dorothy C. Bass in *Practicing Our Faith*

❧ [One] reason we have difficulty praying is that we are unable to quiet down enough to become sensitive to the movements of the Spirit. This usually happens because we have been living our lives at too fast a pace. Rushing from one activity to the next, we lose touch with the Spirit. We are not moving against the Spirit in a sinful way, but we are not allowing the Spirit to infuse our activities, enabling us to perform them in peace and joy. Finding ourselves anxious and worried both about the result of our work and about getting it all finished within the allotted time, we come to prayer restless and find it almost impossible to quiet our minds in a way that allows us to be sensitive to the movements of the Spirit. Since we cannot allow the Spirit to bring us to the Lord, we begin composing our own monologue to the Lord, expressing our own needs and concerns, often in a rushed and rather compulsive way. It often seems that we could be using our time more effectively by skipping prayer and finishing the work we left undone. Prayer will remain difficult until we develop a rhythm of life that enables us to work in tune with the Spirit, thus experiencing the peace and joy that flows from the Spirit's presence. If we are living

in tune with the Spirit during the day, it is easy to allow the Spirit to unite us to the Lord during prayer.
—From *In His Spirit* by Richard J. Hauser

❧ If I am not at home with myself I won't feel at home anywhere else. It is such a delight to come home to myself, to become my own friend. I experienced this kind of homecoming once when I was living alone. Under the guise of ministering to others I had become alienated from myself. In my everyday maddening ministerial rush I suddenly discovered myself eating on the run—grabbing a sandwich and eating it while standing up or going out the door. The violence of this great irreverence to myself suddenly occurred to me. I was not at home with myself. It took a while to slow down, but I was finally able to make a decision to spend time with myself. I began to experience the joy of being with *me*. I put a flower on the table, lit a candle, turned on soft music, ate slowly. I learned the joy of simply being with myself without rushing. It was like taking myself out to dinner. It was a kind of coming home to myself. When you can lovingly be present to yourself, your presence to others takes on a deeper quality also.
—From *A Tree Full of Angels* by Macrina Wiederkehr

❧ It is one of the great insights of religion that only God is worthy of the best in one's treasure house and the best in one's treasure house is not worthy. . . . The urge to share as an offering of the heart that which has deepest meaning is at bottom the hunger for God. It is deep calling unto deep. Offerings may be made to other human beings. . . . But such offerings do not satisfy, nor do they bring peace to the spirit. . . . [O]nly when the offering is seen as being made to the Highest, to God, however crude may be the altar upon which it rests, is the deep need in us all satisfied and our spirits come into the great Peace.
—From *The Mood of Christmas* by Howard Thurman

⋅ The action of those whose lives are given to the Spirit has in it something of the leisure of Eternity; and because of this, they achieve far more than those whose lives are enslaved by the rush and hurry, the unceasing tick-tick of the world. In the spiritual life it is very important to get our timing right. Otherwise we tend to forget that God, Who is greater than our heart, is greater than our job too. It is only when we have learnt all that this means that we possess the key to the Kingdom of Heaven.

—From *The Spiritual Life* by Evelyn Underhill

⋅ *The government shall be upon his shoulder* (Isa. 9:6). You are tired, and driven, and worried, and weak, and ill, and depressed, because you have been trying to carry the government upon your own shoulder; the burden is too much for you, and you have broken down under it.

—From *Power Through Constructive Thinking* by Emmet Fox

Twenty-second Sunday after Pentecost (Ordinary Time)
Sunday between October 16 and October 22

51: What Are You Looking For?

Affirmation
The next day John again was standing with two of his disciples, and as he watched Jesus walk by, he exclaimed, "Look, here is the Lamb of God!" The two disciples heard him say this, and they followed Jesus. When Jesus turned and saw them following, he said to them, "What are you looking for?" They said to him, "Rabbi" (which translated means Teacher), "where are you staying?" He said to them, "Come and see." They came and saw where he was staying, and they remained with him that day. It was about four o'clock in the afternoon (John 1:35-39).

Petition
Jesus said to him, "If you are able!—All things can be done for the one who believes." Immediately the father of the child cried out, "I believe; help my unbelief!" (Mark 9:23-24).

Sacred Reading: anthology or other selected reading

Daily Scripture Readings

Sunday	A.	Exodus 33:12-23; Psalm 99; 1 Thessalonians 1:1-10; Matthew 22:15-22
	B.	Job 38:1-7; Psalm 104:1-9, 24, 35; Hebrews 5:1-10; Mark 10:35-45
	C.	Jeremiah 31:27-34; Psalm 119:97-104; 2 Timothy 3:14–4:5; Luke 18:1-8
Monday		John 12:20-26
Tuesday		Acts 1:6-11
Wednesday		Isaiah 51:1-8
Thursday		John 1:35-42

Friday	Hebrews 11:8-12
Saturday	1 John 3:1-3

Prayer: thanksgiving, petition, intercession, praise, and offering

Reflection: silent (listening to God), written (journaling)

God's Promise
Jesus answered, "Do you believe because I told you that I saw you under the fig tree? You will see greater things than these." And he said to [Nathanael], "Very truly, I tell you, you will see heaven opened and the angels of God ascending and descending upon the Son of Man" (John 1:50-51).

My Response
[Andrew] first found his brother Simon and said to him, "We have found the Messiah" (which is translated Anointed). He brought Simon to Jesus, who looked at him and said, "You are Simon son of John. You are to be called Cephas" (which is translated Peter) (John 1:41-42).

Readings for Reflection

❧ What has your attention at this very moment? This reading? Perhaps, but we all know that we can give modest attention to several things at once. We eat, read, and listen for the phone all at the same time. When our search for something consumes all our energy and all our faculties, everything else fades away and disappears. Even a ringing phone goes unanswered when we are seeking to give answer to another call deep within. What are you searching for that consumes all your energy and attention? The quest for God is a search worthy of such all-consuming passion and energy. The biblical record indicates that such a search is always generously rewarded.

Jesus asked two of John's disciples (John 1:38) what they were looking for and invited them to come and see where and how he lived. The desire to know and be near to God has been placed within as an invitation to a lifelong quest for companionship with the divine. And yet, from personal experience we know that sometimes we look in all the wrong places. These disciples of Jesus were invited to continue their search where Jesus was and not where he was not. Our directions are certainly as plain as theirs are.

What are you looking for today and where will your search be successful? The quest for God is always successful when carried out where God is to be found. Where shall we begin the search? The deep inner rooms of our own soul, sacred scriptures, the book of history, current events, the lives of the saints, the poor and oppressed seeking our compassion, and the creation itself offer places where God has been most readily found in the past. Today pay attention to what has your undivided attention and follow the clues to a closer walk with God.

—Rueben P. Job

  ✸ True mystics are not necessarily those who have visions, but rather those who have vision. They see the extraordinary, the mystical, in everyday events. If we desire such vision, we will have to give our brains a bath! Our minds must be cleansed of prejudgments about what God looks like. We will have to take a brush and scrub away all those grade school pictures of God and erase all the statements made by saints about their experience of the Divine Mystery. Only then can we begin to see the true picture.

—From *In Pursuit of the Great White Rabbit* by Edward Hays

  ✸ But neither let it trouble your understanding, that we see the unrighteous having riches and the servants of God straitened. Let us therefore, brethren and sisters, be believing: we are striving in the contest of the living God, we are exercised by the present life, in order that we may be crowned by that to come. No one of the righteous received fruit speedily, but awaiteth it. For if God gave shortly the recompense of the righteous, straightway we would be exercising ourselves in business, not in godliness; for we would seem to be righteous while pursuing not what is godly but what is gainful. And on this account Divine judgment surprised a spirit that was not righteous, and loaded it with chains.

—From "The Second Epistle of Clement"

⊰ You will think, Sisters, that since so much has been said about this spiritual path it will be impossible for anything more to be said. Such a thought would be very foolish. Since the greatness of God is without limits, [God's] works are too. Who will finish telling of [God's] mercies and grandeurs? To do so is impossible, and thus do not be surprised at what was said, and will be said, because it is but a naught in comparison to what there is to tell of God. [God] grants us a great favor in having communicated these things to a person through whom we can know about [God]. Thus the more we know about [God's] communication to creatures the more we will praise [God's] grandeur and make the effort to have esteem for souls in which the Lord delights so much. Each of us has a soul, but since we do not prize souls as is deserved by creatures made in the image of God we do not understand the deep secrets that lie in them.

—From *The Interior Castle* by Teresa of Avila

⊰ There are some who resign themselves, but they attach conditions to it. They do not trust in God completely, so they take pains to provide for themselves just in case. Some offer everything at first, but later, beaten down by temptations, they go back to their old ways and thus make little progress in virtue. People like these will not gain the true freedom of a pure heart nor the grace of a joyful intimacy with me unless they surrender themselves unconditionally and offer themselves as a sacrifice to me each day. Without this total self-surrender a joyful union between us cannot exist, either now or ever.

—From *The Imitation of Christ* by Thomas à Kempis

❧ Who then is a wise [one], and endued with knowledge among you? Let [this person] resolve this day, this hour, this moment, the Lord assisting, to choose in all the preceding particulars the "more excellent way": And let [this one] steadily keep it, both with regard to sleep, prayer, work, food, conversation, and diversions; and particularly with regard to the employment of that important talent, money; let *your* heart answer to the call of God, "From this moment, God being my helper, I will lay up no more treasure upon earth: This one thing I will do, I will lay up treasure in heaven; I will render unto God the things that are God's: . . . all my goods, and all my heart."

—From "Sermon 89" by John Wesley

❧ For a Christian, an economic system is a means to an end—a mechanism for exchanging goods and services. . . . nothing more. We steer our lives by a higher value—the love ethic of Jesus. Central to our bearing the cross is our acceptance of Jesus' love and our attentiveness to the needs of others. Love, not mammon, must be our guiding light.

Each of us can choose to change out of aspiration rather than desperation. We have the choice to live our faith. But living our faith will require "righteousness," that is, a genuine relationship with God. Compassion will be our guiding light, our rule in life. Justice will lead us to faithful stewardship—to care for and work on behalf of others in the global community. Shalom will be our reward.

—From *Climbing the Sycamore Tree* by Ann Hagmann

✌ My dear friend, abandon yourself, and you will find me. Give up your will and every title to yourself, and you will always come out ahead, for greater grace will be yours the moment you turn yourself over to me once and for all.

—From *The Imitation of Christ* by Thomas à Kempis

✌ If we are to experience God, we must be open to God, to the mystical, to the divine, appearing in our lives. And we must have an openness that is free of any preconditions about *how* that will happen. Looking for God in a godly form is the great historical mistake.

—From *In Pursuit of the Great White Rabbit* by Edward Hays

52: *Choose Life*

Affirmation

He called the crowd with his disciples, and said to them, "If any want to become my followers, let them deny themselves and take up their cross and follow me. For those who want to save their life will lose it, and those who lose their life for my sake, and for the sake of the gospel, will save it. For what will it profit them to gain the whole world and forfeit their life? Indeed, what can they give in return for their life?" (Mark 8:34-37).

Petition

Incline your ear, O LORD, and answer me,
    for I am poor and needy.
Preserve my life, for I am devoted to you;
    save your servant who trusts in you.
You are my God; be gracious to me, O Lord,
    for to you do I cry all day long.
Gladden the soul of your servant,
    for to you, O Lord, I lift up my soul (Ps. 86:1-4).

Sacred Reading: anthology or other selected reading

Daily Scripture Readings

Sunday	A.	Deuteronomy 34:1-12; Psalm 90:1-6, 13-17; 1 Thessalonians 2:1-8; Matthew 22:34-46
	B.	Job 42:1-6, 10-17; Psalm 34:1-8; Hebrews 7:23-28; Mark 10:46-52
	C.	Joel 2:23-32; Psalm 65; 2 Timothy 4:6-8, 16-18; Luke 18:9-14
Monday		Matthew 10:34-39

Tuesday	Deuteronomy 30:15-20
Wednesday	Proverbs 8:32-36
Thursday	Romans 6:12-14
Friday	John 3:31-36
Saturday	John 6:35-40

Prayer: thanksgiving, petition, intercession, praise, and offering

Reflection: silent (listening to God), written (journaling)

God's Promise
Above all else, guard your heart,
    for it is the wellspring of life . . . (Prov. 4:23, NIV).

My Response
Teach me your way, O LORD,
    that I may walk in your truth;
    give me an undivided heart to revere your name.
I give thanks to you, O Lord my God, with my whole heart,
    and I will glorify your name forever (Ps. 86:11-13).

Readings for Reflection

❧ Choosing life seems like the reasonable thing to do. If given the choice why would anyone not choose life? It seems foolish to choose anything else, to choose anything less than the best. It remains a mystery to me that we often find ourselves choosing what diminishes life and leaves us less than we were before. But we are often unaware of the consequences of our choices until later, sometimes much later.

Jesus always invites us to choose life by forsaking our way of life for his way of life. It is never an easy choice. Choosing to walk with Jesus in a culture that ridicules faithfulness and glorifies violence is to choose a way with cost attached. When you choose to walk with Jesus in a culture that rewards those who take for themselves before thinking about others, you may end up feeling someone has taken advantage of you. And yet, as the decades pass and we look back, it is clear to see that those who sought advantage by taking advantage have in reality lost life. Those who chose to walk with Jesus in the hard decisions and in the good times have discovered richness to life beyond price. At times it may seem that the cost of choosing life is too high, but when you stop and think about it, choosing life is the only reasonable choice to make.

—Rueben P. Job

❧ Spirituality is about seeing. It's not about earning or achieving. It's about relationship rather than results or requirements. Once you see, the rest follows. You don't need to push the river, because you are in it. The life is lived within us, and we learn how to say yes to that life.

—From *Everything Belongs* by Richard Rohr

❧ What, pray, do you know about dragonflies?
Or what happens when they die?
Yes, what happens when the gazelle expires in the desert after running for miles to escape the jackal?
What happens when a flower withers?
When the lamb enters its death agony under the butcher's knife?
What do you know about it?
What if, at that moment, there were high festival?
What if pain turned into joy?
What if death became life, more life, all life?
This is the only mystery I have left you with in creation; why do you take it so amiss?
It was certainly a cruel thing for human beings to have crucified Jesus and you might well reproach God for having stayed silent over the tragedy of Calvary, and yet . . . Have you experienced the resurrection?
Have you made the transit from the visible to the invisible, to see what happens?
Certainly, if everything ended with death whether

for the dragonfly or for the grass of the field or for my son Jesus, you would be right, but . . .

It isn't like that.

Life goes on.

It not only goes on, it develops, grows, matures.

Life is eternal and you haven't seen the best of it: the kingdom.

—From *And God Saw That It Was Good* by Carlo Carretto

❧ I know that many wiser and better Christians than I in these days do not like to mention heaven and hell even in a pulpit. I know, too, that nearly all the references to this subject in the New Testament come from a single source. But then that source is our Lord himself. People will tell you it is St. Paul, but that is untrue. These overwhelming doctrines are dominical. They are not really removable from the teaching of Christ or of his Church. If we do not believe them, our presence in this church is great tomfoolery. If we do, we must sometime overcome our spiritual prudery and mention them.

—From *Fern-Seed and Elephants* by C. S. Lewis

❧ Wait a little, my soul, wait for the divine promise, and you will have more than enough of all good things in heaven. If your appetite for present things is excessive you may lose eternal and heavenly ones. Use the things of the world, but long for the things of eternity. You cannot be fully satisfied by material possessions, for you are simply not made to enjoy them. Even if you owned every good thing in the world you would not be happy and blessed, for your blessedness and joy is in God, who created all those things. Your happiness is not in what is seen and admired by others but in what the good and faithful followers of Christ seek. Your happiness is in what the spiritual and pure of heart, those whose citizenship is in heaven, sometimes experience in this life, though it is meant for the next.

—From *The Imitation of Christ* by Thomas à Kempis

꙳ O for a spark of heavenly fire,
From the Redeemer's throne,
The pure and permanent desire
Of loving [God] alone!

The pure desire unquenchable
Ev'n now I *seem* to prove,
But only Thou, my God, canst tell
If Thee I *wish* to love.

Vouchsafe me then the wish sincere,
The wish sincere fulfil,
And stamp me with thy character
According to thy will:

Accomplish'd see thine own desires,
And O! be satisfied,
When singing with th'immortal quires
I triumph at thy side.
—From *The Unpublished Poetry of Charles Wesley*, Vol. 3

꙳ To the degree that we Christians surrender ourselves freely to the leadership of Jesus Christ through the mystical oneness we enjoy with him and in him, to that degree we can say we are Christians, living members of his body. We will know experientially that we live in his light by the gentle love we have toward each person whom we meet in each moment.

Thus we will be led from moment to moment into greater light as we see, by increased faith, hope and love, God's loving presence in all events. Complete abandonment and childlike trust are the Holy Spirit's gifts to those who are ready to die to their false selves and begin to live in the truth of the new creatures that they are and have always been in the eyes of the heavenly Father.

—From *In Jesus We Trust* by George A. Maloney

ॐ God is, above all else, a being of immense beauty. It is this beauty that continues to draw us and enfold us in eternal goodness. This mysterious Beloved is forever wooing us, longing for us to be totally immersed in love of the purest kind. As I look at my life, I count as my greatest blessing the gift of God's own essence. Being able to know this wondrous God of beauty, being embraced and welcomed home time and again, all of this is truly powerful.

I see this immense goodness of God reflected in every variety of people and in all the facets of the universe that sing out the goodness of the Creator. Each one mirrors the essence of God's beauty. Each one is a vessel filled with manifestations of the Creator. I know this beauty, also, within myself, in the silent encounters deep within my own being. Every once in awhile, each of us senses, for a moment, this rare blessing of the touch of God. Brief as it is, it is enough to remind us that there is an underlying harmony beneath all the chaos. There is an eternal beauty giving a loving texture to all of life.

—From *The Cup of Our Life* by Joyce Rupp

ॐ But after Paul, in consequence of his appeal to Caesar, had been sent to Rome by Festus, the Jews, being frustrated in their hope of entrapping him by the snares which they had laid for him, turned against James, the brother of the Lord, to whom the episcopal seat at Jerusalem had been entrusted by the apostles. The following daring measures were undertaken by them against him. Leading him into their midst they demanded of him that he should renounce faith in Christ in the presence of all the people. But, contrary to the opinion of all, and with a clear voice, and with greater boldness than they had anticipated, he spoke out before the whole multitude and confessed that our Savior and Lord Jesus is the Son of God. But they were unable to bear longer the testimony of the man who, on account of the excellence of ascetic virtue and of piety which he exhibited in his life, was esteemed by all as the most just of [persons], and consequently they slew him. Opportunity for this deed of violence was furnished by the prevailing anarchy, which was caused by the fact that Festus had died just at this time in Judea, and that the province was thus without a governor and head.

—From "The Martyrdom of James" by Eusebius

  ▸ "It's time," announced the Other One.

"I know," responded the man. "Could you explain the choice to me again?"

"Of course," said the Other One. "I will write one thing in the dust and one thing only. I will write whatever you ask me to write, and whatever it is it will become a part of your life. You may ask for anything: any knowledge, any virtue, any gift, any hope, any dream, any grace, any possession, anything. I will write it in the dust, and it will become a part of you and your life.". . .

Everything good he could think of to ask for was incomplete and flawed in some way. While each choice fulfilled one hope or dream, it left some other hope or dream unprotected and potentially unfulfilled. That was why he had been sitting there for so long.

"It's time," the Other One reminded him again.

"I know," replied the man. "I know."

"What shall I write in your dust?"

The man took a deep breath. He was ready to make his decision.

"Your Name," he declared to the Other One. "Write your Name in my dust."

Suddenly it seemed as if light and song surrounded them as the Other One moved a single finger toward the tabletop.

—From *The Carpenter and the Unbuilder* by David M. Griebner

* "The Lord is near to brokenhearted, and saves the crushed in spirit" (Ps. 34:18).

"Religion's for old people," my buddy declared as we drove through the countryside. I found his comment a little insulting: I was a churchgoer, age nineteen. Was that so wrong? I lost touch with him; now it's been twenty-five years since we've spoken. But he was on to something. At twenty, the road looks clear all the way to forever. We arrogantly waste time, try a hundred new jobs or relationships or ideologies, believe any fool thing. The heart is not yet broken, not in the way it is when time crashes down on it—soured dreams, career missteps, divorce, illness, the death of loved ones, the passing of so much we love. By old age the ghostly procession of the once-was can be unbearable.

My heroes include any elderly persons who keep the flame lit, who still feel inspiration and outrage at ideas, current events, history, movies, books, national tragedies, spring flowers, the passing parade. Somehow they take it all in. Life enlarges their spirit, becomes fuel for the remaining journey, seasoned with humor, not bitterness. They age with dignity. Part of the dignity is keeping the inevitable heartbreak framed by larger perspectives and by going deeper into the grief, not denying it.

—From *A Turbulent Peace* by Ray Waddle

Twenty-fourth Sunday after Pentecost (Ordinary Time)
Sunday between October 30 and November 5

53: From Doubt to Belief

Affirmation
Take care, brothers and sisters, that none of you may
have an evil, unbelieving heart that turns away from the
living God. But exhort one another every day, as long
as it is called "today," so that none of you may be hard-
ened by the deceitfulness of sin. For we have become
partners of Christ, if only we hold our first confidence
firm to the end (Heb. 3:12-14).

Petition
Jesus said to him, "All things can be done for the one
who believes." Immediately the father of the child cried
out, "I believe; help my unbelief!" (Mark 9:23-24).

Sacred Reading: anthology or other selected reading

Daily Scripture Readings

Sunday	A.	Joshua 3:7-17; Psalm 107:1-7, 33-37; 1 Thessalonians 2:9-13; Matthew 23:1-12
	B.	Ruth 1:1-18; Psalm 146; Hebrews 9:11-14; Mark 12:28-34
	C.	Habakkuk 1:1-4; 2:1-4; Psalm 119:137-144; 2 Thessalonians 1:1-4, 11-12; Luke 19:1-10
Monday		John 20:24-28
Tuesday		John 10:22-30
Wednesday		John 10:31-42
Thursday		Mark 11:20-25
Friday		Matthew 14:22-33
Saturday		John 1:10-13

Prayer: thanksgiving, petition, intercession, praise,
and offering

Reflection: silent (listening to God), written (journaling)

God's Promise
Then Jesus said to his disciples, "Truly I tell you, it will be hard for a rich person to enter the kingdom of heaven. Again I tell you, it is easier for a camel to go through the eye of a needle than for someone who is rich to enter the kingdom of God." When the disciples heard this, they were greatly astounded and said, "Then who can be saved?" But Jesus looked at them and said, "For mortals it is impossible, but for God all things are possible" (Matt. 19:23-26).

My Response
[The woman said], "He told me everything I have ever done." So when the Samaritans came to him, they asked him to stay with them; and he stayed there two days. And many more believed because of his word. They said to the woman, "It is no longer because of what you said that we believe, for we have heard for ourselves, and we know that this is truly the Savior of the world" (John 4:39-42).

Readings for Reflection

⌘ We move away from doubt at our own pace and with our own set of doubts and beliefs to master. While our first step is a matter of belief and ultimate trust in God, there are many other and some even more diffi-cult steps to take in our movement from doubt to belief.

One step along this journey that causes many peo-ple to stop and struggle is the step of actually believ-ing God loves them and that they can be lovable in God's sight. This more than any other step along the journey makes men and women, young and old, stum-ble and fall from faith to doubt. Why is it so hard for us to believe that God's love really is unconditional and that we should imitate God's love not only for others but also for ourselves?

Perhaps we have regarded self-centered behavior too harshly. We are unwilling or unable to give ourselves the same gentle grace that God offers us and that we believe should be offered to others. Leap from doubt to belief and remember that God loves you, delights in you, and yearns for your response of faith in God and in God's creation.
—Rueben P. Job

෴ Faith is such a necessary virtue: unless you teach your moods "where they get off," you can never be either a sound Christian or even a sound atheist, but just a creature dithering to and fro, with its beliefs really dependent on the weather and the state of its digestion. Consequently one must train the habit of Faith.

The first step is to recognize the fact that your moods change. The next is to make sure that, if you have once accepted Christianity, then some of its main doctrines shall be deliberately held before your mind for some time every day.
—From *Mere Christianity* by C. S. Lewis

෴ You called, shouted, broke through my deafness;
you flared, blazed, banished my blindness;
you lavished your fragrance, I gasped,
    and now I pant for you;
I tasted you, and I hunger and thirst;
you touched me, and I burned for your peace.
—From *The Confessions* by Saint Augustine

෴ I have always marveled at how plants unconsciously seek the light and warmth of the sun and how persons unconsciously seek the light and warmth of God's Love. As persons, we do this at the level both of our roots and of our fruits—at a level of both our being and our doing. When we become aware that our roots have been reaching for God all along and that God's Love has been sustaining us throughout, we begin consciously and willingly turning inward toward God in

prayer. This moment of prayerful turning marks a major conversion in our life and growth as persons.
—From *The Art of Passingover* by Francis Dorff

❧ Faith is not belief in an afterlife based on today's moral litmus test. To the contemplative "bad" and "good" make no matter. Each has the capacity to become the other. Out of bad much good has come. It is often sin that unmasks us to ourselves and opens the way for growth. Mature virtue is tried virtue, not virtue unassailed. Great good, on the other hand, whatever its effects, has so often deteriorated into arrogance, into a righteousness that vitiates its own rightness. But both of them, both bad and good, lived in the light of God, blanch, are reduced to size in the face of the Life that transcends them.
—From *Illuminated Life* by Joan Chittister

❧ Life is not a game we win, and God is not a trophy we merit. No matter how "good" we are, we are not good enough for God. On the other hand, no matter how "bad" we are, we can never be outside of God. We can only hope in each instance to come to such a consciousness of God that no lesser gods can capture our attention and no trifling, self-centered gods can keep us from the fullness of awareness that is the full-ness of Life. It is the project of life, this coming to Wholeness, this experience of Purpose beyond all pur-poses, this identification with everything that is.
—From *Illuminated Life* by Joan Chittister

❧ Life, the contemplative knows, is a process. It is not that all the elements of life, mundane as they may be, do not matter. On the contrary, to the contemplative everything matters. Everything speaks of God, and God is both in and beyond everything.

Having the faith to take life one piece at a time—to live it in the knowledge that there is something of God in this for me now, here, at this moment—is of the essence of happiness. It is not that God is a black box full of tests and trials and treats. It is that life is a step on the way to a God who goes the way with us. However far, however perilous.

—From *Illuminated Life* by Joan Chittister

❧ Love without trust has no foundation and will not last unless it is compassionate, merciful love. Compassionate love is given for someone simply because that person is in need. It is God's life-giving love: *agape*, expecting nothing in return. It is not a covenantal relationship in which both parties commit to each other.

Trust without love may simply be admiration or dependency. It receives without an impulse to give back. It does not offer itself in response. It has no cost. It is not a part of covenant or commitment.

When Luther pledged his heart in trust, it was to the one to whom he owed his life, to the Lord of goodness and grace who had captured his heart. It was a response to the one who claims each one of us, not because we deserve it, but simply because we are cherished.

—From *Faith, the Yes of the Heart* by Grace Adolphsen Brame

❧ At four in the afternoon I came to Oxford, and to a small company in the evening explained the nature and extent of that salvation wherewith, "by grace we are saved through faith." The next evening I showed, what it is to believe; as well as, more largely, what are the fruits of true believing; from those words of the Apostle, "This is the victory that overcometh the world, even our faith."

—From "Journal, Nov. 12, 1739" by John Wesley

❧ After we had wandered many years in the *new path*, of salvation by *faith and works*; about two years ago it pleased God to show us the *old way*, of salvation by *faith only*. And many soon tasted of this salvation, "being justified freely, having peace with God, rejoicing in hope of the glory of God," and having his "love shed abroad in their hearts." These now ran the way of his commandments: They performed all their duty to God and man. They walked in all the ordinances of the Lord; and through these means, which he had appointed for that end, received daily grace to help in time of need, and went on from faith to faith.

—From "Journal, June 22, 1740" by John Wesley

❧ The more healing I experience, the more I understand one of the most magnificent truths of the Christian faith: God can turn our worst pain into the source of our giftedness. It is no accident that my life's work involves helping people invite Jesus into the worst moments of their lives.

—From *Ashes Transformed* by Tilda Norberg

54: *Claim Your Inheritance*

Affirmation

So if you have been raised with Christ, seek the things
that are above, where Christ is, seated at the right hand
of God. Set your minds on things that are above, not on
things that are on earth, for you have died, and your life
is hidden with Christ in God. When Christ who is your
life is revealed, then you also will be revealed with him
in glory (Col. 3:1-4).

Petition

O God, plead my cause and redeem me;
   give me life according to your promise
      (Ps. 119:154).

Sacred Reading: anthology or other selected reading

Daily Scripture Readings

Sunday:	A.	Joshua 24:1-3, 14-25; Psalm 78:1-7; 1 Thessalonians 4:13-18; Matthew 25:1-13
	B.	Ruth 3:1-5; Psalm 127; Hebrews 9:24-28; Mark 12:38-44
	C.	Haggai 1:15–2:9; Psalm 98; 2 Thessalonians 2:1-5, 13-17; Luke 20:27-38
Monday		Matthew 6:25-34
Tuesday		Luke 12:32-34
Wednesday		Acts 20:31-38
Thursday		Ephesians 1:3-14
Friday		1 Thessalonians 4:1-12
Saturday		Luke 10:25-37

Prayer: thanksgiving, petition, intercession, praise,
and offering

Reflection: silent (listening to God), written (journaling)

God's Promise
Ask of me, and I will make the nations your heritage,
   and the ends of the earth your possession (Ps. 2:8).

My Response
Let me abide in your tent forever,
   find refuge under the shelter of your wings.
For you, O God, have heard my vows;
   you have given me the heritage of those who fear
   your name (Ps. 61:4-5).

Readings for Reflection

❧ We would be very upset with millionaires who lived in life-robbing poverty because of ignorance or personal choice. We would be very disappointed in someone who had enormous wealth but refused to spend any of it for even the simple resources to sustain life. Why then are we not outraged about Christians by the millions who live as though God were dead and God's grace were exhausted? Could it be because we live that way so often ourselves?

The good news we share with one another is the gospel's declaration that no matter where we are in life, we are the recipients of God's limitless grace. We can have peace, joy, assurance, comfort, hope, tranquillity, confidence, and companionship with our Creator and beyond that, life eternal. With a life bank full of such gifts we are indeed rich. And yet, so often I permit myself to slip into poverty thinking and poverty living. I feel anxious, alone, fearful, faithless, without joy, and sometimes without hope. I feel this way because I have forgotten and lost grip on the inheritance that God gives me anew every morning.

Many of us live in spiritual poverty because we have forgotten who we are as God's children and who God is as our loving and almighty Creator. The fact that

you are reading these words suggests that you are reaching out even now to claim your full inheritance as a child of God. May God grant grace and wisdom to do so more and more today and every day of your life. Claim your inheritance and live as God's beloved child today.
—Rueben P. Job

ȝ♦ We talk about God in the third person. We teach about God. However, we don't teach about our spouses or about good friends. We introduce them, not teach about them. Too often we relate to God as a myth or a theorem to be talked about and not as a friend.
—Norman Shawchuck

ȝ♦ Jesus invited Peter and his brother, Andrew, to forsake their business in order to string along with him, and "immediately they left their nets and followed him" (Matt. 4:18-20). Soon Jesus called two other brothers to follow him. "Immediately they left the boat and their father, and followed him" (Matt. 4:22). The Gospel writers reveal a sense of immediacy accompanying Jesus' call. They recognize a sense of timing. Jesus' call to our lives is both immediate and timely.

Not only does Jesus call us to join ranks with him; he also names us. In recruiting Peter, Jesus said to him, "You are Simon, . . . you are to be called . . . Peter" (John 1:42). Gospel vignettes remind us that we must name Jesus for ourselves. Nathanael named Jesus "the Son of God . . . the King of Israel" (John 1:49). In the early chapters of the Gospels, so many people are naming and being named. We too might allow Jesus to name us, to tell us who we really are. Naming someone defines the person, allows the person to take on an entirely new identity. When Jesus lays claim upon our lives, we are given a new name.

Why is all this naming necessary? For one thing, the ancients felt that a person had no distinct identity until he or she was named. This thought prevails among Native Americans today. I once named a young Native

American man. The process of choosing the right name for this young man took two years, so carefully must the family discern who he will be—for the family and for the tribe. His name determines his destiny.

When John's disciples broke ranks to follow after Jesus, he asked them, "Who are you looking for?" They responded, "Where do you live?" Jesus asked *who*, they responded *where*. Their spirituality was unformed. They looked for grace in "things and places." Jesus offered them grace in a living, loving relationship. Jesus still asks the "who" questions—not merely "what." "What are you?" is a *doing* question with a *doing* reply: I am a teacher, a machinist, a physician, and so forth. But "who" you are invites a *being* response. "Who" inquires into the soul of us. Who are you? What name has Jesus given you? What name have you given Jesus?
—Norman Shawchuck

> ❧ Turn again, thou trembling Reed
> To thine everlasting Rest,
> Lean on [Christ] thy languid head,
> Sink on the Beloved breast;
> Lifting there the streaming eye,
> Tell [Christ] all thy wants and fears:
> He shall all thy wants supply,
> He shall dry up all thy tears.
—From *The Unpublished Poetry of Charles Wesley*, Vol. 3

❧ I am! Here is the home of the spirit, where we can hear and say, "I am," a kingdom of persons, a life larger than life. When God says "I am," all nature replies "Thou art," according to Christopher Smart, the mad poet of the eighteenth century, but then Jesus says "I am" and we too can say "I am," I have learned, and God says "Thou art," as if to say
> You are,
> You are known
> And you are loved.
—From *The Homing Spirit* by John S. Dunne

᠁ For a long time, I prayed the words, "The Lord is my shepherd; there is nothing I shall want. Fresh and green are the pastures where he gives me repose. Near restful waters he leads me to revive my drooping spirit." I prayed these words in the morning for half an hour sitting quietly on my chair trying only to keep my mind focused on what I was saying. I prayed them during the many moments of the day when I was going here or there, and I even prayed them during my routine activities. The words stand in stark contrast to the reality of my life. I want many things; I see mostly busy roads and ugly shopping malls; and if there are any waters to walk along they are mostly polluted. But as I keep saying: "The Lord is my shepherd. . . ." and allow God's shepherding love to enter more fully into my heart, I become more fully aware that the busy roads, the ugly malls, and the polluted waterways are not telling the true story of who I am. I do not belong to the powers and principalities that rule the world but to the Good Shepherd who knows his own and is known by his own. In the presence of my Lord and Shepherd there truly is nothing I shall want. He will, indeed, give me the rest my heart desires and pull me out of the dark pits of my depression.
—From *Here and Now* by Henri J. M. Nouwen

᠁ You are the object of all good, the apex of life, the depth of wisdom. Your servants' greatest consolation is to hope in you above all things. I turn my eyes to you. In you, my God, Father of mercies, I place my trust. Bless my soul and make it holy with your heavenly blessing; let it become your holy dwelling, the place of your eternal glory. Let nothing be found in your temple that may offend the eyes of your majesty.

According to the greatness of your goodness and your many mercies, look down on me and hear the prayer of your poor servant, exiled far off in the land of the shadow of death. Protect and keep the soul of your servant, traveling amid the many dangers of life.

By your grace, direct him along the path of peace until he is back home in the land of everlasting brightness. Amen.

—From *The Imitation of Christ* by Thomas à Kempis

❧ Do you then, my son, diligently apply yourself to the reading of the sacred Scriptures. Apply yourself, I say. For we who read the things of God need much application, lest we should say or think anything too rashly about them. And applying yourself thus to the study of the things of God, with faithful prejudgments such as are well pleasing to God, knock at its locked door, and it will be opened to you by the porter, of whom Jesus says, "To him the porter opens." And applying yourself thus to the divine study, seek aright, and with unwavering trust in God, the meaning of the holy Scriptures, which so many have missed. Be not satisfied with knocking and seeking; for prayer is of all things indispensable to the knowledge of the things of God. For to this the Saviour exhorted, and said not only, "Knock, it shall be opened to you; and seek, and ye shall find," but also, "Ask, and it shall be given unto you." My fatherly love to you has made me thus bold; but whether my boldness be good, God will know, and Christ, and all partakers of the Spirit of God and the Spirit of Christ. May you also be a partaker, and be ever increasing your inheritance, that you may say not only, "We are become partakers of Christ," but also partakers of God.

—From "Letter from Origen to Gregory"

A Special Time for New Beginnings
Sunday between November 13 and November 19

55: A New Beginning

Affirmation
O sing to the LORD a new song,
    for he has done marvelous things.
His right hand and his holy arm
    have gotten him victory (Ps. 98:1).

Petition
I will extol you, my God and King,
    and bless your name forever and ever.
Every day I will bless you,
    and praise your name forever and ever.
Great is the LORD, and greatly to be praised;
    his greatness is unsearchable (Ps. 145:1-3).

Sacred Reading: anthology or other selected reading

Daily Scripture Readings

Sunday	A.	Judges 4:1-7; Psalm 123; 1 Thessalonians 5:1-11; Matthew 25:14-30
	B.	1 Samuel 1:4-20; Psalm 16; Hebrews 10:11-14, 19-25; Mark 13:1-8
	C.	Isaiah 65:17-25; Psalm 98; 2 Thessalonians 3:6-13; Luke 21:5-19
Monday		Isaiah 43:14-21
Tuesday		Revelation 21:1-5
Wednesday		2 Corinthians 3:1-6
Thursday		2 Corinthians 5:16-21
Friday		John 13:31-35
Saturday		Jeremiah 31:31-34

Prayer: thanksgiving, petition, intercession, praise, and offering

Reflection: silent (listening to God), written (journaling)

God's Promise
Such is the confidence that we have through Christ toward God. Not that we are competent of ourselves to claim anything as coming from us; our competence is from God, who has made us competent to be ministers of a new covenant, not of letter but of spirit; for the letter kills, but the Spirit gives life (2 Cor. 3:4-6).

My Response
I will sing a new song to you, O God;
      upon a ten-stringed harp I will play to you
          (Ps. 144:9).

Readings for Reflection

❧ We often think of a new day as a point of new beginning. However, we know that new beginnings are available all the time. Life itself provides a constant opportunity to grow, and to grow is to become new, to have a new beginning. How is God calling you to begin anew today? Think for a moment about those areas in your life where new life is waiting to be born.

There is always opportunity for a new beginning in our relationship with God. Because God is infinite, unlimited possibility for growth and starting anew exists. No matter how intimate the companionship we share with Jesus Christ today, there is room for growth and new beginnings.

While our relationships with others do not have the range or depth of opportunity for growth, there is nevertheless room for fresh beginnings with family, friends, colleagues, coworkers, neighbors, caregivers, and those strangers who serve us day by day in shop, gas station, and restaurant. We have in our possession the key to changing—making new—each of these relationships. What slight or radical change is God calling you to make in relationship with God and with those

persons who cross your life path every day? Follow the promptings God gives and launch a new beginning in this new day.
—Rueben P. Job

❧ Two millennia ago at an early morning breakfast by the Sea of Tiberias, Jesus had only one question for Peter: "Simon son of John, do you love me?" (John 21). Jesus did not ask him about his effectiveness, or his skill, or anything but his love. Three times Jesus asked, "Simon, do you love me?" Peter struggled for an adequate response to that probing query. Finally, he blurted out, "Lord, you know everything; you know that I love you." Assured of his heart, Jesus gave Peter work to do: "Feed my lambs."

The same question is asked of us. The same work is given to us.
—From *Prayer: Finding the Heart's True Home* by Richard J. Foster

❧ If any doctrines within the whole compass of Christianity may be properly termed fundamental, they are doubtless these two,—the doctrine of justification, and that of the new birth: The former relating to that great work which God does *for us*, in forgiving our sins; the latter, to the great work which God does *in us*, in renewing our fallen nature. In order of *time* neither of these is before the other; in the moment we are justified by the grace of God, through the redemption that is in Jesus, we are also "born of the Spirit;" but in order of *thinking*, as it is termed, justification precedes the new birth. We first conceive [God's] wrath to be turned away, and then [God's] Spirit to work in our hearts.
—From "Sermon 45" by John Wesley

❧ My God, every fiber of my being vibrates at the touch of your grace—whereby I am given the privilege of being your child. My joy at your overwhelming gestures of love and the high privilege you extend to me of entering into your life invades my being with an acute sense of your ever-nearness. In response to this, my Lord, I offer praises to you.

Yet, my Lord, I am often cold toward you. I forget to love you for long periods of time—and this to my own harm and regret. Forgive me, Lord! Everloving God, set my life aflame with love for you only. O my God, I long to reflect your image throughout the world so that others might observe your doing in me and themselves be convinced that you love them also.
—Norman Shawchuck

☙ Contemplative spirituality would agree with the devotional school of spirituality in saying that constant change or conversion, the biblical reality of *metanoia*, is a necessary imperative of the spiritual life. But whereas devotional spirituality would want to think of such change primarily in terms of behavior, contemplative spirituality, without being unmindful of this kind of change, would tend to stress the need for a change in consciousness. *It is not enough that we behave better; we must come to see reality differently.* We must learn to see the depths of things, not just reality at a superficial level. This especially means we need to see the nonseparateness of the world from God and the oneness of all reality in God: the Hidden Ground of Love in all that is. Prayer is a kind of corrective lens that does away with the distorted view of reality that, for some mysterious reason, seems to be my normal vision, and enables me to see what is as it really is.
—From *Silence on Fire* by William H. Shannon

☙ "Being in the world without being of the world." These words summarize well the way Jesus speaks of the spiritual life. It is a life in which we are totally transformed by the Spirit of love. Yet it is a life in which everything seems to remain the same. To live a spiritual life does not mean that we must leave our families, give up our jobs, or change our ways of working; it does not mean that we have to withdraw from social or political activities, or lose interest in literature and art; it does not require severe forms of asceticism or long hours of prayer. . . . What is new is that we have moved from the many things to the kingdom of God. What is new is that we are set free from the compulsions of our world and have set our hearts on the only necessary thing. What is new is that we no longer experience the many things, people, and events as endless causes for worry, but begin to experience them as the rich variety of ways in which God makes his presence known to us.

—From *Making All Things New* by Henri J. M. Nouwen

❧ What deadens us most to God's presence within us, I think, is the inner dialogue that we are continuously engaged in with ourselves, the endless chatter of human thought. I suspect that there is nothing more crucial to true spiritual *comfort*...than being able from time to time to stop that chatter including the chatter of spoken prayer. If we choose to seek the silence of the holy place, or to open ourselves to its seeking, I think there is no surer way than by keeping silent.

God knows I am no good at it, but I keep trying, and once or twice I have been lucky, graced. I have been conscious but not conscious of anything, not even of myself. I have been surrounded by the whiteness of snow. I have heard a stillness that encloses all sounds stilled the way whiteness encloses all colors stilled, the way wordlessness encloses all words stilled. I have sensed the presence of a presence. I have felt a promise promised.

I like to believe that once or twice, at times like those, I have bumbled my way into at least the outermost suburbs of the Truth that can never be told but only come upon, that can never be proved but only lived for and loved.

—From *Telling Secrets* by Frederick Buechner

Reign of Christ Sunday

We began the seasons of the church year with antici-pation, and we end the seasons of the church year declaring a certainty. In Advent we waited for the needed and longed-for definitive and ultimate self-disclosure of God in the birth of Jesus of Nazareth. On Reign of Christ Sunday we celebrate the fulfillment of the biblical revelation of God in Christ.

Once again the church has listened to, reflected upon, rehearsed in worship, and tried to live in daily experience the redemption story. We come away from this last Sunday of the church year soaked to the core in the revelation of God in Christ. For us, as for those first disciples, there can be no turning back. Here in the light of Christ's triumphant presence we find our voice and declare once again, Jesus Christ is Lord of all and shall reign as Lord in my life. So committed, we are ready to face every eventuality of life because we now know the One in whom our life is found, redeemed, and kept secure. Our radical trust is in the One who is completely trustworthy (2 Tim. 1:12). Life in Christ is good and complete.

Reign of Christ Sunday
Sunday between November 20 and November 26

56: *When All Is Said and Done*

Affirmation
All that is to be, now is!
The reign of God is now with us.
Return to God's way,
And live out the Good News.

Petition
O LORD, remember in David's favor all the hardships
he endured; how he swore to the LORD and vowed to
the Mighty One of Jacob, "I will not enter my house or
get into my bed; I will not give sleep to my eyes or
slumber to my eyelids, until I find a place for the LORD,
a dwelling place for the Mighty One of Jacob." . . . Rise
up, O LORD, and go to your resting place, you and
the ark of your might. Let your priests be clothed
with righteousness, and let your faithful shout for joy
(Ps. 132:1-5, 8-9).

Sacred Reading: anthology or other selected reading

Daily Scripture Readings

Sunday	A.	Ezekiel 34:11-16, 20-24; Psalm 100; Ephesians 1:15-23; Matthew 25:31-46
	B.	2 Samuel 23:1-7; Psalm 132:1-12; Revelation 1:4-8; John 18:33-37
	C.	Jeremiah 23:1-6; Luke 1:68-79; Colossians 1:11-20; Luke 23:33-43
Monday		Zechariah 14:1-11
Tuesday		Acts 3:17-26
Wednesday		Romans 14:10-12
Thursday		Hebrews 9:23-28

| Friday | John 12:20-26 |
| Saturday | 2 Thessalonians 1:5-12 |

Prayer: thanksgiving, petition, intercession, praise, and offering

Reflection: silent (listening to God), written (journaling)

God's Promise
John to the seven churches that are in Asia: Grace to you and peace from him who is and who was and who is to come, and from the seven spirits who are before his throne, and from Jesus Christ, the faithful witness, the firstborn of the dead, and the ruler of the kings of the earth. To him who loves us and freed us from our sins by his blood, and made us to be a kingdom, priests serving his God and Father, to him be glory and dominion forever and ever. Amen.
Look! He is coming with the clouds;
    every eye will see him,
even those who pierced him;
    and on his account all the tribes of the earth will wail.
So it is to be. Amen. "I am the Alpha and the Omega," says the Lord God, who is and who was and who is to come, the Almighty (Rev. 1:4-8).

My Response
Take my life! Lord, put me to doing your work and your will in the world so that lost and hungry souls may be attracted to your love and mercy and be drawn into the embrace of your love.

Readings for Reflection

❧ Every United Methodist preacher since the time of John Wesley has been asked a series of questions before being admitted into full membership in an annual conference. The first question is, "Have you faith in Christ?" The second question is, "Are you going on to perfection?" Seventeen more questions follow, and every candidate is to be led in discussion and understanding of the questions by the resident bishop of the area.

Once during the turbulent sixties, Bishop Gerald Kennedy was asking these historic questions of candidates standing before him in the presence of the annual conference session. When asked if he was going on to perfection, one candidate responded, "No!" Bishop Kennedy quickly replied, "Then where are you going?" It was an appropriate question then, and it is an appropriate question now—not only for preachers but also for all Christians.

Where are you going? If you continue on the course you have charted, where will it all end? So often we discount Christ's return, forgetting that in many ways Jesus Christ has never left. Or we begin reasoning that since Christ has not returned yet, why think about it? But the truth is that at the very best, our lives are short and soon we will have reached our destination, whether Jesus Christ will have returned in a cosmic unfolding or not. Are you going on toward God? If not, where are you going? It is always a good time to review and if necessary redirect your life toward God.
—Rueben P. Job

   ✒   Wherefore if thou canst fail,
Then can thy truth and I: but while rocks stand,
And rivers stir, thou canst not shrink or quail:
Yea, when both rocks and all things shall disband,
      Then shalt thou be my rock and tower,
      And make their ruin praise thy power.
      —From "Assurance" by George Herbert

   ✒   The life that the God of the gospel wills for human beings—"abundant," "eternal" life—contains as such no hint of ambiguity, no dialectic of light and darkness, yes and no. It is all light, all affirmative (2 Cor. 1:19-20; James 1:17). But the question is, how can *we*, who *are* full

of ambiguity and duplicity, who *are* children of darkness, who *are* "being-towards-death" (Heidegger)—
can we come to this light, affirm this affirmation, enter
this life? Clearly, it is not a simple matter: purity in
exchange for sin, light for darkness, life for death—like
Aladdin's "new lamps for old." The Scriptures know
that it is much more difficult than that. There is a cost
involved (Matt. 19:23), a narrow path to be trod (Matt.
7:14), an "impossibility" to be encountered (Matt.
19:26). This is not because the authors of the Scriptures
. . . enjoy making things difficult. . . .

To begin to move towards real life means, for us,
to come face-to-face with that within and around us
which bars us from life. Not because God is who—in
biblical perspective—God is, but because we are who
and what we are, ". . . facing the God who is really God
means facing also the absolute threat of non-being."
The good news that *life* is available to those who sit in
darkness and the shadow of death has as its corollary
the less enticing news that in order to avail ourselves
of this life we shall have to know ourselves numbered
among those who sit in . . . the shadow of death! . . .

The gospel calls us to a great and profound seriousness about our condition as human beings, and
there are many who would prefer to avoid that seriousness. For to enter reflectively and earnestly into
the reality of one's (fallen) creaturehood is certainly the
first step in "taking up one's cross."
—From *God and Human Suffering* by Douglas John
    Hall

❧   Lord I have invited all,
        And I shall
    Still invite, still call to thee:
    For it seems but just and right
        In my sight,
    Where is all, there all should be.
    —From "The Invitation" by George Herbert

❧ In some of his final words to Timothy, Paul talks about his death, that the time has come for his departure. The word *departure* is a nautical term; it suggests a ship which has been moored to the shore, the rope flung off, the anchor lifted, and the ship moving out of harbor in the wide and boundless sea.

Paul sees death as a moment for new adventure, not a time for defeat or sadness. It is not like an old half-ruined wreck of a ship putting into port; rather, it is a ship which has cast off the ropes which bind us to this world to sail into unknown waters where God becomes present. Only on the sea can the ship fulfill the possibility of its own being, and fulfill the purpose for which it was made.

The apostle John made this clear when he wrote, "Beloved, we are God's children now; what we will be has not yet been revealed. What we do know is this: when he is revealed, we will be like him, for we will see him as he is" (1 John 3:2).

What a blessed departure! May John's words give us strength to fight the good fight, and persistence to keep the faith.

—From *Autumn Wisdom* by Richard L. Morgan

Index of Readings

Eusebius, 174, 262, 387

Farnham, Suzanne G., et al., 93, 231

Farrer, Austin, 108

Fénelon, François, 319, 328, 338, 346

Foster, Richard J., 274, 404

Foster, Ron, 203, 242

Foucauld, Charles de, 104, 239

Fox, Emmet, 71, 83, 90, 103, 207, 270, 279, 373

Gregory Nazianzen, 108, 109

Griebner, David M., 386

Groff, Kent Ira, 232

Grove, William Boyd, 158

Guyon, Jeanne, 220

Hagmann, Ann, 31, 288, 378

Hall, Douglas John, 408

Harnish, James A., 60, 166

Harper, Steve, 92

Hart, Russell M., 271

Hatch, Edwin, 170

Hauser, Richard J., 221, 371

Hays, Edward, 376, 379

Herbert, George, 408, 409

Hick, John, 116

Hinson, E. Glenn, 270, 326

Howatch, Susan, 114

Howell, James C., 152, 245, 297

Ignatius (Saint), 133, 237

Indermark, John, 275

Iredale, Simon Peter, 343

Jenkins, J. Marshall, 159, 297

Jerome, 258

Job, Rueben P. (excluding essays original to this volume),
    43, 208, 252, 264, 265, 266, 293, 296, 306, 353, 360

John of the Cross (Saint), 364, 365

Johnson, Ben Campbell, 83

Jonas, Robert A., 98, 138, 164

Jones, Alan W., 151, 182

Origen, 401
Patrick (Saint), 226
Paulsell, William O., 76
Pearson, Helen Bruch, 54, 86, 330, 347
Pennington, M. Basil, 78
Philokalia, The, 320
Polycarp, 189
Prevallet, Elaine M., 337
Puls, Joan, 187, 207, 266
Redding, Mary Lou, 32
Rice, Howard L., 285, 327, 329
Richardson, Jan L., 280
Richter, Don C., 167
Rohr, Richard, 32, 70, 102, 176, 181, 188, 206, 252, 300, 307, 315, 370, 382
Rolle, Richard, 77, 237
Rowlett, Martha Graybeal, 303
Rupp, Joyce, 72, 78, 138, 164, 207, 351, 385
Saliers, Don E., 201
Sellner, Edward C., 91
Shannon, William H., 403
Simons, Menno, 24
Sinetar, Marsha, 71, 207, 212
Steere, Douglas V., 288, 309
Stein, K. James, 111
Svoboda, Melannie, 25, 295
Teresa, Mother, 53, 192, 200, 201, 206, 256, 257, 350
Teresa of Avila (Saint), 377
Theodoret, 180
Thérèse of Lisieux (Saint), 99
Thomas à Kempis, 316, 377, 379, 383, 398
Thomas, Gary, 201
Thompson, Marjorie J., 43, 46, 196, 279, 280, 302, 306
Thurman, Howard, 37, 52, 286, 372
Tozer, A. W., 228

The publisher gratefully acknowledges permissions to reproduce the following copyrighted material.

John Ackerman: From *Spiritual Awakening*. Copyright © 1994. Reprinted with permission from The Alban Institute, Inc. 7315 Wisconsin Ave., Suite 1250W, Bethesda, MD 20814-2311. All rights reserved.

Ray S. Anderson: From *Unspoken Wisdom: Truths My Father Taught Me*. Augsburg, 1995.Used by permission of the author.

Wilkie Au: From *The Enduring Heart*. Copyright © 2000 by Wilkie Au. Used with permission of Paulist Press. Available at bookstores or www.paulistpress.com or 1-800-218-1903.

Augustine (Saint): From *The Confessions*, trans. by Maria Boulding. © Augustinian Heritage Institute 1997. Used by permission of New City Press; from *Journey with the Fathers, Year A*. © 1992 New City Press. Used by permission.

Jeannette A. Bakke: From "Glory of the Trinity," an unpublished work. Used by permission of the author; from *Holy Invitations*. Grand Rapids, MI: Baker Books, a division of Baker Book House Company. Copyright © 2000 by Jeannette A. Bakke. Used by permission.

William Barclay: From *The Mind of Jesus*. Harper & Brothers, 1960, 1961. Used by permission of the Estate of William Barclay.

Dorothy C. Bass, ed.: From *Practicing Our Faith*. © 1997 by Jossey-Bass Inc., Publishers. Used by permission of John Wiley & Sons, Inc.

Dorothy C. Bass and Don C. Richter, eds.: From *Way to Live*. © 2002 by Dorothy C. Bass and Don C. Richter. Used by permission of Upper Room Books.

Jean M. Blomquist: From *Wrestling till Dawn*. Copyright © 1994 by Jean M. Blomquist. Used by permission of Upper Room Books.

Roberta C. Bondi: From *In Ordinary Time*. © 1996 Abingdon Press. Used by permission.

Dietrich Bonhoeffer: From *Life Together*, trans. by John Doberstein. English translation copyright © 1954 by Harper & Brothers, copyright renewed 1982 by Helen S. Doberstein. Reprinted by permission of HarperCollins, Publishers, Inc.; from *Meditating on the Word.* Copyright © 1986, 2000 David McI. Gracie. All rights reserved. Used by permission of Cowley Publications, 907 Massachusetts Ave., Cambridge, MA 02139. www.cowley.org (800-225-1534); from *A Testament to Freedom: The Essential Writings of Dietrich Bonhoeffer,* ed. by Geffrey B. Kelly and F. Burton Nelson. Copyright © 1990 by Geffrey B. Kelly and F. Burton Nelson, Rev. ed. 1995. Reprinted by permission of HarperCollins Publishers, Inc., Geffrey B. Kelly, and F. Burton Nelson.

Grace Adolphsen Brame, Ph.D.: From *Faith, the Yes of the Heart.* Minneapolis: Augsburg, 1999; from *Receptive Prayer.* Copyright © 1985 CBP Press. Used by permission of the author.

Howard L. Brown: From "Follow, I Will Follow Thee." Copyright © Singspiration. Admin. Brentwood-Benson Music Publ. 741 Cool Springs Blvd. Franklin, TN 37067. 615-261-3342. Used by permission.

Anne Broyles: From *Journaling: A Spiritual Journey.* © 1999 by Anne Broyles. Used by permission of Upper Room Books.

Frederick Buechner: From *The Magnificent Defeat.* Copyright © 1966 by Frederick Buechner. Copyright renewed 1994 by Frederick Buechner. Reprinted by permission of HarperCollins Publishers, Inc., and Harriet Wasserman Literary Agency; from *Telling Secrets.* Copyright © 1991 by Frederick Buechner. Reprinted by permission of HarperCollins Publishers, Inc.

Elizabeth J. Canham: From *Heart Whispers.* © 1999 by Elizabeth J. Canham. Used by permission of Upper Room Books; from "Sing a New Song" in *Communion, Community, Commonweal,* ed. by John S. Mogabgab. © 1995 by The Upper Room. Used by permission of Upper Room Books.

Carlo Carretto: From *And God Saw That It Was Good.* English translation Copyright © 1989 by St. Paul Publications. Used by permission of St Pauls, UK; from *The Desert Journal: A Diary 1954-55.* English translation © 1991 by HarperCollins Publishers, Used by permission of Zondervan; from *Journey Without End.* Trans. by Alan Neame (Ave Maria Press, 1989). Copyright © 1986 by Cittadella Editrice, Assisi, Italy. Used by permission of Cittadella Editrice; from *Letters to Dolcidia: 1954–1983.* English translation © 1992 by HarperCollins Publishers. Used by permission of Zondervan.

Michael Casey: From *Toward God*. Copyright © 1989, 1995 by Michael Casey. Used by permission of Ligouri/Triumph.

Paul W. Chilcote: From *Praying in the Wesleyan Spirit*. © 2001 by Paul W. Chilcote. Used by permission of Upper Room Books.

Joan Chittister: From *Illuminated Life*. Copyright © 2000 Joan Chittister. Used by permission of Orbis Books.

Mary Conrow Coelho: From "Participating in the New Creation" in *The Weavings Reader*, ed. by John S. Mogabgab. © 1993 by The Upper Room. Used by permission of Upper Room Books.

Jim Cymbala: From *Fresh Faith*. Copyright © 1999 by Jim Cymbala. Used by permission of Zondervan.

Kenda Creasy Dean and Ron Foster: From *The Godbearing Life*. © 1998 by Kenda Creasy Dean and Ron Foster. Used by permission of Upper Room Books.

Gerrit Scott Dawson et al.: From *Companions in Christ: Participant's Book*. © 2001 by Upper Room Books. Used by permission of the publisher.

Jean-Pierre de Caussade: From *The Sacrament of the Present Moment*. English translation copyright © 1981 by William Collins Sons & Co., Ltd. Introduction copyright © 1982 by Harper & Row, Publishers, Inc. First published in France as *L'Abandon a la Providence Divine* by Desclee de Brouwer, © Desclee de Brouwer 1966. Reprinted by permission of HarperCollins Publishers, Inc. and HarperCollins Publishers, Ltd.

Anthony de Mello: From *Contact with God* (Gujarat Sahitya Prakash, 1990) Used by permission of Gujarat Sahitya Prakash, Anand, India; from *Taking Flight*. New York: Doubleday, 1988.

Francis Dorff: From *The Art of Passingover*. Copyright © 1988 by Francis Dorff. Used with permission of Paulist Press. Available at bookstores or www.paulistpress.com or 1-800-218-1903; from *The Journey from Misery to Ministry*. Copyright © 2000 by Francis Dorff, O. Praem. Used by permission of the author.

Stephen V. Doughty: From *Discovering Community*. © 1999 by Stephen V. Doughty. Used by permission of Upper Room Books.

Maxie Dunnam: From *Alive in Christ*. © 1982 Abingdon Press. Used by permission.

John S. Dunne: From *The Homing Spirit*. Copyright © 1987 by John S. Dunne. Used by permission of the author;

from *Love's Mind*. Copyright © 1993 University of Notre Dame Press. Used by permission.

Craig R. Dykstra: From *Vision and Character*. © 1981 by Craig R. Dykstra. Used with permission of Paulist Press. Available at bookstores or www.paulistpress.com or 1-800-218-1903.

Rebecca A. Ellenson: From "Ordinary Elements: Sacramental Ministry" in *Ordinary Ministry: Extraordinary Challenge*, ed. by Norma Cook Everist. © 2000 Abingdon Press. Used by permission.

Suzanne G. Farnham et al.: From *Listening Hearts: Discerning Call in Community*. Copyright © 1991 by the Christian Vocation Project, Inc. Reprinted by permission of Morehouse Publishing, Harrisburg, Penn.

Austin Farrer: From *A Celebration of Faith*. Copyright © 1970 by Katherine Farrer. Reproduced by permission of Hodder and Stoughton, Ltd.

François Fénelon: From *The Royal Way of the Cross: Letters and Spiritual Counsels of Francois de Salignac de la Mothe-Fénelon*, trans. by H. Sidney Lear. © 1982 The Community of Jesus, Inc. Used by permission of Paraclete Press.

Richard J. Foster: From *Prayer: Finding the Heart's True Home*. Copyright © 1992 by Richard J. Foster. Reprinted by permission of HarperCollins Publishers, Inc., and William Neill-Hall, Ltd.

Charles de Foucauld: From *Spiritual Autobiography of Charles de Foucauld*, ed. Jean-Francois Six, trans. H. Holland Smith (New York: P .J. Kenedy & Sons, 1964) as reprinted in *Charles de Foucauld: Writings Selected with an Introduction by Robert Ellsberg*. Copyright © 1999 by Orbis Books. Used by permission of Orbis Books.

Emmet Fox: From *Power Through Constructive Thinking*. Copyright 1940 by Emmet Fox. Copyright renewed 1968 by Kathleen Whelan. Reprinted by permission of HarperCollins Publishers, Inc.

Gregory Nazianzen: From *Journey with the Fathers, Year A*. Copyright © 1992 New City Press. Used by permission.

David M. Griebner: From *The Carpenter and the Unbuilder*. © 1996 by David M. Griebner. Used by permission of Upper Room Books.

Kent Ira Groff: From *Journeymen*. © 1999 by Kent Ira Groff. Used by permission of Upper Room Books.

William Boyd Grove: "We Are Yours, O God Most Holy." Used by permission of the author.

Jeanne Guyon: From *Experiencing the Depths of Jesus Christ*. Copyright © 1975 by Gene Edwards. Used by permission of SeedSowers.

Ann Hagmann: From *Abiding Hope: Encouragement in the Shadow of*

Death. © 2002 by Ann Hagmann. Used by permission of Upper Room Books; from *Climbing the Sycamore Tree: A Study on Choice and Simplicity.* © 2001 by Ann Hagmann. Used by permission of Upper Room Books.

Douglas John Hall: From *God and Human Suffering.* Minneapolis: Augsburg, 1986.

James A. Harnish: From *What Will You Do with King Jesus?* © 1986 by The Upper Room. Used by permission of Upper Room Books.

Steve Harper: From *Prayer and Devotional Life of United Methodists.* © 1999 Abingdon Press. Used by permission.

Russell M. Hart: From *Crossing the Border.* Copyright © 1993 Russell M. Hart. Used by permission of Templegate Publishers (www.templegate.com), Springfield, IL.

Richard J. Hauser: From *In His Spirit.* Copyright © 1982 by Richard J. Hauser. Used with permission of Paulist Press. Available at bookstores or www.paulistpress.com or 1-800-218-1903.

Edward Hays: From *In Pursuit of the Great White Rabbit.* Copyright © 1990 Forest of Peace Publishing, Inc., 251 Muncie Rd., Leavenworth, KS 66048. Used by permission.

George Herbert: From *George Herbert: The Country Parson, The Temple.* Copyright © 1981 by The Missionary Society of St. Paul the Apostle in the State of New York. Used with permission of Paulist Press. Available at bookstores or www.paulistpress.com or 1-800-218-1903.

John Hick: From *The Center of Christianity* (Harper & Row, 1968, 1978). Used by permission of the author.

E. Glenn Hinson: From *Spiritual Preparation for Christian Leadership.* © 1999 by E. Glenn Hinson. Used by permission of Upper Room Books.

Susan Howatch: From *Absolute Truths* (New York: Alfred A. Knopf, 1995).

James C. Howell: From *Servants, Misfits, and Martyrs.* © 1999 by James C. Howell. Used by permission of Upper Room Books; from *Yours Are the Hands of Christ.* © 1998 by James C. Howell. Used by permission of Upper Room Books.

Ignatius of Loyola: From *The Spiritual Exercises of St. Ignatius,* vol. 7, trans. by David L. Fleming. Copyright © 1978 by The Institute of Jesuit Sources. Used by permission.

John Indermark: From *Neglected Voices.* © 1999 by John Indermark. Used by permission of Upper Room Books.

Simon Peter Iredale: Adapted from *The Interior Mountain.* © 2000 Abingdon Press. Adapted by permission.

J. Marshall Jenkins: From *A Wakeful Faith.* © 2000 by J. Marshall Jenkins. Used by permission of Upper Room Books.

Rueben P. Job, comp.: From *A Guide to Spiritual Discernment.* © 1996 by Upper Room Books. Used by permission of Upper Room Books; from *Spiritual Life in the Congregation.* © 1997 by Rueben P. Job. Used by permission of Upper Room Books; from *A Wesleyan Spiritual Reader.* © 1998 Abingdon Press. Used by permission.

John of the Cross (Saint): From *Ascent of Mount Carmel.* Image Books, 1958, published by special arrangement with The Newman Press.

Ben Campbell Johnson: From *Pastoral Spirituality.* The Westminster Press, 1988. Used by permission of the author.

Robert A. Jonas, ed.: From *Henri Nouwen: Writings Selected with an Introduction by Robert A. Jonas.* Copyright © 1998 by Robert A. Jonas. Used by permission of Orbis Books. Published in the United Kingdom under the title *Beauty of the Beloved.* Used by permission of Darton Longman & Todd.

Alan W. Jones: From *Soul Making.* Copyright © 1985 by Alan W. Jones. Reprinted by permission of HarperCollins Publishers, Inc.

W. Paul Jones: From *The Art of Spiritual Direction.* © 2002 by W. Paul Jones. Used by permission of Upper Room Books; from *A Season in the Desert.* © 2000 by W. Paul Jones. Used by permission of Paraclete Press.

Julian of Norwich: From *Julian of Norwich: Showings.* Copyright © 1978 by The Missionary of St. Paul the Apostle in the State of New York. Used with permission of Paulist Press. Available at bookstores or www.paulistpress.com or 1-800-218-1903.

Thomas Keating: From *Intimacy with God.* © 1994 by St. Benedict's Monastery, Snowmass, CO. Used by permission of The Crossroad Publishing Company.

Carole Marie Kelly: From *Symbols of Inner Truth.* Copyright © 1988 by Carole Marie Kelly. Used with permission of Paulist Press. Available at bookstores or www.paulistpress.com or 1-800-218-1903.

Thomas R. Kelly: From *A Testament of Devotion.* Copyright 1941 by Harper & Row Publishers, Inc. Renewed 1969 by Lois Lael Kelly Stabler. New introduction copyright © 1992 by HarperCollins Publishers, Inc. Reprinted by permission of HarperCollins Publishers, Inc.

Thomas A. Langford: From *Practical Divinity.* © 1983 Abingdon Press. Used by permission.

C. S. Lewis: From *Fern-Seed and Elephants.* Copyright © C. S. Lewis Pte. Ltd. 1975. Reprinted by permission of The C. S. Lewis Company; from *Mere Christianity.* Copyright © C. S. Lewis Pte. Ltd. 1942, 1943, 1944, 1952. Reprinted by permission of The C. S. Lewis Company.

James E. Loder: From *The Transforming Moment*. Colorado Springs: Helmers & Howard, 1989. Used by permission of the publisher.

Max Lucado: From *God Came Near*. Copyright © 1986 by Max Lucado. Used by permission of Multnomah Publishers, Inc.

George Macdonald: From *Creation in Christ*. Copyright © 1976. Ed. by Rolland Hein for Harold Shaw Publishers. Used by permission of WaterBrook Press, Colorado Springs, CO. All rights reserved.

George A. Maloney: From *In Jesus We Trust*. Ave Maria Press, 1990. Used by permission of the author.

Brennan Manning: From *Abba's Child*. Copyright © 1994 by Brennan Manning. Used by permission of NavPress/Pinon Press. All rights reserved. For copies call 1-800-366-7788; from *Lion and Lamb*. Copyright © 1986 by Brennan Manning (Chosen Books, a division of Baker Book House Company). Used by permission of Baker Book House Company and Hodder and Stoughton, Ltd. (British title *Relentless Love of Jesus*); from *Reflections for Ragamuffins*. Copyright © 1998 by Brennan Manning. Reprinted by permission of HarperCollins Publishers, Inc.

Dom Marmion: From *Union with God*. St. Louis, MO: B. Herder Book, Co., 1934.

Thomas Merton: "The Road Ahead" from *Thoughts in Solitude*. Copyright © 1958 by the Abbey of Our Lady of Gethsemane. Copyright renewed 1986 by the Trustees of the Thomas Merton Legacy Trust. Reprinted by permission of Farrar, Straus and Giroux, LLC and Curtis Brown, Ltd.

Metropolitan Anthony of Sourozh: From *Meditations on a Theme*. Copyright © 1971, 1980 Metropolitan Anthony. (A. R. Mowbray & Co., Ltd., 1980). Used by permission of The Continuum International Publishing Group, Ltd.

Wendy Miller: From *Learning to Listen*. © 1993 by Wendy Miller. Used by permission of Upper Room Books.

John S. Mogabgab: From "Editor's Introduction" in *Weavings: A Journal of the Christian Spiritual Life* (September/October 1993). © 1993 by The Upper Room. Used by permission; from "Editor's Introduction" in *Weavings* (November/December 1995). © 1995 by The Upper Room. Used by permission; from "Editor's Introduction" in *Weavings* (March/April 1998). © 1998 by The Upper Room. Used by permission; from "Editor's Introduction" in *Weavings* (September/October 2000). © 2000 by The Upper Room. Used by permission; from "Editor's Introduction" in *Weavings* (September/October 2001 and November/December 2001). © 2001 by The Upper Room. Used by permission; from "Editor's Introduction" in *Weavings*

(July/August 2002). © 2002 by The Upper Room. Used by permission.

Richard L. Morgan: From *Autumn Wisdom*. © 1995 by Richard Morgan. Used by permission of Upper Room Books.

Robert F. Morneau: From *From Resurrection to Pentecost*. © 2000 by Robert F. Morneau. Used by permission of The Crossroad Publishing Company.

Danny E. Morris: From *Yearning to Know God's Will*. Copyright © 1991 by Danny E. Morris. Used by permission of Zondervan.

Danny E. Morris and Charles M. Olsen: From *Discerning God's Will Together*. © 1997 by Danny E. Morris and Charles M. Olsen. Used by permission of Upper Room Books.

M. Robert Mulholland Jr.: From *Shaped by the Word*. rev. ed. © 1985, 2000 by M. Robert Mulholland Jr. Used by permission of Upper Room Books.

Susan Muto and Adrian van Kaam: From *Divine Guidance*. Pittsburgh, PA: Epiphany Books, 2000. Used by permission of the authors.

Robert Cummings Neville: From *The God Who Beckons*. © 1999 Abingdon Press. Used by permission.

Tilda Norberg: From *Ashes Transformed*. © 2003 by Tilda Norberg. Used by permission of Upper Room Books.

Henri J. M. Nouwen: From *Bread for the Journey: A Daybook of Wisdom and Faith*. Copyright © 1996 by Henri J. M. Nouwen. Reprinted by permission of HarperCollins Publishers, Inc., and Darton, Longman & Todd, Ltd.; from *Can You Drink the Cup?* Copyright © 1996 by Ave Maria Press, P.O. Box 428, Notre Dame, IN 46556, www.avemariapress.com. Used with permission of the publisher; from *¡Gracias!: A Latin American Journal*. Copyright © 1983 by Henri J. M. Nouwen. Reprinted by permission of HarperCollins Publishers, Inc.; from *Here and Now*. © 1994 by Henri J. M. Nouwen. Used by permission of The Crossroad Publishing Company; from *The Inner Voice of Love* (New York: Doubleday, 1996); from *Life of the Beloved*. © 1992 by Henri J. M. Nouwen. Used by permission of The Crossroad Publishing Company; from *Making All Things New: An Invitation to the Spiritual Life*. Copyright © 1981 by Henri J. M. Nouwen. Reprinted by permission of HarperCollins Publishers, Inc.; from *Our Greatest Gift*. Copyright © 1994 by Henri J. M. Nouwen. Reprinted by permission of HarperCollins Publishers, Inc., and Hodder & Stoughton, Ltd.; from *Reaching Out*. New York: Image Books, 1975; from *The Return of the Prodigal Son*. New York: Image Books, 1994; from *Sabbatical Journey*. Copyright © 1998 by the Estate of Henri J. M. Nouwen. Used by permission of The Crossroad Publishing Company; from *The Way of the Heart*. Copyright © 1981 by Henri J. M. Nouwen. Reprinted by permission of HarperCollins Publishers, Inc.; from *With Burning Hearts*. Copyright © 1994 by Henri J. M. Nouwen. Used by permission of Orbis Books, Claretian Publications (India).

Marilyn Brown Oden: From *Abundance: Joyful Living in Christ*. © 2002 by Marilyn Brown Oden. Used by permission of Upper Room Books. From *Wilderness Wanderings*. © 1995 by Marilyn Oden Brown. Used by permission of Upper Room Books.

Gabriel O'Donnell: Adapted from "Getting Ready to Pray: The Practices of Spiritual Disciplines" in *Spiritual Traditions for the Contemporary Church*, ed. by Robin Maas and Gabriel O'Donnell. © 1990 Abingdon Press. Adapted by permission.

Max Oliva, S.J.: From *Free to Pray, Free to Love*. Copyright © 1994 by Ave Maria Press. Used by permission of the author.

Charles M. Olsen and Ellen Morseth: From *Selecting Church Leaders*. © 2002 by Charles M. Olsen and Ellen Morseth. Used by permission of Upper Room Books.

William O. Paulsell: From "Ways of Prayer: Designing a Personal Rule" in *Weavings: A Journal of the Christian Spiritual Life* (September/October 1987). Used by permission of the author.

Helen Bruch Pearson: From *Mother Roots*. © 2002 by Helen Bruch Pearson. Used by permission of Upper Room Books.

M. Basil Pennington: From *Living in the Question: Meditations in the Style of Lectio Divina*. Copyright © 1999 by Cistercian Abbey of Spencer, Inc. Reprinted by permission of The Continuum International Publishing Group, Inc.

The Philokalia: The Complete Text, volume 1, compiled by St. Nikodimos of the Holy Mountain and St. Makarios of Corinth, trans. by G. E. H. Palmer, Philip Sherrard, and Kallistos Ware. Translation copyright © 1979 by The Eling Trust. Reprinted by permission of Faber & Faber, Inc., an affiliate of Farrar, Straus and Giroux, LLC. and Farrar, Straus and Giroux, LLC.

Elaine M. Prevallet: From "Living in the Mercy" in *Weavings: A Journal of the Christian Spiritual Life* (September/October 2000). Used by permission of the author.

Joan Puls: From *Every Bush Is Burning*. Copyright © 1985 World Council of Churches. Used by permission of Twenty-Third Publications; from *Seek Treasures in Small Fields*. Copyright © 1993 by Joan Puls. Used by permission of Twenty-Third Publications.

Mary Lou Redding: From *While We Wait*. © 2002 by Mary Lou Redding. Used by permission of Upper Room Books.

Howard L. Rice: From *Reformed Spirituality: An Introduction for Believers*. Copyright © 1991 Howard L. Rice. Used by permission of Westminster John Knox Press.

Jan L. Richardson: From *Sacred Journeys*. © 1995 by Jan L. Richardson. Used by permission of Upper Room Books.

Richard Rohr: From *Everything Belongs*. © 1999 by Richard Rohr. Used by permission of The Crossroad Publishing Company.

Richard Rolle: From *The Fire of Love*. Trans. by Clifton Wolters. Copyright © 1972 Clifton Wolters. Reproduced by permission of Penguin Books, Ltd.

Martha Graybeal Rowlett: From *Praying Together*. © 2002 by Martha Graybeal Rowlett. Used by permission of Upper Room Books.

Joyce Rupp, O.S.M.: From *The Cup of Our Life: A Guide for Spiritual Growth*. Copyright © 1997 by Ave Maria Press, P.O. Box 428, Notre Dame, IN 46556, www.avemariapress.com. Used with permission of the publisher.

Don E. Saliers: From "Sanctifying Time, Place, and People" in *The Weavings Reader*, ed. by John S. Mogabgab. © 1993 by The Upper Room. Used by permission of Upper Room Books.

Edward C. Sellner: From *Mentoring: The Ministry of Spiritual Kinship*. Copyright 2002 Edward C. Sellner. Cowley Publications, 907 Massachusetts Ave., Cambridge, MA 02139. www.cowley.org (800-225-1534).

William H. Shannon: From *Silence on Fire*. © 1991 by William H. Shannon. Used by permission of The Crossroad Publishing Company.

Menno Simons: From *The Complete Writings of Menno Simons c. 1496-1561*, ed. by J. C. Wenger, trans. by Leonard Verduin, Herald Press, Scottdale, PA 1956, 1984. Used by permission.

Marsha Sinetar: From *Ordinary People as Monks and Mystics*. Copyright © 1986 by Dr. Marsha Sinetar. Used with permission of Paulist Press. Available at bookstores or www.paulistpress.com or 1-800-218-1903.

Douglas V. Steere: From *Dimensions of Prayer*. © 1997 by Dorothy Steere. Used by permission of Upper Room Books.

K. James Stein: From *Spiritual Guides for the 21st Century*. © 2000 by K. James Stein. Used by permission of Upper Room Books.

Melannie Svoboda: From *Abundant Treasures*. Copyright © 2000 Melannie Svoboda. Used by permission of Twenty-Third Publications.

Mother Teresa: From *Mother Teresa: A Simple Path*, comp. by Lucinda Vardey. Copyright © 1995 by Lucinda Vardey. Used by permission of Ballantine Books, a division of Random House, Inc., and Random House Group, Ltd., Ebury Press; from *My Life for the Poor: Mother Teresa's Life and Work in Her Own Words* by José Luis González-Balado and Janet N. Playfoot. Copyright © 1985 by José Luis González-Balado and Janet N. Playfoot. Reprinted by permission of HarperCollins Publishers, Inc.

Teresa of Avila: From *The Interior Castle,* trans. by Kieran Kavanaugh and Otilio Rodriguez. Copyright © 1979 by the Washington Province of Discalced Carmelites, Inc. Used with permission of Paulist Press. Available at bookstores or www.paulistpress.com or 1-800-218-1903.

Thérèse of Lisieux: From *Collected Letters: St Thérèse of Lisiuex.* Copyright © 1949 by Sheed & Ward, Ltd. Reprinted 1977, 1979. Used by permission of The Continuum International Publishing Group, Ltd.

Thomas à Kempis: From *The Imitation of Christ,* trans. by William C. Creasy. Copyright © 1989 by Ave Maria Press, P.O. Box 428, Notre Dame, IN 46556, www.avemariapress.com. Used with permission of the publisher.

Gary Thomas: From *Seeking the Face of God.* Harvest House, 1999. Used by permission of the author.

Marjorie J. Thompson: From *Soul Feast: An Invitation to the Spiritual Life.* Copyright © 1995 by Marjorie J. Thompson. Used by permission of Westminster John Knox Press; from *The Way of Forgiveness: Participant's Book.* © 2002 by Upper Room Books. Used by permission.

Howard Thurman: From *The Mood of Christmas and Other Celebrations.* Friends United Press, 2001. Used by permission of the publisher.

A. W. Tozer: From *The Pursuit of God.* Copyright © 1948 by Christian Publications, Inc. Used by permission.

Frank X. Tuoti: From *Why Not Be a Mystic?* © 1995 by Frank X. Tuoti. Used by permission of The Crossroad Publishing Company.

Evelyn Underhill: From *The Spiritual Life.* Copyright © 1937, 1938, 1955 Hodder & Stoughton. Reproduced by permission of Hodder and Stoughton Limited and Morehouse Publishing, Harrisburg, PA.

Carlos G. Valles: From *Faith for Justice* (Gujarat Sahitya Prakash, 1988). Used by permission of Gujarat Sahitya Prakash, Anand, India.

Dwight W. Vogel and Linda J. Vogel: From *Sacramental Living.* © 1999 by Dwight W. Vogel and Linda J. Vogel. Used by permission of Upper Room Books.

Linda J. Vogel: From *Rituals for Resurrection.* © 1996 by The Upper Room. Used by permission of Upper Room Books.

Ray Waddle: From *A Turbulent Peace: The Psalms for Our Time.* © 2003 by Ray Waddle. Used by permission of Upper Room Books.

Charles Wesley: Adapted from *The Unpublished Poetry of Charles Wesley,* vol. 1, ed. by S T Kimbrough and Oliver A. Beckerlegge.

© 1988 Kingswood Books. Adapted by permission of Abingdon Press; adapted from *The Unpublished Poetry of Charles Wesley*, vol. 3, ed. by S T Kimbrough and Oliver A. Beckerlegge. © Kingswood Books. Adapted by permission of Abingdon Press.

Robert J. Wicks: From *Everyday Simplicity*. Copyright © 2000 Sorin Books, Notre Dame, IN.

Macrina Wiederkehr: From *A Tree Full of Angels*. Copyright © 1988 by Macrina Wiederkehr. Reprinted by permission of HarperCollins Publishers, Inc.

Dallas Willard: From *The Divine Conspiracy*. Copyright © 1998 by Dallas Willard. Reprinted by permission of HarperCollins Publishers, Inc.; from *The Spirit of the Disciplines: Understanding How God Changes Lives*. Copyright © 1989 by Dallas Willard. Reprinted by permission of HarperCollins Publishers, Inc.

Patricia Wilson: From *Quiet Spaces*. © 2002 by Patricia F. Wilson. Used by permission of Upper Room Books.

David Winter: From *Forty Days with the Messiah*. © 1999 Abingdon Press. Used by permission.

Nicholas Wolterstorff: From *Lament for a Son*. Copyright © 1987 Wm. B. Eerdmans Pub. Co., Grand Rapids, MI. Used by permission.

Wendy M. Wright: From "Passing Angels: The Arts of Spiritual Discernment" in *Weavings: A Journal of the Christian Spiritual Life* (November/December 1995). Used by permission of the author; from *The Time Between*. © 1999 by Wendy M. Wright. Used by permission of Upper Room Books.

Flora Slosson Wuellner: From *Feed My Shepherds*. © 1998 by Flora Slosson Wuellner. Used by permission of Upper Room Books; from *Forgiveness, the Passionate Journey*. © 2001 by Flora Slosson Wuellner. Used by permission of Upper Room Books; from *Release*. © 1996 by Flora Slosson Wuellner. Used by permission of Upper Room Books.

At the time of publication all Web sites referenced were valid. However, due to the fluid nature of the Internet some addresses may have changed or the content may no longer be relevant.

Additional permissions for scripture quotations

Scripture noted NIV is taken from the *Holy Bible, New International Version. NIV.* Copyright 1973, 1978, 1984 by International Bible Society. Used by permission of Zondervan Publishing House. All rights reserved.

Scripture noted JB is from The Jerusalem Bible, copyright © 1966 by Darton, Longman & Todd, Ltd., and Doubleday, a division of Random House, Inc. Reprinted by permission.

Additional Resources from Upper Room Books

A Guide to Prayer for Ministers and Other Servants
by Rueben P. Job and Norman Shawchuck
leather edition ISBN 0-8358-0460-7
paperback ISBN 0-8358-0559-X

A Guide to Prayer for All God's People
by Rueben P. Job and Norman Shawchuck
deluxe edition ISBN 0-8358-0613-8
paperback ISBN 0-8358-0710-X

UPPER ROOM SPIRITUAL CLASSICS series offer selections from great Christian thinkers compiled and introduced by Keith Beasley-Topliffe. Each series is available as a set, and individual titles are also available separately.

SERIES 1 (5 titles in slipcase) ISBN 0-8358-0832-7

A Longing for Holiness: Selected Writings of John Wesley (80 pages)
ISBN 0-8358-0827-0

The Soul's Passion for God: Selected Writings of Teresa of Avila (80 pages)
ISBN 0-8358-0828-9

The Sanctuary of the Soul: Selected Writings of Thomas Kelly (72 pages)
ISBN 0-8358-0829-7

Hungering for God: Selected Writings of Augustine (96 pages)
ISBN 0-8358-0830-0

Making Life a Prayer: Selected Writings of John Cassian (72 pages)
ISBN 0-8358-0831-9

www. upperroom.org